A PLUME BOOK

RED

AMY GOLDWASSER, a graduate of Ernest W. Seahoim High School in Birmingham, Michigan, has edited and written for publications including *Elle*, *Seventeen*, *The New Yorker*, *Vogue*, *Runner's World*, *The New York Times*, Salon.com, *New York*, and *Outside*. She teaches editing in the Columbia Publishing Course and writing at the Lower Eastside Girls Club. She lives in New York City with her husband, illustrator Peter Arkle. Read her blog—and the authors'—at www.redthebook.com.

Praise for *Red*

Newsweek Book of the Week
Family Circle Book of the Month

"It's high time people stopped writing, talking, and worrying about teenage girls and just let those girls speak for themselves."
—Elizabeth Gilbert, author of the
#1 *New York Times* bestseller *Eat, Pray, Love*

"A must-have." —*Teen Vogue*

"Unsparingly frank and perceptive, the essays in *Red* take on politics, pop culture, and body image—and, oh yeah, they're written by teenage girls. Long underestimated and undervalued by society, they emerge as literature and society's great hope." —*Vanity Fair*

"This book is amazing. Amy Goldwasser has gathered a perfect blend of raw and original voices. Honest, hysterical, heartbreaking, uplifting—these essays come straight from the true teenage soul. Read this book!"
—Paul Feig, creator of the TV series *Freaks and Geeks*; author of *Kick Me*, *Superstud*, and *Ignatius MacFarland: Frequenaut!*

"*Red*: Spread the word." —*US Weekly*

Real Reviews from Real Girls

"After *Red* I was not the same. *Red* rocked, gave joy, inspired, and healed. This book is a revolution."　　　　　—Justine Kayumba, 16, New York

"Finally, here is a book from our generation telling it like it is."
　　　　　—Annalena Barrett, 13, Massachusetts

"*Red* is empowering. These stories made me laugh and cry, all at the same time. I could connect to them so deeply."
　　　　　—Amber Gibson, 17, Illinois

"I am delighted and inspired by the ability of my peers to write such intelligent, clear-sighted assessments of that inscrutable subject: the Teenage Girl. These stories, self-aware but not self-involved, with dramatic realities but without drama queens, overcome stereotypes with refreshing, witty honesty, and prove that our generation is not a *de*generation."
　　　　　—Caroline Smith, 18, Pennsylvania

"*Red* is the most truthful book on my shelf. These girls' stories are potent, there is no watering down, and everybody can find a piece of her (or his) self in here."　　　　　—Bari Saltman, 16, New York

"I'm the type of girl that absolutely hates to read. But when my teacher assigned us *Red*, I read the whole book, honestly! I loved this book. I related to it in many ways, and that is what interested me—to know that it's not just me going through these things. Every teenage girl should own *Red*!"　　　　　—Molly Mayo, 15, Louisiana

"My mom gave me *Red* as a Christmas present, and I will be forever in her debt for picking out such an amazing bundle of words. I think the best part of the book was you really knew that these were real girls. They're brilliant and brave, and I envy their courage to make so public some very intense and delicate subjects."
　　　　　—Veronica Pacentrilli, 17, Alberta, Canada

"For every girl who has read books for teenagers before but come away unhappy, your book is finally here: It's relevant, it's funny, and it's true!"
　　　　　—Anja Brandon-Drevitch, 14, Washington

"Frank, moving, and unsparingly original—a wonderful collection for *anyone* to own."   —Jane Crile, 19, New York

"This is a great book for all ages, and it connected my mom and me a little more. (Life for us girls can be pretty difficult, and now there is this wonderful book to prove just that.) Once we finished reading all the funny, sad, and interesting essays together, I think my mom better understood young girls today. And I realized how different girls can be and why they act the way they do. I know I will read this book again when I get older. I love *Red*!"   —Hadley O'Brien, 12, Michigan

"Thank you so much for publishing this book! It has so many different voices—and they're all true and original. I am amazed at the courage it took for these girls to put their stories out there."
                                                        —Winta Bairu, 14, California

"*Red* is a really awesome book, and the authors seem to fly out of the pages! It's heartwarming, laugh-out-loud- and OMG-worthy. I ELLE OH VEE EEE *Red*!!!! Like sometimes, life feels like it's pointless, routine after routine. But when I read *Red*, I was excited to see who I would meet each day."   —Cassandra Tran, 15, Louisiana

"Essays range from the hilarious to the darkly poignant and lend the collection as a whole a relevance I have rarely felt from the genre of teen lit."
                                                        —Laura Jensen, 19, Minnesota

"*Red* was such an inspiration. It's nice to know that I'm not alone in the struggles of growing up."   —Amanda Oakley, 14, Oregon

"Eye-opening, heartfelt, and insightful. Girls don't just read *Red*. They relate to *Red* because the stories are REAL!"
                                                        —Brittany Mathews, 18, North Carolina

"*Red* recognizes real teen girls, not stereotypes of what they should be. My favorite essay is 'Curve'—some details aside, it is my story. And I have no doubt that any teen girl who reads *Red* will be able to find a reflection of herself in at least one, if not every one, of these incredible essays."   —Allie Jones, 19, Texas

Red

TEENAGE GIRLS in America Write On What Fires Up Their Lives Today

edited by amy goldwasser

A PLUME BOOK

PLUME
Published by the Penguin Group
Penguin Group (USA) Inc., 375 Hudson Street, New York, New York 10014, U.S.A. •
Penguin Group (Canada), 90 Eglinton Avenue East, Suite 700, Toronto, Ontario, Canada
M4P 2Y3 (a division of Pearson Penguin Canada Inc.) • Penguin Books Ltd., 80 Strand,
London WC2R 0RL, England • Penguin Ireland, 25 St. Stephen's Green, Dublin 2, Ireland
(a division of Penguin Books Ltd.) • Penguin Group (Australia), 250 Camberwell Road,
Camberwell, Victoria 3124, Australia (a division of Pearson Australia Group Pty. Ltd.) •
Penguin Books India Pvt. Ltd., 11 Community Centre, Panchsheel Park, New Delhi – 110
017, India • Penguin Group (NZ), 67 Apollo Drive, Rosedale, North Shore 0632, New
Zealand (a division of Pearson New Zealand Ltd.) • Penguin Books (South Africa) (Pty.)
Ltd., 24 Sturdee Avenue, Rosebank, Johannesburg 2196, South Africa

Penguin Books Ltd., Registered Offices: 80 Strand, London WC2R 0RL, England

Published by Plume, a member of Penguin Group (USA) Inc. Previously published in a
Hudson Street Press edition.

First Plume Printing, November 2008
10   9   8   7   6   5   4   3   2   1

Copyright © Amy Goldwasser, 2007
All rights reserved

Each selection is the copyrighted property of its respective author and appears in this
volume by arrangement with the individual writer.

Handwriting by Peter Arkle

 REGISTERED TRADEMARK—MARCA REGISTRADA

The Library of Congress has catalogued the Dutton edition as follows:

Red : the next generation of American writers-teenage girls-on what fires up their lives
today / edited by Amy Goldwasser.
p.   cm.
ISBN 978-1-59463-040-8 (hc.)
ISBN 978-0-452-28983-3 (pbk.)
1. Teenagers' writings, American.   2. American essays—21st century.
I. Goldwasser, Amy.
PS683.T45R43   2007
814.6—dc22   2007027247

Printed in the United States of America

For the hundreds of girls who shared their words
and everyone who led me to them.

And in memory of my father, James Goldwasser, who taught me
to always respect a young person—no matter
how monstrously she's behaving—and what writing can do.

Contents

What Can Be Learned at School

Friendships: Gone Well, Gone Poorly, Just Gone

Crushes Sweet and Excruciating, Sex, and a Love That Ends in Desert Rehab

Contents

Anything Extracurricular: The Beach, the Horse, the Bee, the Lousy First Job, the Stellar Future Career, etc.

Media, Pop Culture, Johnny Depp, Freakdom and Fandom

The World and What's Wrong (Sometimes Even What's Right) with It: Battle Cries

Introduction

~~~~~~

About six months into putting together this book, I was having lunch with a friend—a very grown-up, indulgent kind of lunch, nearly two hours out of the office in a new steakhouse that had corn as an ice cream flavor—and telling her about the essays that were coming in, by then tens a day. These girls can *write*, I'm sure I said. They crack me up, they make me cry on airplanes. They're so much more original and less cynical to work with than adult writers. The eating disorders and cutting are out of control since you and I were in school, and by *far* the majority of essays I got were about body image. Where's it headed? I worry. One girl wrote, "Someone once said that I should kill myself I'm so fat." Then again, another sent me nine pages titled "The Depth of Depp," on how Johnny Depp determines everything in her life. And you wouldn't believe what even the thirteen-year-olds are coming up with. (She's fourteen now, but I still can't get my head around that about Kelly Otterness or, for that matter, that Elizabeth Metzger is only eighteen.)

I went on and on, and my friend was with me—until she went all quiet. I saw her almost recoil a bit, like I'd violated her confidence, turned out not to be the person she'd thought I was. She looked at me with suspicion and asked, "Did you actually *like* being a teenager?"

My mother thought that was the funniest thing she'd ever heard. I still haven't given her my friend's e-mail address.

No one *likes* being a teenager, at least not in such an uncomplicated way—and that's what this book is about. I'm blown away by the talent of these writers, their willingness not to self-censor like the rest of us, their trust. It's a brave thing they're doing, writing their bloody red hearts out (in the perfect words of Emma Considine) like this and getting up and going to school the next day. A lot's been said about nothing being private or sacred to this generation, that the kids blog about *everything*, blah, blah, blah. But it's one thing to blog about your crush on the star of the soccer team or your suicide attempt or what a bitch your mom is under a screen name that only your friends search for, in a world of your peers, where everyone traffics in secrets: You tell them something they didn't know, and you expect the same in exchange.

It's another thing to commit your personal essay to paper, forever with your full name on it, in a book that your parents, your grandparents—your *kids*—your principal, the college admissions committee, the star of the soccer team, the entire soccer team, will have every opportunity to read. I am in awe of this act. Please note that adult writers are only as confessional as they dare to be without having to eat in the school cafeteria or at their parents' dinner table.

Red is a place for the freshest, most fearless young voices out there to explode the puffy pink stereotype of the American teenage girl. These writers reveal their complicated interior lives and intelligence—vividly, emphatically, sometimes terrifyingly—and always in their own words. It's not a series of quotes from teenagers run through an adult filter and called an oral history, and it's not their ideas, only rewritten to suit some grown-up the-culture-of notion of what kids today are thinking. Often the original work called for little to no editing. When it did, I only edited as much as I asked the girls questions—in some cases a year-and-a-half's worth of them—which they worked amazingly hard to respond to. What you're reading are their answers, 100 percent their writing. This book is meant to be a true portrait of teenage girlhood in America today, via 58 of the country's finest, most credentialed authors on the subject.

It's a generation, perhaps the first, of writers. If you're one of the 33 million Americans between the ages of thirteen and nineteen, you are a writer. It's how you conduct your friendships, get to know people, break a heart, manage your family, flirt, lie, make plans, cancel them, announce big news, and, most important, present yourself to the rest of the world. You're fluent in texting, e-mailing, and IM'ing. You're blogging and constantly amending your profile on sites like Facebook and MySpace (which, on average, thirty of your friends will visit every day). Regularly, often late at night, you're generating a body of intimate written work. You're used to writing about yourself. In fact, you choose to write about yourself, on your own time, rather than it being a forced labor when a paper's due in school. You're a reporter embedded in your parents' home, your school, your own head.

Your writing challenges prepackaged concepts and quick-cut TV edits of what it means to be a teenager today. This book is an antidote to the chilling, media-driven sense that teens care about nothing more than shopping, celebrities, supermodeldom, all things expensive and fabulous—and that we, as Americans, have produced the most vapid, unconscionable generation to date.

Truth is, these girls' delights and concerns are as existential as any adult's. They're just freer, more honest documentarians. They had the luxury of devoting their essays to absolutely whatever they wanted to, whatever they personally deemed urgent and important. They wrote about what they're preoccupied with, which is largely themselves (no break in the continuum here). Yet it's an overwhelmingly wise, sophisticated sense of who they are in a larger context. They're engaging, articulate storytellers who have a lot to say—and a lot to teach adults. And even when their subjects are girly, their writing isn't. This generation just happens to live in a world that's saturated with pop culture and consumerism; of course it informs their experiences. They know more about style, music, and culture than any young people in history. A crush smiles like Jimmy Fallon, friendships are forged on *Yu-Gi-Oh!*, jeans are expensive. When Kanye West's "Gold Digger" plays loudly on the ride home, they're aware it's from the guy who said, on live national TV, "George Bush doesn't care about black people."

The authors of *Red* are fascinating and impossible to typecast. They can be hopeful and grave and funny all at once. They're simultaneously confronted with the realities of siblings fighting in Iraq and Ashlee Simpson's nose jobs. They discuss fashion and politics in a single breath. Obesity is an epidemic and so are eating disorders. They set up photo shoots at home for fun and launch indie-music magazines. They know their cities can flood and that reality TV is scripted. They're concerned about the country. They've seen torture photographs and students shooting students. Their doctors can prescribe the morning-after pill; there's a vaccine that could wipe out cervical cancer.

To them, music is downloadable and playlists are of their own design. They may think the greatest threat to their civil rights is the liberals robbing Americans of prayer in school—or the conservatives opposing stem-cell research. They're the most racially diverse generation this country has seen, with whites comprising only 58 percent of the teenage demographic. They're apt to have gay friends. The Gay-Straight Alliance (GSA) came up so many times in these essays that I had to double-check with one of the writers to make sure I didn't have it wrong and they weren't all talking about some new student government association.

These girls were raised with, not impressed by or trying to keep up with, technology: They keep their phones on all night in case a friend needs them. The IT guy of the house is likely an IT girl. For the rest of her life, her checklist before running out the door in the morning will be (or at least begin with): wallet, keys, cell phone. She determined the number-one site on the Internet—of MySpace's more than 70 million American users, roughly a quarter of them are teenage girls—and knows her power. She will vote for the first time in a presidential election whose candidates debated on YouTube.

She respects the ways that sex can change a relationship—but not everything about a relationship. As Caro Fink tells it, "I'm not sure what I thought would happen after, but whatever it was, it didn't happen. I didn't suddenly become a different (or diseased) person, and he didn't either." She's well versed in both the importance of using condoms and the stupid terror of not using them. Often too well versed. "I think that if toddlers were taught about the world the way we're taught about sex in school, they would never leave their cribs," writes Eliza Appleton.

The authors of *Red* see that the world is full of Paris Hilton and loneliness and doubt and heartbreak—and aren't afraid to speak out. They believe they can effect change, stop cutting themselves, stop global warming, be president. (I challenge anyone to read thirteen-year-old Dani Cox's essay and doubt what she's capable of.) These are the best shades of red: a little bit angry, a lot passionate, blood-burning, organ-on-the-table invested in their causes. These girls are on fire, and their essays speak well for the future. It's heartening, inspiring, possible.

The day of that lunch with the steak sauce prepared tableside and the selection of homemade ice creams, I reassured my friend that I'd been as miserable a teenager as any—and that she probably knows me well enough to see clearly who I was in high school.

This book speaks to the fact that the experiences, insights, understandings, and misunderstandings of that stretch between thirteen and nineteen play no small part in determining the people we will always be. And what a good thing that is, to remember and honor that part of ourselves, no matter how much it scares us. The writers of *Red* have.

A Quick Note About Making Red, and Its Contributors

This book started with an e-mail I sent, just to test the waters, to a few dozen friends and colleagues in March 2006, with the subject line "teen girl writers?" I asked them to invite any girls they knew, ages thirteen to eighteen, to submit a piece of personal nonfiction for consideration in a potential collection. Those were the only guidelines. The girls could write on any subject at any length. Their essays could already exist (from a blog, a school assignment, an e-mail to a friend, college applications) or be original works written for this purpose—as almost every one of them turned out to be. Their essays could be important or fun, as long as they were true.

The essays I received, about eight hundred in the end, were thrillingly beyond what I could have imagined, in both quantity and quality. Somehow this generation's great comfort level with new media has organically come around to reviving the old, in the unlikely form of personal essays on paper. These young writers are creating terrific reads—and an exciting new body of American literature.

As opposed to a collection held together by adult writers on a single theme, the essays in *Red* have, really, only one thing in common. It's their heart. From there, in selecting essays for final inclusion, my criteria were: range of subject, voice, age, and geography. I didn't impose chapter categories—the writing organically fell into the eight areas you see here. Within each chapter, essays are simply arranged by age, youngest writer to oldest.

It was really important to me that *Red* not be based on the stories of a privileged few in large cities on the coasts. This book is a true representation of girls across the country, writing across the spectrum of geographic, socioeconomic, political, racial, and religious upbringings. I'm proud to say that the *Red* contributors come from Park Avenue to rural Nevada and twenty-four states in the United States (West Virginia to Hawaii, Kentucky, Michigan, New Jersey, Connecticut, Florida, and so on).

Where necessary, the writers and I had to change names and identifying characteristics of their subjects—schools, boyfriends, girlfriends, racists, mentors, criminals, the boss, gym teachers. Mostly gym teachers. After all, it was the decision of the writers to mercilessly expose whatever they wanted to expose about themselves; other characters didn't have that choice to make.

But the writers' names and stories are absolutely, without exception, real. And the beauty is they keep evolving. I'm delighted to report that as of this summer, Amy Hunt had lost thirty pounds; she's not really sure how, but she's happy. And the move Deborah Kim's parents imposed on her, to San Diego this time, wasn't the cataclysmic event she'd expected. "It changed my life substantially, in the best of ways," she wrote about a month ago:

I had the choice of learning seven different languages instead of three. I took Japanese. I renewed my love affair with books, and went to the first concert of my life (Brand New: utterly amazing). I gawped repeatedly at the iridescent scales of fish, dug my toes into wet gritty sand, and forged new friendships with people who are all vibrant in their own ways and have taught me too many things to name.

She's even made two moves since—the first on her own initiatives—to Los Angeles for college, then to study in England. With life going on in all its primary colors though, the news isn't always good. Tiffani Hortman's friend Andrew, who she wrote about so lovingly, died in late July after a long battle with cancer. It's an honor to have a very alive portrait of him in this book, and I can only hope he would have liked what he read.

You can catch up on the continued stories of the *Red* contributors as well as check out their other work (novels, blogs, drawings, photos), video interviews, readings, and music they've chosen to go with their essays at www.redthebook.com.

This is a book that never ends, and that's a thrilling thing. As Carla Perez-Gallardo says, "I am EXCITED."

The Body and Various Thoughts on Beauty

Amy Hunt, 16

Sleeves

~~~~~~

You'd be surprised at what a girl can hide beneath her sleeves of skin: Truths lies secrets screamshoutlisten CRAZY. She's all CRAZY! CRAZY and forgotten what she'd like to say to do to know to listen to for hours on end music television computer screens and magazines, all adds up to the CRAZINESS, drenched in celebrity gossip and LiveJournal friends' page drama—global addictions made better when you're CRAZY.

But besides the point, she's only CRAZY because you've driven her to be faceless and listless, only wants to *please* and *fit*. What drives her to be so maniacal CRAZY afraid of herself and her friends her grades dreams school goals, her everyday and everything?

Fat.

Self-consciousness, insecurity, weariness, inability: "But these pants fit last week," "Oh honey, that won't look good on you," "Are you *sure* you want to wear that?"

It's weight, it's body. It's absolutely pathetic how girls our age act as if being skinny is what makes the world go round.

Magazines filled with supermodels and gorgeous clothes. Abercrombie, The Gap, American Eagle, Hollister, and I can't shop there. I'm *overweight*, have to say it like it's a curse word. I don't believe in labels, but sometimes I wish that I could be labeled. Nothing looks good on me, though, not punk goth prep loser geek nerd freak, anything, because of a little weight a little skin a little fat. Only the skinny can joke about how fat they are because they know how much they aren't; all they want are the compliments. I know I won't get compliments:

"Oh no you aren't!"

Don't lie to me, I'm two hundred pounds.

"N-no you're not, Amy."

It's the stutter that gives it away.

Funny how there's always the fat chick surrounded by pretty girls, girls with clothes that fit, who can wear tank tops and short skirts and are allowed to dress provocatively because they have the figures. They are my friends and they mean well. But still they say, "Man I'm so fat," while they clench the tummyskin that is perfect, which causes me to wonder, *If they're fat, then what could you call me?* And how is it that I'm overweight yet the most invisible one of all? Sometimes I truly wouldn't mind being shallow and giggling and talking about boys and clothes and nail polish and who has what, when the next party is. Being invited to parties. I wouldn't mind having many shallow skinny Evil friends, even though this would mean good-bye to those who mean so much to my life right now.

And then, even with the friends that are there, they're all skinny, pretty. The Evils still talk to them. Why do they befriend the fat chick anyway? Sometimes I feel as if they only pity me. We went shopping at the mall once, three of us, and the other two tried on prom dresses as I sat in the dressing room, wishing.

They'd say, "Amy, try on pretty dresses, too!"—"Oh, they won't fit me."—"You don't know that!"—but no, the largest size is only 13. They commented on their own sizes and I wanted to spit and scream at them. But I acted the friend and said, "It looks good on you, I promise." *And it did, it did, I wouldn't lie!*

All I think about now is, *What is wrong with me?* And every time it's the same answer. I hate that word. I hate it with more passion than I've felt toward anything else in my life. It's the reason I'm nobody to so many people, because it's the reason I'm nobody to myself.

Feel as if the world is attacking: fat jokes and unheard laughter hiding behind every eye and pair of lips. It's the inability to say a speech, read out loud, audition for anything important to my heart. Fear of being laughed gawked pointed at because it's a fat girl trying to be a part of something ha ha ha! Fat girl has opinions? Fat girl wants to make something of herself? Tried out for the play but can't do the physical stuff. What if the fat chick looks funny? I want to be a part of so much, but it's all so out of reach. I think about it all the time. Getting teary-eyed now, wondering what-if what-if what-if. All I can do is think, *If I were skinny this, if I were skinny that, then they would have liked me.* I would have confidence woulda woulda coulda shoulda—no.

I can't even raise my hand in class anymore, can't earn any of my participation points. Remember that mock senate project, when we were supposed to speak a total of fifteen times over five or so days? Remember how I spoke not once? Not a single time?

Fat.

Someone once said that I should kill myself I'm so fat. Not to my face, no, but they meant for me to hear it. I've tried so hard to block it from my mind, but it's not something that can ever leave me. It's always there, behind my eyelids, every time I see him in the hallway, when my heart runs to the back of my chest. So afraid of him now.

I don't even remember direct quotes—except for the one. But here, it went a little something like this:

Biology, he (we'll call him Jerk-1) and his lab partner (Jerk-2) working on dissecting beans. Except that Jerk-2 was an obvious cheat, staring over my head at my partner's, one of my best friend's, paper. So I say (I admit, a little rudely, but Jerk-2 was never polite to me in any way), "Um, could you move over?"

"Hey, I'm just working with my group here, don't you tell me to move."

"Well, you're invading my personal space."

"You don't have personal space."

Any ability to say what needs to be said vanishes, and all I can manage is, "Yes I do!" Mentally slap myself, *What was that? What? Yes I do? Amy, just keep your mouth shut.*

And Jerk-1 tells his lab partner, "Just move, she's a fatass." Stifled laughter, Jerk-2 walks over to the other side of Jerk-1's chair and sits down. "She was trying to truck you or something, telling you to move."

"Haha, *her* trying to truck me. She can't truck me."

"She's just a fat bitch. She should kill herself she's so fat."

And they laugh.

Singled out, I hate being singled out. Why should I kill myself for being fat? Why should it matter to them, why act like I'm unworthy of sharing a classroom with because I'm fat? I just don't want people copying the work of my lab partner, my *friend*.

I'll bet they don't even remember anymore.

But I do.

Fat.

Fluctuate between 198 and 201, it never really changes. I seem to feel different, think to look different, but those doctor visits ruin everything, meaning frequent runs to the friendly neighborhood scale, no reason to have one at home. Sure, we own one. But as far as I know it's broken, and with three females living in the house, isn't it bad for a girl's self-esteem to constantly be checking her weight? So we hope and wait until those doctor visits.

Fat.

Will a boy ever like me? I think one did once, and I thought that I liked him but then came to the realization that it was the thought of being liked. I was too afraid of actually being noticed. What if he notices the bad things? I'm full of them, after all. They're boys and sometimes they're friends, sometimes want them to be more than friends, but they never feel the same. Is it because of the weight the looks the imperfections galore? Nobody seems to realize that the fat chick wants somebody, too. Then I feel ridiculous. All those surrounding me, they must think it hilarious: Who would like a fat girl? Let these thoughts keep me from wanting anything, afraid of what everyone thinks. Everyone except those who actually matter.

I went a month then a summer, once, obsessing over someone I

had seen from afar—thinking and writing about him but never talking to him. He made my decisions for me, although he didn't know it:
where to sit at lunch, which hallways to take to classes, hell, even
which music to listen to and books to read. What to say and when to
say it. I went crazy for him, wrote about him for over forty pages even
though I knew it was pointless. I wanted forever and a day, every day,
to see his golden-luscious hair, his vibrant eyes. But I kept my distance because I was fat and stupid and he had friends and a life of his
own. Friends and a life that could never involve me.

Fat.

I hide behind the computer the Internet online journals and typed
messages, words that mean everything because there are no pictures
to accompany them unless I want for there to be. Words directed to
and only read by people unknown. I would rather have those who are
strangers, those who are creatures of the computers be a part of my
life. Anything anybody other than those who are truly there, those
who are within reach, who are within laughing distance. Who are the
girls I'd like to be.

I want to learn how to love myself. Not just learn how to lose this
mass that is my body fat but how to love it while I have it and how to
stop crying every time I return home after shopping. I want to know
how my mind works, why I continue to torture myself with these
demons, splurges of chips and candy and chocolate. I want to learn
how to jump out. But I can't do it alone. I need people, people who
know what I feel. Imagine, a school fat club of sorts, overcoming obesity together! Because my friends don't need the diets like I do. I
want the willpower and the teamwork that I see on TV but never in
my own life. Is there anyone out there like me? Is there anyone else
who needs help, who needs encouragement, love, friends? Is there
anyone out there who would want to join this fat club?

I don't want to be alone. It's nice to think about not being alone.
It's nice to dream about not being alone. It's nice to not be alone.

Alison Smith, 16

Curve

〰〰〰

My whole life I've been told I'm too skinny. I've always had the opposite problem of everyone else. The bones stick out from every joint, my clothing hangs awkwardly—nothing is average, regular, *normal* about it.

My mother pokes me, saying, "You need some meat on your bones." My grandmother is determined to "fatten" me up. But worst of all is when my friends complain about their weight. If I join in, saying that I wish I could gain some, they shout at me and tell me to "just shut up." They tell me that I'm making them feel bad—that my problem is like having a "too pretty" problem.

In my mind, it's being healthy-looking that's the too-pretty problem. Being underweight or overweight isn't. But I never get to have a say over my body; instead I'm judged meanly or with unfair jealousy.

I'm always the Skinny Girl, the one with no athletic talents, the girl who doesn't try hard enough, the girl who apparently never eats enough. The girl excluded from the conversation because of her weight or lack thereof, the girl who never made it past 104 pounds.

Last month I was at a friend's house, laughing at her diaries from eighth grade. As we were flipping through, we stopped at a page on which she'd summed up each of our friends. Everyone else's descriptions spoke in detail about their personalities. Mine only said, "It hurts to hug Alison."

But isn't that what society wants? Isn't the girl with little to no body fat, the girl who looks like it hurts to hug her, the American ideal? It's debatable, but generally, yes. (Not to say that *I'm* the American ideal, because that's certainly not true.) Is it my ideal though? No. Does anyone care what the Skinny Girl thinks? No, not particularly. It probably doesn't even occur to many people that she may not like her body to be so angular and thin. If every time I mentioned my unhappiness with my weight and someone replied, "I hate you," I ate a Super Sized McDonald's meal, there would be no reason for me to complain anymore.

I've always yearned for a curve, a sweet separation from the straightness of my body. The closest I've gotten to that dream is my hips, my favorite part of me. They start so high and sweep out past the boundaries of my body, then return through my thighs. They have little fat on them, but they are curves nevertheless. They are my pass to join in conversations about jeans not zipping or dresses not fitting. They are my superficial excuse to be normal. They're so mine. They're so me. They stick out just right, they fit just right, they take me away from being the Skinny Girl. I can customize them, tattoo them, tan them, dress them—make them mine because they are my happiness.

My curve.

The Jewish Hair

I t takes a lot more effort than you might think.
Look closer.

I can only brush my hair right after the shower, when it's still wet.
Make sure it isn't behind my ears, or there will be a crease. Pulling
the Jewish Hair back is out of the question unless it's completely dry.
I can only use those *thick* bands on my hair, my big hair, my frizzy
hair, my curly hair, my wild hair, my sometimes-sexy hair, my long
hair, my dark hair. It does everything in its power to make me mad—
to turn me into the hot-tempered Jew I am by nature.

For a not-so-limited time, the Jewish Hair comes with the following: a light blue wide-tooth comb, Matrix Vavoom calming gel, anti-
frizz serum, split ends, an umbrella, my father's baseball cap, my
mother's silk scarf, a ceramic steam straightening iron, a lace *kipa*.
Full curls, messy curls, no curls at all. John Frieda smoothing sham-
poo and conditioner. A bad attitude.

The Jewish Hair is composed of DNA, poof, and *tzuris*, the Yiddish
word for annoyance. The longer it is, the more time it takes. It can be
found on men and women, and is also known as the Jewfro. In Orthodox households it is the custom for women to shave it all off and wear
a wig. Its sole purpose, it seems, is to get in the way.

When I was thirteen years old, I stood before my family and
friends and spoke Hebrew. I chanted ancient prayers and read from
the scrolls of the Torah. The bat mitzvah is a nerve-wracking occasion, especially when it comes to the Jewish Hair. Usually one goes to
a salon. Usually it takes a team of professionals to tame her monster.

All different kinds of up-dos and crazy hair-sprayed experiments can be seen on this special day. *Lecheim*, everybody.

The Jewish Hair has two styles: up and down. There are slight variations—buns, twists, half-ponytails, low ponytails—but in the end it's one or the other, up or down. You may use certain styling products, but be careful not to use too much, or you will make your hair crunchy. Don't get carried away with the straightening iron—you do not have smooth silky-shiny blond hair, and you never will. Don't try the sexy finger run-through to impress; you'll just get stuck. And please, please, PLEASE, *never* attempt bangs.

The Jewish Hair gets ripped off at fashion shows. Tall, slender figures parade under big frizzy balls of teased and sprayed extensions as if in costume. The models can try our look on for however long it takes to walk down the runway, without having to experience the true wonders and trials of actually living with the Jewish Hair. It has been known to resemble a hairy animal. It's very good at scaring small children.

But, when flipped in a certain way, the Jewish Hair can, believe it or not, be attractive. When there isn't any moisture in the air, it can be styled just so, resulting in a smile-provoking look. It can actually aid in making a person look pretty and draw in the opposite sex. Occasionally.

The Jewish Hair makes the boys who they are and the girls who they would never want to be. A Jewish girl spends hours at a time in front of her bathroom mirror, shaking and twisting, twirling and pulling. A Jewish boy, however, rolls out of bed in the morning, glances into a mirror, and heads off to school. His giant hair adds to his personality. He is witty and cute, original and friendly.

Funny how that works.

Muscle

~~~~~~

Being a teenager is never easy, but just think: If you had an illness or disability it might be even harder, right? As a high school senior living with muscular dystrophy, I can tell you that sometimes it is. But you can always change that. My name is Tiffani Hortman. I am someone—like you are someone—who could feel sorry for me. I don't.

At the age of five I was diagnosed with a very uncommon form of muscular dystrophy called dermatomyositis. It causes my muscles to hurt and gives me something called a butterfly rash on my face—a little red rash that doesn't itch or anything; it just shows up sometimes. My disease mostly affects girls, and researchers still aren't sure how many have it. I know of only four other girls with my form of MD. I met them at a muscular dystrophy camp here in Georgia called Camp Walk-n-Roll. My friend Sierra and I are very close because we can relate to each other about our condition; we understand.

I've always told myself that I can do anything I want to. And guess what, I can! I have girl time and go to school. I also love singing, being crazy, and just being myself. I have some friends who are sick and others who are not. I've met tons of people at school and online who are amazing and don't care that I have something wrong with my health.

Over the years, I've also had to deal with people who weren't so accepting. Between second and eighth grades, I was in a wheelchair pretty much full-time due to muscle weakness; inevitably there were the kids who'd call me a "cripple." Then there would be some days when I felt strong enough not to use the wheelchair, and kids would say really rude things like, "You're not sick, you just want a lift" or "attention" or "sympathy." I never really let it get to me, because I knew the truth about my condition and wasn't going to let anyone bring me down. You know?

Another great thing in my life is Starbright World. It's an online social network, kind of like MySpace or Facebook, except the only members are kids with serious illnesses and their brothers and sisters. We all have different conditions, but in a bigger way everyone understands what it's like to be young and sick, and they don't make you feel bad for it. I sign on almost every day.

My best friend on Starbright World is Andrew, one of the strongest, most spirited people I have ever met. We have the closest friendship, even though he lives across the country in Seattle. The weird thing is, under any other circumstances it would be way different. If Andrew and I went to the same school we probably would have never spoken. Were we both healthy high school kids, what are the chances we would have taken the time to stop and talk and find we had something in common?

Andrew has cancer. He was diagnosed two years ago, at the age of sixteen. He went into a short remission, but then the cancer came back. Last December he gave us all a very big scare because he had a bad reaction to the chemo and had to be put in the hospital. Right now all is going smoothly. He keeps fighting and he keeps me updated with IMs. It all depends on the day, but he never fails to report something positive. "Always keep your head high," he'll write after a diagnosis that will take both of us days online to process. "God has a reason for everything."

Andrew's right, and one of the things my illness led me to is swimming. I started in the pool when I was seven, as physical therapy. The doctor wanted to help keep my muscles moving since, at that time, I was always in my wheelchair. I really didn't like it at first because I was one of the slowest kids imaginable. But my heart for the sport just got bigger because it gave me a different kind of mobility.

I kept at it and became faster. In sixth grade, I joined BlazeSports.

It's all over America—swimming, track and field, and basketball teams for kids who have disabilities, in and out of wheelchairs. My swimming classification, determined by your ability to use your arms and legs, was a 9-10-9, which meant I'd be competing with people who were mostly missing a single limb or who couldn't use their legs and had to rely on their (amazingly well-developed) arms. It was hard for me to do strokes like the butterfly, but I went on to junior nationals with a bunch of other disabled swimmers. And soon I set a record in the 50 freestyle. I don't remember what my time was, but it was fast, and I am very proud of that. I could have gone to the Paralympics, but they don't recognize MD. I don't know why not, so I really don't think I can say if it's fair or not.

When Blaze was over for the year, I swam on an able-bodied team. I was still doing well, with kids who didn't have anything wrong with them. I'm happy that I was swimming for so long, because if I hadn't gotten into it, I know I probably wouldn't be able to even walk today. I'm now completely out of my wheelchair unless I'm going to the mall or something in that range. I've had the privilege or luck of being able to see the world from two places: being in a wheelchair and not.

Today I'm riding horses at least three days a week. I've been the leader of my town's 4-H drill team for two years, and it's been so much fun. In 2005 we placed third in regionals; in 2006, we placed second. Right now we're preparing for our next show to see if we'll be able to go to nationals in Texas. You would not believe these shows. You have so much fun with your friends, and of course you also get to ride your horse, which is one of the most wonderful things. For a while an instructor's daughter loaned me her barrel horse. Bunny is so amazing. She minds so well, most of the time. But I'm now on a horse they call Vernie, a gorgeous bay—which is brown. I've only ridden her a couple of times, and she's really nice and calm. Vernie has white socks that come halfway up her legs and a white blaze on her face. If I fall off Vernie I always get right back on.

It's so cool to be able to run a horse, because four or five years ago

I wouldn't have been strong enough to at all. In my early days of riding, I was having flair-ups with my disease. When I go into a flair-up, I'm placed back in my wheelchair, and they up my medications to get me out of it. Flair-ups are never fun because they mean you're right back on the meds—and more of them—that they'd been trying so hard to bring you off of. But soon after I started to feel better, I signed up for lessons with a lady who had me jumping my second or third day. And then I fell off. But, as someone who's been thrown from a wheelchair, I can tell you that being thrown from a horse is much more fun.

If I were to give advice to other teens, I would say: If people don't listen to you about whatever makes you different from them, you should come out and tell them as directly as possible about it. Let them know, from wherever you sit, that you want to be their friend. Let them know there's no need to be afraid of you.

Ode to My Breasts

~~~~~~~~

I am not a tall girl; in fact, I would go as far as to say that I'm a short girl. Just under the respectable five-foot line, everything about me is miniature. I have baby feet and baby hands and a little squishy baby face. Surprisingly, though, most people I meet do not choose *small* as their first word to describe me. Usually I find they take a more direct route: *voluptuous* or *broad* or sometimes simply *breast-o-rific*! Yes, there is something about me (besides my personality, of course) that makes me very large—mammoth, in fact.

I remember approaching fifth grade: carefree, joyous, happy. Little did I know that the end of my elementary school career would also be the end of my innocence. I like to refer to the following event as my fall from grace, considering there were apples involved (so to speak). See, now, in my seventeenth year of life, the bra has become something very lackluster. It summons no excitement. It goes on every morning, it comes off every night, and occasionally it will make a small cameo somewhere in between. When the concept was introduced to me, though, it was formal, foreign, and frightening. It was *brassiere*, and it was not standing with its arms open to welcome me.

My mom and I were having a conversation at the kitchen table—most likely about soccer, or dolls, or *The Sound of Music*, or something else sickeningly adorable like that. All of a sudden, the attention sank out of her face. Her eyes lowered farther and farther beneath my chin, and, yes, I believe she went a bit slack-jawed. She came closer, stooped to my level, and proclaimed, "Well, I hate to say it, but I think you're going to need a brassiere soon."

Only moments later it seemed, my mother and I were in the department store. Apparently she'd meant I needed some support NOW. As we trekked through the cornfields of cotton, I avoided eye contact with her, all other customers, and myself in any mirror we happened to pass. The more my mother tried to bond over which brands were her personal favorites, the more appealing death looked to me. I was embarrassed, plain and simple. I didn't want to begin that awkward transition into womanhood, and least of all did I want the other girls to see me in the lingerie department and know I was a frontrunner in the race of puberty. I anxiously declared to my mom that we would be out of there in fifteen minutes. Preferably less.

My mother was determined to make the trip thorough, though, and did so by offering as much help as she could, which unfortunately involved a lot of pointing at advertisements and saying, "See, don't her breasts looks lovely?" Her assistance also included loading my arms to the ceiling with various options (everything from push-up and black lace to minimizing and 24-hour comfort) and then nudging me into a fitting room. Of course she offered to come in and, "you know, adjust things and take a look around." But the thought of me, my mother, and a bra in such close proximity made me feel faint. I pretended to try on her selections—which meant I took a bit of time to noisily hold each up, rustle my clothes around, and then proclaim surely, "Nope, no good."

Finally, two long hours later, I knew it was time to compromise. I reached out for the last available choice: the sports bra, as close to a cotton undershirt as possible. It looked safe, comforting, almost like my tea-party bears baby blanket (which, I should mention, I was still sleeping with at the time). I opened the door with my new friend in hand and allowed my mother to purchase it for me. I knew I would never wear it. Maybe she did, too. But the smile on her face as she pulled out the credit card told me that I'd done something good.

The thought of pleasing my mother, however, was not enough to get me to use the damn thing. It sat in my drawer for the next few months. I expected my mother to question why I wasn't wearing it, but I guess we were on a don't ask, don't tell kind of plateau. I also ex-pected to remain braless and free for the rest of my life.

Until we saw the Movie, that is. We were reaching our final few weeks of fifth grade, and the teachers were getting more and more anxious to send us up to middle school. So one fateful afternoon, they pulled out that VHS that's been adored by generations of students. This one piece of cinema was supposed to prepare us for the rest of our lives, asking such elusive and philosophical questions as:

Why do I smell so funny?

What's that thing in Johnny's pants?

And:

What's the deal with bras?

The video came to a close, the lights were turned back on, and suddenly, all was clear! Bras, helpful and reliable, had been invented for our benefit! They were there to keep us modest and supported, but also to make us perky and mouthwatering. The girls started chat-tering and the excitement rose, bras almost instantly replacing Poké-mon cards in the position of the cool thing. Many of my classmates were lamenting how their mothers wouldn't let them get one, or that they didn't have anything to put into one.

That was when I spoke the words I never thought I would: "I al-ready have one." What was this? I was now bragging about the very thing I'd so vehemently kept hidden in my dresser? The room went silent for a moment. And then there was a tornado. I had girls on all sides of me, asking what the mechanism was like. I was getting high-fives and compliments. Who knew so much could change over the course of one film? That is the beauty of the Movie, I suppose.

When I got home that day, I did not stop for milk and cookies. No, that time of my life was over. I went straight to my room and put on the bra. And there it has stayed ever since. Of course the style has changed a bit. The size, too. Like I said, I'm a small girl in stature. I didn't grow much taller after that initial shopping trip. My breasts, on the other hand, took off on a race to I-don't-know-where, and they still haven't reached the finish line. As I move toward the end of high school and the end of available cup sizes, I occasionally get frustrated with my gigantic girlfriends: a backache here, a stretched-out shirt there. And there's always the nuisance and the risk of poking out an eye when I'm running in gym class. Sometimes I find myself wishing I wasn't so breast-o-rific.

Then I recall that day, my short reign as queen of the class. While my breasts have at times been obstacles—you could say they were mountains to climb during adolescence—mostly, now, I live with them with a smile. When you're as petite as I am, you can't expect people to ignore the twins. But now that I've realized the beauty of these things on my chest, whatever they are, I'm not ashamed to get the attention. Naturally, it doesn't beat scholastic achievement, true love, or life success. But the compliments (and the desire of my female friends to poke them) never hurt. Of course, there are some issues that you never outgrow. I still don't let my mother into the fitting room, although she will always offer.

Caro Fink, 17

Lucky

~~~~~~~~

I sang through most of what this story is about, even when it's not documented here. Between voice lessons, my a cappella group, and what I choose to do in my spare time, my life revolves around music. Singing and music influence most, if not all, of my emotions.

The dates here will not be accurate. They go from Valentine's Day—which is also my birthday—in seventh to eleventh grades. By Valentine's Day I do not mean February 14th. I mean events that occurred around that day, possibly at my birthday party, sometimes memories jumbled from a few different dates. So please excuse my inaccuracy.

In seventh grade, when I was going to turn thirteen, I invited many girls whom I'd met very recently to my party. My best friend since kindergarten, Bella, had introduced me to Cara and Maggie, who would change my life drastically because of our love for the new television show *Yu-Gi-Oh!* (We'd just broken free from our Pokémon obsession.) Also, I had begun to make friends with the girl down the street, Nessa, and the girl I sat with in homeroom, Julie. Everything was perfect in my short-sighted seventh-grade view. I had friends and was popular. Not the popular of blond hair and lip gloss, but the popular I'd always wanted—a comfortable circle of close friends who understand me and accept me no matter what.

This perfection I describe is my pitiful way of trying to make what happens next sound almost reasonable. To be able to say, See, it really isn't my fault! There's a good reason for my actions, not just insanity and chemical imbalances. Of course I was never really insane.

But it's kinder to plead insanity than to know I consciously did what I did.

The next winter, eighth grade, I can clearly remember two distinct days, though not the actual dates. Maggie and I had become virtually inseparable; I went to her house almost every day after school. She'd convinced me to join her dance class, and I'd convinced her to come to at least a few of my karate classes. We wrote notes to each other during classes we weren't in together, just to pretend the other was there. We were completely dependent on each other.

Then I fell in love with her. I was passing one of our famous notes-between-classes and mentioned that I was attracted to a girl. All of my friends are big supporters of gay rights, and Maggie's sister had started a GSA at her college, so I wasn't worried about homophobia. Maggie asked me who the girl was, and on the two-hour car ride to my black-belt test I wrote her a letter, explaining it was her. Looking back, this was probably not the smartest move on my part. A thick tension grew between us.

Maggie and Julie quickly became the best of friends, similar to how Maggie and I had been. Only Julie was so excited by the new embrace that she agreed with Maggie on everything. Since Maggie was uncomfortable around me, Julie not only wouldn't go near me but convinced all of our common friends (my only friends) I must be shunned. Maggie and Julie would make a scene out of switching seats in classes so that everyone would know I was not acceptable to be in their presence. Once, during a long block of chem, I finished the lab early and cried in the corner for two hours. Maggie and Julie came to the closest bench to me and started talking, extra loudly, about how stupid people have no friends. The worst was when I asked one of them for help with my life because, as you'll soon read, it got a little out of my hands. Her response: "The only thing that will help you is suicide."

The saving grace about that time was that I was in the best singing Valentine group in our middle school. There were about six groups that year, performing at assemblies and in classrooms at the request of teachers, and ours was the most in demand. We had a pretty sophisticated routine for eighth graders and arranged an entire background and simple choreography—pointing when singing "you" or blowing fake kisses. I soloed in "Kiss Me" by Sixpence None the Richer twenty-nine times.

During one of the last of these performances was the first time I can remember thinking seriously about how horrible I actually was/am. I felt as if I were sitting in the back row, watching myself and my friends—if I could still call them that at this point—perform. I remember my dissociated self thinking, You horrible girl, get off the stage. You look ugly, even more so singing than normal, and you sound like SHIT. Get off the fucking stage!

The next day was my birthday party. I invited the usual crowd, despite my better judgment: Maggie, Nessa, Julie, Cara, Mark (a boy Maggie, Julie, and Nessa had become close with), and Lily, a girl I'd met at summer camp. I'd only been around most of these people at rehearsals for *Grease* and singing Valentines. The whole thing was more to give my "friends" a chance to hang out with each other, and for my parents to think everything was all right in my life so they wouldn't worry, than any kind of celebration on my part.

Maggie made the announcement at that party, while we were watching FLCL (*Fooly Cooly*), that she and Mark were dating and in complete and mature love with each other. This was, of course, news to me, and it forced open wounds I'd been trying desperately and with wasted effort to close. I left my own party early, retreating to my room to find a pair of scissors. I took the scissors and scraped the blade against my forearm. I was amazed at how rewarding it felt. I've read many memoirs of women cutting, which probably gave me the idea, although I don't remember actively thinking about it when I started. They'd all said it was painful, a way to feel something other than numb. For me it was the complete opposite. A guilty pleasure, cutting was not at all painful (even a small paper cut hurts, how does that work?) but a twistedly beautiful release of the pain inside of me.

It was almost cleansing, a morose baptism. It gave me a short-lived, wonderful numbness. I imagined death to be like this absence of feeling, saying it often to myself and anyone who happened to overhear. Killing myself was not my goal, though. In fact, I was trying to save myself. Cutting was a desperate and disastrous effort to feel better.

I never used bandages to hide the cuts. Much too obvious, not my style. Instead I just wore long sleeves, which occasionally showed more than I was comfortable with but were much less conspicuous. Thankfully, the cutting started in the winter.

After that night, whenever anything bad happened, even something like a slightly lower grade on a paper than I'd hoped for, I would cut it out of me, always on my arms. I was able to hide the damage for a while, but eventually Julie told her mom I was cutting and talking about suicide. Her mom, of course, told mine, and my mom and I had a fabricated teary confrontation. Fabricated on my part, at least. I told her everything she wanted to hear. "No Mommy, I never meant to hurt you." "Yes Mommy, I know it was wrong." "No Mommy, I'll never do it again." "Yes Mommy, of course I want to get better." I never did mean to hurt her or my father. Neither of them had done anything to deserve a daughter with such a severe disorder. The talk of me having to go "see someone" scared me. It was OK for me to know I had a problem, but it was a whole other issue to proclaim it to the world by going into therapy. So I took a drastic measure that almost no one knows about, even now.

To try to avoid therapy and life in general, I swallowed half a bottle each of ibuprofen, aspirin, and any other medication I could find. (My logic was that I wouldn't swallow any full bottles, in case my attempt failed and I had to explain why all the drugs in the house had suddenly disappeared.) I do realize now that the approach had a very low probability of actually killing me and that there are much better ways of going about suicide. But I wasn't exactly thinking clearly at the time.

Obviously, since I'm here and able to write this, the attempt failed. I ended up passing out on the floor of my room with my head on my futon. I woke early the next morning and threw up for what felt like forever. I told my mom I had a stomach bug that was going around school, and she didn't question it. I never felt the need to try suicide again.

I had virtually gotten over my cutting addiction by the next year. Going to therapy didn't help, because I've studied psychology and was easily able to trick the shrink into thinking I was "making significant progress." I quit therapy over the summer of 2006. And I quit cutting mostly because I went away to camp and it was impossible to pull it off there without getting caught. I also thought going into high school in the fall would be a good time to start anew.

Quitting was one of the hardest things I've ever done. I threw out all my razors. I'm ashamed to admit I didn't shave for most of that summer, but it was worth it.

Freshman year my home life slipped, and my mother and I fought an insane amount about nothing. It was a horribly painful time, and I feel extremely proud to be able to say that I did not relapse into cutting and instead sought the help of friends. After I told them I was no longer in love with Maggie and that I'd stopped cutting myself, they just accepted me again. It was awkward and fake to begin with, but we all eventually grew somewhat back into our old friendships.

Despite the home issues, I pretty much felt on top of the world. I hadn't cut myself for about two months. Then February vacation rolled around. Lily, whom I'd ended up dating until we broke up at camp that summer, came to stay with me for the break. She'd gotten together with Frank, a freshman in college who was racist—and to me, the worst person in the world. She asked me if, when we went shopping for the day, she could invite him to drive down and meet us. I said no. She told him yes anyway.

I separated from Lily and Frank at the mall, meeting back up with them when it was time to get picked up and go home. Not wanting to have to talk to Frank, I started walking ahead to the parking lot. When I noticed Lily wasn't following me, I turned around, just in time to see them pull away from a make-out session in the middle of the crowded mall. Lily, reluctantly, left with me.

Back at my place she talked to Frank on the phone for three hours, while I sat in my room and cut up my arms. It was my first and only relapse that year and it eroded what was left of my self-esteem.

This year I had someone on Valentine's Day. His name is Devin. I met him through a mutual friend in the center of town, and we exchanged screen names. We ended up having all our lunch blocks together, and since I was still slightly uneasy with my friends, I ate with him every day. One major reason we became so close was because I could tell him everything about me, even my cutting addiction, and he still respected me. He's seen me through a lot of difficult things, and I eventually got to repay the kindness. I was the only person he told about his parents' divorce for a month after it happened, and I helped him through it, seeing him every day, reassuring him.

It was weird, because before I met Devin, I'd always classified myself as a lesbian and appropriately so. I'd never felt attraction to a guy before. So it took me three or four months to admit to myself I'd fallen in love with Devin, let alone to anyone else. I've decided not to classify myself sexually now. Maybe because it's just too annoying. Maybe because I don't actually know. I'm Carosexual; I like who I like and that's it.

I hadn't cut for seven months. I relapsed then, mostly because I hadn't been able to tell Devin I'd fallen in love with him, even though we would cuddle on my couch, occasionally kissing each other's hands. I cut again three weeks before he flew away for a weekend to see Kelly, a friend from his French-immersion camp who I knew he'd had a crush on. These relapses were odd because I refused to go back to cutting my arms. Instead I would cut my stomach and shoulders, mercilessly. Mostly my stomach. I cut my stomach fifty-six times one night—the night I thought Devin was never going to come back from visiting Kelly and would leave me there to die without him.

When he did come back, I told him about my encounter with the

razor. But I never did tell him why. He was worried but didn't disre-
spect me for it, for which I am insanely grateful. He showed genuine
concern, as opposed to the concern many people show: the concern
they feel they must show or it reflects poorly on them. He held my
hand and let me talk about it to my heart's content, even though he
was visibly uncomfortable, tightening his muscles and flinching
while he listened. I gave him my knife, and by the time he gave it
back three months later we were dating. He returned it to me saying
he trusted me to call him before I'd consider hurting myself again. I
do. I have not cut since then, last December, and am still working
hard to suppress the urges. I've found rubbing ice on my arm helps
to create a physical numbness, and if I concentrate on that sensation
long enough, the comfort is almost the same.

I'm not sure how Devin got through to me, but somehow he did.
He's helping me regain my shattered sense of self ever so slowly, yet
ever so persistently. Although he would occasionally ask, I made him
wait a whole year to have sex because I was so disgusted with my
body. I assumed he would have the same reaction when he saw it.

That Valentine's Day was special. I mixed him a CD—"Accidentally
in Love" by Counting Crows, "Entwined" by Lacuna Coil, "Gravity of
Love" by Enigma, "Kiss Me" with my solo, and so on with the love
songs. I bought him twelve roses. Eleven of them were real, and one
was made of silk with a note attached saying, "I'll love you until every
last rose dies." The trick of this, of course, being that the fabric rose
will never die and I will always love him. I know it's a pretty unpre-
dictable claim for a seventeen-year-old, and I accept that maybe our
romantic love will die one day. But Devin has been such a part of my
life that I will always love him as at least a friend loves another friend.

This November 9th was our year anniversary. We celebrated by
going out to a fancy restaurant in Boston, and it was an amazing
night. We had sex. In health class recently, we'd been talking about
the big taboo topic of teen sex and how horrible it can be if you do it

too early. But in reality, it wasn't anything like what they teach you. Neither of us has some horrible STD, nor am I pregnant. I'm not emotionally damaged by it or anything like that. I'm fine. I enjoyed it. And Devin wasn't thoroughly repulsed by my body.

That isn't to say that I would suggest sex to everyone my age. I'm in a very loving, stable relationship, and we were both ready because we feel comfortable talking about anything with each other. I know it sounds cliché, but I could never have known how emotional it would be, in a positive way, until I did it. Not much actually changed, I guess, but it's like we have a closer connection. I feel silly writing a whole entry on sex because, yes, it was important, but it doesn't change much in the rest of my life. I'm not sure what I thought would happen after, but whatever it was, it didn't happen. I didn't suddenly become a different (or diseased) person, and he didn't either. I have the same morals and ideals, and I'm no more or less mature than I was. It just seems like it's not worth making a huge deal out of.

At least not compared to everything else. Do not be fooled—this is not a story that ends in happily-ever-after. Things are stable for me now, but I'm aware that that also leaves more room for me to fall. These experiences will stay with me for the rest of my life, the angel and the demon sitting on my shoulders, whispering that going back to my razor blade is a justifiable act. Telling me that it would be noble, even, to prove to the world that I am someone who had to go through a time so bad that I had no choice but to resort to methodically destroying myself—and that I lived through it.

But the least noble thing I have done in my life was to turn to a razor blade. I have cut out and warped my supposed angel and fueled my devil so that neither of them will be the same. Mine is more of a neutral ending. It's not an entirely happy one, but not a suicide either. It is an ending of hope and worry. Not yet a conclusion, but an end to my troubles for now.

The Weather Report

Over the past few years, I have come to master the art of the slouch. I can adjust it to suit any situation. I exhibit my signature semi-slouch position daily—while signing a receipt at the checkout counter, taking a shower, or assessing my reflection in the locker-room mirror. The maneuver shaves off a good two or three inches and is just discreet enough to keep people from noticing. I even do it when I'm being measured at the doctor's office. My semi-slouch is stealthy and inconspicuous enough to preempt even a professional's order to "Stand up straight."

In addition to my semi-slouch, I take great pride in my periodically applied full slouch. The full slouch—one knee bent at a nearly 90-degree angle, hips jutting to the side opposite the bent knee, shoulders pulled down and forward, arms akimbo—is strictly for special occasions. I resort to it if I'm in the front row at a standing-room-only concert or when I actually want to look one of my many five-foot-tall friends in the eye.

I've always hated being tall. When I was a little girl, I would constantly get comments about how "big" I was, making me feel like some massive behemoth. I have never been able to purchase jeans without exposing nearly three inches of ankle, and I usually resort to sleeping in the fetal position because I get fed up with my feet hanging off the end of the bed. I graduated last from eighth grade because the order was determined by height. I've seen far more encroaching roots and dandruff-ridden scalps than most.

Plane rides can be challenging—even the inch-long increase in legroom on American Airlines hasn't solved my problem. If I were to sit normally, my knees would nearly penetrate the seat in front of me, making the flight objectionable for two people. Luckily I'm extremely flexible, so I can assume the butterfly position (provided I'm seated next to a family member) or I can twist my body into a pretzelesque configuration, which tends to be the most comfortable.

But it's the amount of clichéd commentary I get that really bothers me. People often feel compelled to inform me how tall I am. I usually reply, in the nicest way possible, that "yes," I am extremely tall, and "yes," I have been spitefully aware of that fact for seven years or so. I've been asked how the weather is up here. I've been told I'm destined to become or marry a basketball player. But the comment I get the most is "You'll appreciate your height when you're older." I never tell them that thus far, my height has refused to grow on me (pun intended).

Still, I have started to find a few ways to look at my height optimistically. As the tallest athlete at my all-girls school, I play center on the varsity basketball team; I care more about basketball than disproving the cliché. I can reach the top shelf in my closet and qualified at age seven for admission onto upside-down theme park rides. However, the single greatest advantage of my vertical loftiness is my personality. It's as if, since being welcomed into the world at my twenty-four-inch length, I've felt this intrinsic obligation to match my height with my presence in a room.

At four feet tall in kindergarten, I knew I was different. Not only were my fuchsia leggings and denim overalls shorter than those of the other girls, but I also noticed that I was more outspoken in class. I starred in *Cinderella*, the first of many musical theater performances, at age five. Each of my normal-size parents has acute stage fright, but I've always loved giving speeches (particularly handy during student council election season). My friends volunteer me, the outgoing one, to ask for directions, and I have never been known to turn down an opportunity to sing Spice Girls at karaoke.

This is not to say I've fully come to terms with my height—I doubt that will happen until I begin the process of age-induced shrinkage. However, I have finally realized that my personality is largely determinant on my height. And I have even found two instances where I can stand up straight: yoga class (impeccable posture is greatly encouraged), and at formal events where the majority of female attendees wear heels, making most of them (as well as my date) level with me in ballet flats.

Last year, when trying to decide on a college, I opened one of those voicey, tell-it-like-it-is guidebooks. I flipped to the page about the top school I was considering and read the sole quote about the student body: "Girls over 5' 8" beware, this school breeds midgets." Although I finally decided on attending the school, I haven't really had any problems. They even found me an extra-long twin bed.

Meike Schleiff, 19

The "Beautiful" Cause of Death That Had Me Dying for a While

~~~~~~

Our world is on the edge. So many things are out of proportion. So many of us no longer have families, no longer eat together, and are no longer satisfied with enough stuff. Many people have too little and many have more than they need. We're wrapped up in having clothes and cars. Young people pay outrageous amounts for a pair of jeans or invest in nurturing an iPod over real friends, generosity, and true love. Priorities continue to shift from qualities like leadership, kindness, and honesty to the extremes of ownership, personal property, and being thin.

I have noticed this, and it has deeply affected me. For a while I just observed and pondered. The world looked sad, suffering, tortured, judgmental, and unrelenting. I was at college beginning my sophomore year when the situation began to get out of hand.

Going from a fit, healthy self, I lost nearly a third of my body weight. I no longer wanted to eat, especially with people. I dreaded the cafeteria and each meal. I started going when I knew it would be quiet, for fresh fruit or a salad. I would only sit with friends who had been proven not to notice (or at least not to comment on) what I ate, or with people I didn't know at all. I counted calories fanatically and was constantly on the verge of collapse or tears. I ate less and less until it was just half a banana in the morning and some steamed vegetables or lettuce with vinegar on it in the evenings. The vinegar gave me stomachaches and acid reflux, but it was the only thing I would put on stuff anymore, because I knew it to contain no calories and no salt. Eating salt would mean gaining the weight in water my body would retain to metabolize it.

I felt unworthy of everything I had or needed, including food. My heated room, my pairs of expensive jeans that kept getting looser and looser, and my chance to study at a college where everything from my laundry to my meals were taken care of were all luxuries that I didn't deserve. I withdrew into my single dorm room, studied, exercised in the gym, or went running outside, running for hours, even when I was exhausted and my joints were hurting all the time. In the dead of winter, I would go on three- or four-hour hikes along the country roads around the campus in snow and on ice. I'd be falling and freezing and getting sick all the time. I couldn't relax enough to sit down and have a really nice, open conversation with a friend. I couldn't sleep at night because of hunger, nausea, headaches, and heart-wrenching dreams of loss, pain, and sadness. I was running away from snakes, the past, and myself constantly. I felt a core-deep confusion and despair.

No amount of weight loss was enough; any flesh or soft spot was too much. Part of me wanted to obliterate myself—becoming smaller was sometimes not satisfying enough. I would pick at any perceived bodily imperfections, like a freckle or a bug bite, until my thighs, upper arms, and face were bleeding and never got a chance to heal. I was out of control. I could suddenly understand why people would slash themselves, torture themselves, or destroy their bodies: why they would commit suicide.

Many of my relationships suffered or died because of my inability to be part of life. My friends got worried and started hovering, judging me and what I ate, which changed what we did together. I no longer wanted to have parties, watch movies and eat popcorn, go out to dinner, or even just stay up late hanging out.

I'd had a boyfriend the year before, and it was a very rough relationship. He was the one who started me on the ideas of working out and dieting to be like models and movie stars. He got more and more controlling and violent until he raped me. Later, when my eating disorders were out of hand, that was all over, but he was still on the same campus. He started expressing interest in me again during this time, at my sickest. He'd follow me down the halls, whistling and calling me "hot," telling me things like, "You look so sexy lately, you should really keep it up."

Everything hurt—physically and emotionally. Just sitting on a chair without cushioning was torture. By Thanksgiving, after a semester of teetering, I was at the bottom. I felt no love for myself, for my family and friends. I was completely removed from the life I'd known, and worse, I had no idea how it had changed so much so quickly. My mother sent me to doctors who could find nothing seriously wrong. They said I was really thin and that they could feel a lot of things that you couldn't feel in most people (like my vertebrae through my stomach), but they let me go. They did blood work, which came out borderline or low in some cases, but nothing to be really worried over.

I was missing my menstrual cycle, my skin was yellowing, my hair was falling out. Everything ached, and I was cold all the time. I insisted I was fine, didn't tell or show anything that was not demanded. My mother threatened to not let me go back to school if I didn't get better. She said, "It's nice to be thin, but not this thin." My father tried to talk me out of the place I was stuck in and told me that I was "not a very nice person to live with," meaning I was no longer my old bright, happy kid-self. My parents had brought me up to know what society expects of a young lady: thin, pretty, smart, but not sticking-out funny, not in disagreement with the status quo. I remember little things they'd said and done through the years, like telling me to hold in my stomach and not to make faces that weren't attractive, to reinforce those messages. They had always wanted me to succeed in the world, to have an easy way, to be prepared, and now it had all backfired. Perhaps, I reasoned, gaining control over my body, growing smaller and withdrawing, would help. I wanted no one and nothing except a way out of myself. Sometimes dying seemed like an easier path than facing this life.

Being at home that Christmas broke the pattern and gave me a chance to reevaluate. My family had all meals together, I could cook again, and I got to care for the animals on our farm. I had many friends and got a lot of attention because of how I looked and the rumors that had circulated that I was sick. I started wanting people to see that something was bothering me. I was so tired. Maybe someone else could fix this for me. I struggled, thought, and listened to others for a while. Could I maybe be somebody with a laugh and some love again? I tried the smallest spoonfuls of chocolate and peanut butter, and they tasted so good! I switched colleges so that I could start over. I made new friends, and I ate better. I thought it was over.

Then I began to have a different problem. Every once in a while I would binge on sweets and other foods I loved and craved. The binge-ing got worse, and I started finding ways to hide it, to throw it up, and to fast later to make up for it. At first it wasn't too bad, but I got into a pattern and it felt horrible. Compared to how I'd been eating, even, this seemed extreme and terrible. I gained weight back and felt less in control than I had before. The problem was still there, but now it didn't show as much outwardly, so I no longer got the attention or support.

I remember taking ipecac syrup, and even swallowing laundry soap on one occasion, to make myself throw up. It was torture and I could no longer tell anything about what my body needed because it was so confused and poisoned. I would have terrible mood swings, blood sugar ups and downs. I blacked out at work once over the sum-mer, and I could not sleep. And the weight didn't come off.

I finally had to lay it out honestly to some people I trusted. I told an old family friend who's a doctor, I told some close peers, and I told my parents enough that they could attempt to understand. Saying it out loud was a battle. Everything until then had relied on hiding and secrets, so the truth came out haltingly, painfully, in bits and pieces.

So at the beginning some people, including me, underestimated the problem. Perseverance in bringing out the whole truth was the hardest part because it hurt me and those I was trying to tell.

However, once it was out in the open, the issue—that I was suffering from anorexia and bulimia—looked different. It wasn't solved, but it was no longer me fighting with myself and my body and the world all alone. It's a slow process to heal and change, and sometimes it's still so overwhelming that I don't know if it's worth the fight. The feelings and some behaviors are not gone, but they do not rule my life anymore. I still have harder days and worry sometimes what others think or that I am still not perfect. It does get better, though, through conscious effort, group support, and the desire to do something good for the world. On my path to recovery I threw away my scale, which used to be the measure of how worthy I was, and I vowed never to own one or to step on one again. I haven't yet.

I get strength from those who have gone before me and overcome this. I've had to stop trying to live up to the ideals that society sets for young people. There is no integrity in the clothes and makeup you wear. There is no true love in the TV scenes between the ideal cast man and the ideal cast woman. And, most important, who really wants to be miserable, weak, sick, and at risk of dying to look a certain way and get attention? Just think how much more you could contribute to the world by being healthy and able to energetically pursue a career and a life doing something you're passionate about.

What makes me the saddest is to see the many others who struggle with the same feelings. Celebrities, models, my friends, classmates, so many people get and promote the message that you have to be thin to be beautiful, to be perfect, to be loved. Anorexia can kill you, seriously. Models faint on the runway and die from it. Celebrities cannot have any time or space to think, heal, or bond with their new babies instead of their trainers. These are only the ones we hear about; there must be so many more.

The good news is that my eating disorder—others are the same—was an invading lie about what I had to do in order to feel better, be special, fit in. It was not my true self speaking, so it lost much of its power when I let who I really was step forward. The lie can be very strong if you feed it, but it remains only a lie. The truth is much stronger and makes for a lovely life.

I try to hang on to the high moments, when the old feelings are overcome and the world feels happy and hopeful. It takes time, sometimes years, experiments, and mistakes to find the right path. And it takes help. Trying to stand alone in this for so long, to spare others the pain or to hide what was going on, was probably my biggest mistake.

Now that I feel the freedom of living, I suddenly understand how wrong it is to be miserable. Deep, delicious inhales of fresh air and a sense of gratitude for everything that exists are the best feelings in the world—and they do come. I want to reach out so that someone somewhere will breathe more easily because I have lived. Then I will feel that I have succeeded, which is something that my eating disorders have never and will never be able to do for me.

People You Have to Live with and Other Family

Alicia Davis, 13

Country

~~~~~~~

I won't sugarcoat the truth, I won't dramatize reality. If you're looking for a story overflowing with sentiment and dripping with sorrow, then you'd better stop reading now. I write only my feelings, only how I perceive my life and others.

Family is important to me; it is my top priority. My dad, though, is the furthest thing from my mind. I tell all of my friends and family that I love them, and I say it with the utmost sincerity. I've never told my dad that and been honest.

I have no real reason not to like him. There is no tale of horror, of abuse or foul treatment, behind this. Plainly and simply, I just don't like him. He thinks he is always right and that he can do no wrong. He is short-tempered, robotic, rude.

I would give many things to say that he is my stepfather. Then it would be OK for me to detest him. However, this is my real dad, and I know only too well how wrong it is for me to dislike him. A child is supposed to love her parents, just as the sun is supposed to shine. It is wrong to not love a parent. Well, then, I guess I'm wrong.

And I guess things sometimes change in time—time, music, and love.

Family is important to me; it is my top priority. My mom, sisters, cousins—my dad—everyone is included. I tell all of my friends and family that I love them, and I say it with the utmost sincerity. I really do care for each and every one of them.

I like my dad now. There is no wall of animosity between us, just a small cloud of irritation that comes and goes. Plainly and simply, we are companions. He is intelligent though cocky. He takes care of his family. He tries to control his temper, but it can get the better of him. He does have a heart, although at times it becomes hidden.

I would give many things to say that I love my father uncondition-ally. But then life would be perfect, and we all know that's impossible. However, our relationship has gone from dislike and anger to some odd form of love. It is correct for a child to cherish her parent. Well, then, I guess I'm halfway there.

My dad forced me to start singing with him. He plays in a band—him and a few of his friends. Their music is country, a genre that I don't like. At first I resisted and despised the act, but sometimes I wouldn't be able to find an excuse and I'd have to participate. I'd sing. Over time, however, I gave in and actually enjoyed myself. It became fun enough, because I liked the connection it created be-tween me and my dad. It was then that I realized he really does love me. He'd just been struggling to find something for us to do to-gether, allowing us to close the canyon that had formed. It has in-deed shrunk, but it still has a way to go. All the makings of a good country song.

Claudia Berger, 14

The News

~~~~~~~

It was the day after Christmas, so I opened my eyes to see a pile of new things—CDs, clothes, books, and much more. I remember thinking I couldn't wait to try out my new tarot set. But I was too hungry to do that. I went downstairs to get some breakfast. I saw my parents. They looked worried. They weren't saying anything, just sitting there in silence watching the TV, their faces tense. The TV was showing all of these pictures of water and destruction. I asked what it was; it didn't look like the movie we'd rented the night before.

"The news. There was a tsunami and an earthquake," one of my parents, I'm not sure which, replied.

"Where?"

Then my mom, in a shaky voice: "Thailand."

My sister was in Thailand, on vacation with her friend and her friend's family. Wait, where in Thailand was she? Where was the tsunami? That last picture, of the wave hitting the hotel, makes it seem pretty serious. They just said it was the biggest in one hundred years. Serious. What if Nathalie is not OK? If she is OK, why isn't anyone telling me? Oh my god, she could be dead. I might never see my sister again. What if they don't find the body? There would be no closure to her life or anything.

I went numb. I had no body. I felt like I was just a head. I knew I had a head, because horrible thoughts were filling it to the bursting point. I couldn't watch the news with its wall of water—knocking down this building and killing these people, flooding a town, tearing down trees and drowning animals. But I couldn't look away for fear of missing an important detail. My mom told me Nathalie was in the area. She'd called home right after the first wave—she was OK—but before the second. That was hours ago.

When my grandparents (who were staying with us for the holidays) woke up we all just huddled an inch from the TV; its pictures seemed to come straight out of a horror story. Snippets from home videos showed the terrible wave hitting the beach while people just stood there, taking pictures, not realizing their fate until way too late. Images of dead people and animals floating in the mess the water left behind were played over and over again as a voice told the terrible stories and the miracle stories. Some people had gone out toward the wave in boats, hoping to meet it and ride it out before it became all-powerful. Scuba divers inadvertently underneath had survived. People desperately tried to hold on to pieces as their houses floated away.

In my house, no one seemed to remember I was there. I forgot, too. I felt numb and invisible, even to myself. I was hoping that all of a sudden the newscasters would shout out, "Just kidding!" But no. Or I wished that I would wake up in my bed and be like, I had the weirdest dream but I can't really remember it.

My sister was in Thailand. There was a tsunami there. Millions had died. She was only sixteen. I put two and two together and came up with no sister. When was the last time I'd talked to her? We'd had a fight about some stupid thing, like what to do for dinner or something, and we didn't really say good-bye. We didn't hug or anything. She just sort of left. It was as if she'd be gone for the morning, not for all of December. Oh my god. I may never see my sister again, and one of the last things I'd said to her was "I hate you and I'm glad you're leaving." I am an awful sister. Karma was going to get me sometime. Maybe it was getting me now.

Days went by, blended together. Why isn't anyone telling me anything? She's dead, that's why; she's dead because the second wave got her. They don't know how to tell me. I woke up on one of those mornings. I stormed right into the kitchen and demanded, "Is she dead?"

"No," my mom said, an empty breakfast bowl in front of her for the first time in ages. "We just heard from her. She's fine!"

You know the saying "It felt like a ton of bricks were lifted off me"? Well, finding out your sister's alive when you thought she was dead feels like a 100-ton bag of them just goes away. I was floating. Then I crashed when I realized that she could be seriously traumatized. She still had to find her way home; she could get lost.

For the next few days, no one said much to me. I didn't do much. I watched the news, trying to find out all I could. We didn't really ever sit down as a family. We ate on our own, and during the day we were just there. My grandmother would try to make sure I performed the daily functions—eating, sleeping, showering—but otherwise no one paid me any attention. I understood that they were worried about Nathalie and had sort of forgotten about me, but I still didn't really know what was going on.

Tons of people, family and friends, called to find out if she was all right. My parents told the callers more than they told me. They spoke to each person for forty minutes to an hour and to me for no more than ten minutes. I tried to listen but gave up after three calls. I found out most of what I knew, like that Nathalie was in Bangkok trying to get home, through my grandparents. They wanted me to be OK, but of course I wasn't. I was terrified. I couldn't sleep. Pictures from the news would go through my mind day and night. I would see my sister's body floating, or I would hear her screaming. I felt like I was going crazy, like I'd lost my mind. I could already tell so much had changed.

A few days later, about a week after the tsunami, Nathalie walked in our front door. I gave her the longest hug I've ever given someone. I told her I loved her and how scared I'd been. My mom made her favorite meal, fatty noodles. My sister told us she'd lost most of what she'd packed, not in the wave but in the wave of thefts after it. At dessert she gave me a dress and some bangle bracelets that she'd bought in one of the Thai markets and hung on to.

In the following months, everyone was worried about my sister— her grades and any lasting psychological effects of the trauma. I understood, of course. At first she couldn't stand water. She wouldn't even go near our grandparents' house on the bay. And she had terrible nightmares. But not once did my mom ask me if I was all right. I went into a sort of depression, and the sense of helplessness never ceased. Whenever I tried to do homework or anything else, I felt like I wasn't good enough. I kept to my room, and I couldn't focus on anything. I hated school for the first time.

Finally, when my mom noticed, we talked. I can't remember what was said, but I remember I had waited so long to just cry on my mom's shoulder that I forgot how to do anything else for a few minutes. We realized that the tsunami had affected more than one person in the house. I needed a fresh start, because everything at school reminded me of that time and that feeling of hopelessness. So my mom and I started to look at schools. Once I switched, I found it easier to go back to the way I was.

Now, in our house, it seems as though we just cut that winter break right out of our lives. We don't talk about what happened, and none of us are closer or further apart because of it. But what doesn't kill you makes you stronger. Nathalie has gotten over her fear of water. She went away to college in New Orleans, just a year after Katrina. I was proud of her, thrilled to see her move on. But in the months after she left, I kept thinking about another storm hitting, and I still sometimes have dreams of that wave that washed everything away.

Hannah Morris, 15

The Two of Us

~~~~~~~

Sarah is my twin sister. She's my best friend, my inner mirror. Think about that for a moment. *Inner* mirror? Aren't twins, like, identical on the outside? Well, you would think. We are biologically identical twins, even if it takes convincing for other people to see it. But Sarah is definitely the better looker, and I only wish I could catch up. In truth, though, it doesn't bother me all that much. When the time comes that I want to get serious about my looks, I'll change. End of story.

We're a pair. A match. Life is better when we're together. More fun. More exciting. More challenging. More heartfelt. It's tougher. Stranger. Sadder. More wonderful.

Sure, we argue, we yell, we annoy each other on a daily basis. Though we can never stay mad for long. Being teenagers, the bulk of our disagreements involve who owes who money—not cash, but things like whose turn it is to pay for Starbucks. Our parents will come running into the room, thinking from all the screaming that we're ready to kill each other. But then we laugh and we try to explain. People usually don't understand.

I can tell Sarah anything. It's hard to keep things from each other, and we both know what's said in confidentiality stays that way. Why go through something alone when there's someone you can trust to be with you? Plus, we both play soccer, we both love band, and we're suckers for a chance to hang out with friends.

And I must say, we both love guys. A lot. We're teenage girls!

Our minds are 75 percent guys, 25 percent every girl emotion you can think of. When a hot guy walks by (tall, perfect face, bold eyes, you know the type), all it takes is a quick glance from each other to know we're thinking the exact same thing: WHOA. That is one long conversation in which not even a word is exchanged.

We pretty much have the same friends, too. What does get annoying, though, is a few of our friends see us as a package. If one of us is missing, they can't resist asking the whereabouts of the other.

Have I mentioned that we also have a brother? Yeah, Ben. He's tough to live with and does things the two of us don't approve of. I don't understand how or why he became this way, seeing as we were all brought up together and he's only fifteen months older than we are. Maybe the difference was that Sarah and I had each other. He didn't have anyone. Conflict in our house is always Me vs. Ben or Sarah vs. Ben. Or even our parents vs. Ben. Never has it been Me vs. Sarah. I guess we can blame ourselves for not getting along better with him; it could have made all the difference. We know that if Ben keeps this up he will destroy his life. The worst part is, we try to act like it doesn't bother us when he's smoking or something. But it does, and nothing we say to him—Sarah's partial to "You smell like cancer"—seems to spark a change.

And it's not like what he does is a big secret. The two of us can't go a week without someone from school sharing another story of a certain anonymous "this guy" in another questionable situation. They seem to find whatever he's done hilarious, whereas nothing has ever been so unfunny to me. I hope our brother reads this and understands. I hope his friends read this and get serious about their lives. And I hope the world reads this and stops to think for a moment about what they are doing to themselves, to others, to the ones they care about.

Sarah is my sister. My best friend. My soulmate. If we go away to different colleges we'll never live more than two days without a phone call. When we start our own families, we'll never spend a holiday apart. Our friends, based on what they've seen between Sarah and me, often tell us how much they wish they had a twin. But we know that what we have is completely ours.

To See How They Look
on Me, on You

~~~~~~~

"So, what's it like to have a twin?"

I hear this question and ones similar to it whenever I meet someone new. I usually say that it's "fun," or "like having a best friend who I can yell at and fight with." This answer, for the most part, is suitable to anyone who hears it. They move on to other things from there.

I am fifteen years old, five feet four inches tall. I'm thin, with fair skin and a pretty smile. My twin sister, Hannah, is five feet six inches, same fair skin, a beautiful smile as well, but she's larger by about forty pounds. I wear size 5 jeans, and she wears 15s. I wear small shirts; she's L to XL. The sole difference between us, really, leads many people into awkward astonishment when they find out we're identical twins.

I can't possibly sum up the love and respect I have for my sister. Our inner similarities are uncanny. But our outer differences sometimes bother me. It's not like I wish she looked exactly like me; I enjoy being different and not having to have our own friends play that game of guess who Hannah is and guess who Sarah is. But I care for her so much, and I just don't want her to get hurt or made fun of. Our brother, Ben, often says nasty things about her. I know for a fact that when he talks about us to his friends, Hannah's "the fat one." Just the other day I passed him in the hall at school, and the guy he was with asked if I was his sister, and Ben replied, "Yeah, this is the skinny one."

Except by looks, Hannah is just like me. We don't have our own twin language or telepathy or any other nonsense like that. We have what I like to call an understanding. We basically share a sense of humor. One time we went to see *War of the Worlds* in the theater, and the scene where Tom Cruise throws the peanut butter sandwich at the window made both of us laugh uncontrollably for about five minutes. It wasn't that funny, and while everyone else gave it a little chuckle, we spazzed out. Also, when I see something I like, she likes it too, especially when it comes to guys. We'll sort of rate their hotness just by looking at each other. Usually Hannah is more generous than I am with her rating; I'm a tough person to please.

Our friends think it's weird for two sisters to be so immensely close. We have secrets between us that no one else would trust to even their closest and longest friend. People tend to always have an opinion of someone or something, but they won't say it out loud because it may sound mean or scary or strange. It would be impossible for Hannah or me to freak each other out like this. After a big event, or if something is bothering one of us, it's customary for us to go to my room, close the door, sit on the bed, and talk it through in whispers. Even in the morning, Hannah brings her clothes for school into my room and we get ready together.

I wish Hannah were the same size as me, because she is *so* pretty, and if she just loses the weight, then I wouldn't feel like I had to protect her. I mean, don't get me wrong, she's really not made fun of by anyone, at least not that I know of. She has a lot of friends who love her and would never hurt her. But she hasn't really had a boyfriend, and I know it's horrible for me so say, but I don't think she will have one unless she loses some more weight.

When Hannah and I were younger, we were about the same size. Actually, we were about the same size until sixth or seventh grade. Then, with the pressures of middle and high school coming into view, I decided to start watching what I ate and became more active. I took soccer more seriously and would go out running on my own sometimes. I became aware of what I was putting into my body and gave up a lot of foods when I saw how high the calorie or fat content was. That summer I lost about twenty-five pounds. Hannah, on the other hand, got bigger. I'd tell her often that whatever she was eating had a lot of fat in it, but she usually didn't listen. I don't think she was ready to take such criticism. Every so often I'd step back and look at her, then launch another effort to push her to lose weight. And she'd get angry with me. We'd discovered the one subject we didn't agree on.

One time while we were on vacation in Toronto, I was lying awake in bed thinking about how much I wanted Hannah to lose the weight. I got up and went into the next room to wake her and tell her how strongly I felt. I was so upset and worried about what the future would bring for her that I started crying. I laid it out that if she doesn't lose the weight now, she'll have to lose it later, when it will only be more difficult. That night she agreed with me, and we came up with a diet plan. We'd do it together; I'd offer support and show her that if I could stick to it, then so could she.

After a few days, we both failed on our promise to stay with the plan, and it crashed. I'm saying that it's my fault, too, for not pushing her hard enough and not setting a good example. I know some people would argue that if I really loved Hannah, then I would honor her choices. But it's not enough to just step aside and watch someone you love pretend to be happy.

The good news is that just recently Hannah has taken the initiative to get into shape. She's dropped down to about 160, and she looks amazing. I love to just look at her now and think, Wow! And I'm almost positive that if I can be 125 pounds, so can she.

I really want Hannah to get attention from those boys that we talk about. I want her to be happy and successful in life. I want her to be confident. I want her to be able to wear nice form-fitting clothes, which she can share with me. I want her to get into nightclubs when we get older. I want her to be able to run an eight-minute mile. I want to, just once, confuse people and switch places. I want to look alike because I don't know how that feels.

I want so much. This makes me very selfish, I know, wanting so much. But if Hannah could just want it, too, then I could rest easy.

It's funny, we have this joke that if there's no mirror around and we want to try on a pair of sunglasses or something—even though we don't look alike—we'll ask the other, "Put these on, I want to see how they look on me." Hannah will try anything on for me. Hannah looks out for me.

"So, what's it like to have a twin?" Having a twin is like having a best friend who's your age, lives with you, and is your sister. Are you in the same school and classes? Some. Do you copy each other's homework? No. Do you have your own language or telepathy? No. Would you do anything for each other? Yes. Do you love each other unconditionally and to an end that no other creature on this planet can possibly know? Yes. Will I ever be able to understand this bond? No.

Emma Considine, 16

Bloody Red Heart

~~~~~~

The separated family is a seemingly taboo topic, morally wrong. But look around, everyone's doing it, it's a fucking fad! Take my family, for instance. It is the reason for lost earrings, homework assignments left unfinished because the textbook is at Dad's, and aching legs due to walking from one cramped house to another five times a day. My separated family wouldn't function without twenty phone calls a day, concerning Geico, school tuition, and what Emma wants for Christmas. It smells like stress and is the reason for my unhappy elementary school years. My expensive family, my impractical family, my idiotic family, my depressed family, my dysfunctional family, my embarrassing family.

The basic separation comes with the following accessories: two rent checks, a miserable ten-year-old, a nosy babysitter, unsigned divorce papers, lots and lots of phones (three cell, four cordless), one pissed-off wife, cat food, adultery, one lonely husband, eight confusing Thanksgivings and counting, two guilty parents, a move, a car, a slamming door, a mouth.

The daughter of separated parents is not easy to spot. She can wear expensive jeans and speak English, just like her friends whose parents live under the same roof. Oddly enough, she looks like a regular sixteen-year-old. Her epidermis is still showing, and she has a functioning bloody red heart. However, according to statistics, she may not be able to use it as well as some of her friends.

Getting out of the car, he picked me up and put me on his shoulders like I'd begged him to. In my hands was a book on Helen Keller. Even though I was only four, I loved reading more than anything else. That and when my parents got along.

"Be careful," she warned, lifting grocery bags out of the trunk.

Almost as if in a demented sitcom, he tripped on a stone just as she said it. He fell slowly, landing on his knees and scraping them on the pavement, not able to make his collapse graceful because he was holding so tightly on to my legs. I remember starting to cry, not because I was traumatized or hurt, but because he was bleeding on his hands and knees.

She rushed over. "I told you to be careful!" she hissed at him.

Then she grabbed my hand and opened the door to the house. "Are you OK, sweetie?" she asked. I could hardly look at her. She'd left him outside bleeding on the ground, when it was obvious that I was fine.

"Stop!" I cried and pushed away from her, running.

"Always going to daddy," she said, rolling her eyes. "Never listening to *me*."

The separated family has many uses. It's a way to get more presents, sneak out of the house, guilt-trip parents, become forty dollars richer, get out of a homework assignment, and have a good cry. The separated family is all over the nation, in every 7-Eleven, public school, volleyball tournament, and perfume store.

It splits up friends, ruins Christmas, and makes money tight. People sympathize, and the occasional friend wishes that her parents were divorced, too. No she doesn't. It takes weeks, months, years to get over the fact that you will never have a family that's intact again. Your mom is never going to marry some architect with five kids and start her own little Brady Bunch, and even if she did, you wouldn't be fine with it. You'd cry. You'd ditch the wedding. You'd be sent to a therapist.

Every divorced family contains at least three brains. Handy, but two of those brains are the reason you can't hire a tutor for two hundred dollars a session. (Your parents have to pay twice the rent now.) Those brains ruined second, third, and fourth grades. Those brains agree on the Bush administration, the science department at your school, and cats. Those brains don't agree on what's for dinner, who's going to park the car, and my grandpa's cancer. One has to outweigh the other.

That's why the third brain is so sad, why it feels so cut off. Its parents screwed it over. Some doctors did a lot of tests and determined that brains with divorced parents face a 70 percent greater chance of having a failed relationship when they grow up. It doesn't make sense. It was eight years ago. The times they are a-changin'. How will my mom's stupid mistakes account for my future? What a bitch.

Mascara Wands Are Instruments of War

~~~~~~

Mother-daughter relationships are famous for one thing, really: conflict. It's like war, except personal. Too personal sometimes. Because moms and daughters know each other so well (or think they do), they often don't realize when they've crossed the line from the argument so familiar they could quote both sides of it into something else. You know the drill. The two of you start arguing over that worn-out jacket you just will not get rid of. It's the same discussion you've been having for a year, with her calling you a pack rat and you slamming the door in her face. But then she says something else, something like, "You need to let go of it, honey."

And then? Boom. Does she really think you're holding on too tightly? Does she think you're living *your whole life* in the past tense? This is not a fight anymore, because fights come and go, and the in-between time is fine. It's a war. And in between each battle it nags at you, maybe just a little bit, but a little bit too much.

That my mother and I fight is no exception, but it isn't the sort you think of as oh-so-typical with teenagers and their mothers. Instead of her insisting that "It's what's on the inside that counts" and telling me I focus too much on my appearance, with us it's the opposite. As in, I don't focus enough on my appearance. I inherited my mother's brown eyes, brown hair (even if mine's nearly black), and her skinny gene. But my typical beauty routine consists of lip gloss, a brushed-but-frizzed-out head of hair, cover-up for my, uh, blemishes, and blush when I remember. I don't mess with my hair and makeup as much as my mom would like ("Experiment!" she encourages), and clothes are almost the last thing on my mind.

But her? She actually wears *makeup*—foundation, blush, eye shadow, the whole shebang. Her hair, as much as she claims otherwise, is always done. Then there are the bracelets and handbags that perfectly complement the clothes she loves to shop for, unlike some people.

The thing about it is, at least for me, we're already so entrenched in the war that it stops being about mascara and jewelry at all. Now it's about *us*. And that's scary. Sure, she's just telling me how great I'd look if I "opened up" my eyes a bit, but to me it's more than that. I'm starting to worry that maybe that's all she sees when she looks at me: a girl with no mascara. That's not fair to her, of course, but that's not the point. When it's all I'm thinking, it may as well be true.

She asks, "How are you going to do your hair?" but what I hear is: You're not good enough the way you are. You're not pretty enough. By then the words in translation have sunk deeper and become more powerful than every time she's told me that I'm wonderful or beautiful.

But I can't tell her that. It's not something I could mention oh-so-casually as we're in the car listening to NPR (her station, not mine): "Oh, by the way, you have this knack for making me feel ugly and worthless. I know you don't *mean* to, but you do." At least not without risking something huge—the unspoken balance we have. It's my it-hurts-me-but-I-won't-let-you-know-just-how-bad policy.

The fact is, she just doesn't realize that so often the things she thinks are normal, the little things that make girls feel pretty, I just don't care all that much about. And it's not because I don't think I'm worth it or that I have so much self-esteem that it doesn't even matter. It's just that sometimes those girl-treat things make me feel more flawed, more self-conscious. Other times, to be perfectly honest, it's as simple as *I really just don't care*. And that's the part she doesn't seem to get—when there's no reason I don't want to mess with the curling iron. I just *don't.*

Still, I'm not so wrapped up in myself to think she's the only guilty one in this war. I'm sure I hurt her, too, though she doesn't show it either. Maybe it's the way I bug her when she takes so long to get ready. Maybe it's the way I walk out on her when she's trying her very best to fix my hair (which I messed up, somehow). Maybe when I say I don't feel like wearing makeup she's hearing something like, I don't want to be anything like you. Who knows?

The reality of it is that my mother, cliché as it may be, is the most beautiful woman (on the outside and the inside) I know. When I look at her and think, *she's so beautiful,* it's partly because, well, she is. But it's mostly because she's someone who gets excited about watching chick flicks or black-and-white movies on TCM with me. She's the sort of mom who buys me chocolate when I have my period. The sort of mom who, when I'm in a funk, drives me absolutely crazy wanting to help, even though there's nothing she can do. As much as I want to be like her in so many ways, she's impossible to live up to.

And that's why the simplest comments can hit me at my core. Because she's my *mom,* for crying out loud, and I'm her overanalytical daughter who has problems taking her words at face value. A typical exchange (or fight, if you want to put it that way):

"Why don't you put your hair up?" That's her, and we're standing in her bathroom in front of that huge mirror.

"I don't know," I'll say, shrugging. "I didn't think about it. Should I?"

"Yeah, I think it would look better." She says this as she reflexively curls the stray hairs that won't stay curled.

"Does it look bad?" I look at myself in the mirror and realize that, *yes, my hair does look frizzy and flat and . . . weird.*

"Not bad, just . . . it could look better." My mother is a sugarcoater.

"OK, so you're saying it looks bad?"

"It would look *so cute* if you used one of those big clips I have in that drawer." She points with her toes because she's still holding the curling iron up above her head.

So I'll take the big clip—even though I feel like crying, which, admittedly, is pretty pathetic—and I'll try to do something with my hair. Something that looks halfway decent. It never works, of course, and I end up taking it down, wearing it frizzy and falling around my shoulders. While her hair (and my little sister's) looks perfectly perfect. I hate feeling like a disappointment, even though I know our conversation has been about hair and I'm taking it the wrong way.

That's why I wrote this essay. Because I was mad and because I had to let it all out. But then my mom read it, and there were tears. I hated to see her cry. *Hated it*. Especially since it was all my fault. If I'd chosen to write about almost anything but her, she'd have been fine with it. Except that we'd still fight, and we'd still fight over the same things we do. We always will. Last week she came in my room, gave me a hug, and made a point of telling me I was beautiful on the inside *and* the outside. I believed her. I thanked her. Then she brushed a stray hair out of my face.

The Fourth Floor

~~~~~~~

The elevator thumped rhythmically as the numbers lit up, counting down three ... two ... one ... I flipped the quarter in my pocket in time with the descent until the doors opened onto the deserted hospital lobby. I passed my favorite fountain with hardly a glance. Across the depressingly colorful carpeting, the sliding doors to the cafeteria opened as an important-looking person in a white coat hurried out. The doctor was already partially done with his lunch, eating even as he walked, like my father did when he was the physician on duty.

The cafeteria was quiet except for the hum of coolers and heat lamps, some muffled footsteps, and bits of conversation seeping in from beyond the sliding doors. I dutifully picked out a chicken salad for my mother; I sprinkled the requisite fruits and nuts on top. Then I found the soup of the day—I should know what Wednesday's was by now—for my father and went to the cash register. I waited for someone to come check me out. Finally a sleepy young woman emerged from behind an "Employees Only" door, still holding half of a sandwich. She rang me up, all the while muttering about the useless shift she worked.

I went off to sit on the edge of the fountain to rearrange my armload of food and count my change. I had just enough to buy a cup of soft-serve ice cream. The flavors changed every two weeks, and yesterday the machine label had been switched to "spring mint," a flavor I checked for as often as I was in the cafeteria. I went back in and made myself a cup, just a small one, for its dual purposes of costing less and being quicker to finish. My mother hadn't forbidden me to buy something for myself, but I wasn't ready to go back up to the room just yet. Going back meant reading by the window or playing with the broken old dollhouse from the Child Life ward, half its pieces missing. After three straight days of boredom, in one room with my family, I grasped at even the smallest change of scenery and independence.

I took my ice cream back to the fountain and perched on the side. As I trailed my fingers in the water, I watched the little brass wheel turning, dropping minuscule bucketfuls into a basin. A copper child was climbing up the side of the structure, her skirt permanently blown out by a gust of wind. I knew this fountain by heart and, as much as I loved it compared to a lot of things around, there's only so excited you can get about a fountain in a hospital lobby. Right then my greatest wish (within bounds) was to have unlimited access to explore, with an excuse to do so. Instead I had no access, no reason, and not a lot of time. I wandered over to the elevator and pressed the button.

Inside, it was the smooth feel of ice cream in my mouth that persuaded me. I'd already made one independent decision, and right then I made another. My fingers scanned up the row, past the number-three button where I knew I should get off, and nervously chose four. Such a simple act, yet pushing that button immediately made me feel like a rebel, giddy and tense with adrenaline. I couldn't hold still, bouncing on my toes. The elevator rose excruciatingly slowly.

I don't know what I'd been expecting, but it certainly wasn't what I stepped into. The fourth floor was undoubtedly and by far the most beautiful part of the hospital. There were bright painted murals and an entire wall of full-length windows looking out across the valley. The carpet was a dark pinkish purple, rather than the gray or color mess of so many other corridors, and the wooden floor part was bathed in sun from a peaked skylight. Even the air was better, fresher than the kind down below. I stashed the cafeteria food behind a potted plant and wandered over to the giant windows. Salt Lake City is in a bowl of mountains, and the hospital is perched about halfway up one of the northern rims. On a clear spring day like this, you could see out over the valley, all the way to the purple peaks that form the western and southern arcs of the bowl. Between them, the city lay spread out, grids of houses surrounding our meager excuse for a downtown. Looking up from my height, it was just possible to discern a corner of the helicopter pad on the roof.

It occurred to me that the hospital ranked floors in order of importance. Nothing crucial or interesting ever happened on the first floor, where I routinely went for my brother's appointments. The dirty-white walls were lit solely by fluorescent bulbs, since doctors' offices and clinics had stolen all of the windows. The second floor, where we got surgery briefings and patient-family classes, rated slightly higher. Here they had at least attempted to liven the hallways with paintings of kites and planes and animals, even though a lot of them were obscured by the plastic that isolated areas under construction. The third floor was patient rooms—originally interesting with its maze-like corridors but eventually mundane because I'd spent the last week wandering there.

The fourth floor, with all of its mountain views and sunny entrances and architect-considered skylights, must be the most important. A sign indicated ICU to the left, and NICU to the right. Clearly the inner sanctum of this already exclusive hospital, the fourth floor also made me feel like an intruder. It gave me the distinct sense that the doctors and nurses who hurried past knew that I had no business being there, no matter how hard I tried to look like I belonged—just looking out the window before moving on. I was too clothed and healthy to be a patient, too alone to be visiting family, too young to be an employee. No white coat, no green scrubs, no yellow visitor gown. No reason to be up there. My guilt increased until I could almost feel it pushing me back downstairs. I retrieved my dad's soup and my mom's salad and got in the elevator.

On three, I took my favorite roundabout route, past Child Life and through the weave of hallways until finally I stepped over the dark threshold into my brother's room. I wiped my hands on my skirt and entered. No more than twenty minutes had passed, but it felt like twice as long. I handed my parents their lunches, and my mother asked what had taken so long. I knew they hadn't been worrying much about me, though, because I could see dried blood and rumpled bedclothes—evidence of a recent consciousness in my now-sleeping brother. I shrugged and told her, "There was a line."

My brother's ninth surgery accomplished what the other eight had not. And yet, despite the relief of now having a healthy sibling, some part of me desperately misses those trips to the hospital. I've never been back to the in-patient department or had a chance to re-visit that top floor. But the image remains vivid. And whenever I think of intensive care, especially the NICU with all the babies on ventilators, I imagine them up there in a room filled with sunlight streaming from the windows, breathing rarified air on the most important floor.

Pots and Pans

~~~~~~~

A family gathering at House L in Hialeah, Florida—at least twenty loud, festive Cubans and a drum set consisting of pots and pans—can be quite the scene for any normal person to endure. Normal, of course, meaning anyone who's not my relative. I imagine it's a little like the anxiety you'd feel if you were trapped in a steam chamber with no air vent and a strong scent of rice seasoning.

I often skip family dinners like this. I can't help picturing certain kids in my class watching and judging, and the whole thing can remind me of the most shameful day of my childhood life: sitting with my mother on a park bench at my father's company picnic, the only Hispanics present. My mother spoke only Spanish and wasn't able to communicate with the other mothers. She urged me to play with the blue-eyed children, whose parents all knew each other, but they stared at me from the laps of their pinch-nosed mothers. I simply bowed my head and continued to pick at my melting cherry snow cone. They made me feel ashamed to be different, something I thought I could never overcome.

But on the night of July 30th last year, my mother's birthday, something sparked within me that I would never have believed. I'd decided to join my family, who were wrapped around a long table in the Florida room. Yes, we call it that, even though we live in Florida. The room is adorned with angel statuettes—some giant and glittered, others smaller and at least relatively subtle—in every possible space, because my mother spends most, if not all, of her time and money collecting these figurines.

We had assumed our usual seating arrangements: The elder man of the house, my father, was at the foot of the table. Like nearly every immigrant member of my family, he was dressed in American-brand clothing, loyal to his chosen country. The line of his bifocals was visible in the bright light. My mother was scurrying around, her blue oven mitts in hand, hauling aluminum platters of steaming-hot rice and chicken into the room, followed by a heap of *yuca* and several bowls of *platanos maduros*. Her blonde hair, tied in a soft ponytail at the back of her head, gently swayed as she slipped through the bundle of people. She's a petite five foot one and can do this easily.

Naturally, the men of the family dove into the food first—there's nothing more mind-boggling to me than the stomach capacity of a Regalado male, which, to my knowledge, has yet to be tested to its limit.

At the far end of the table, my mother and godmother discussed life in Cuba versus life in the U.S. I always choose to look the other way when I feel a they-don't-know-how-easy-they-have-it speech coming on, so I never really know just *how* easy I have it. Or how hard they did. *"La juventud de estos dias no saben lo que hemos pasado,"* my mother told my aunt, who nodded her head as she listened to the routine rant. We American-born children know nothing of hard labor and sacrifice.

The voices became louder as they attempted to overspeak Willie Chirino thumping through the stereo. Some of the children let out shrilly giggles, revealing brilliant holes where their baby teeth once were. As I sat at the packed table, the only teenager in the family, I absorbed the deep laughs and the distinctly Cuban slurring of *s*'s.

"Ay, que dia mas bonito hemos pasado," my father contently declared as his eyes twinkled over the many bodies seated around him, all of whom were sporting wide grins and mouths packed with food. My cousins and sisters passed around trays of *arroz con pollo* and *puerco asado*. As a tray reached me, my sister looked at me with her big brown eyes and whispered in English, "I'm glad you finally sat down with us tonight. It means a lot to Mom." I mouthed a quick thank-you to her and began to dig in.

For the first time in eighteen years, instead of wishing myself to be anywhere but the dinner table or the company picnic at the park, I was comfortable with who I am. I was comfortable being the teenage girl with the loud Spanish-speaking, angel-collecting, too proudly Levi's-wearing family, and the pot and pan drum set. I got up to take my plate to the kitchen with an ease I'd never felt before in the company of so many Regalados. I reached into the freezer, grabbed a cherry popsicle, and returned to sit by my mother, who was laughing and telling childhood tales to the full and happy people at the table. I ate my sticky red American treat in the best company.

Annie Littlewood, 13

TLC: Three Days

~~~~~~

The building was not inviting. I'm not sure how it could be, considering the circumstances. Whatever attempts at landscaping were futile; no one entering the building cared about the shrubbery. Even if they saw the brownish bushes and the dying tulips, they would not look past their anger or hate. They would be thinking only, *There's no way this could be happening.*

They were surprised I could spell. One would be amazed at how many illiterate people there truly are in the world. At least how many there were in TLC, a child advocacy program in Kansas. I was handed a piece of paper, blank except for lines numbered one to ten. I took out everything I had in my pockets and put it in a Tupperware box: hair tie, ChapStick, pain medication that some doctor had given me. I didn't really need it, though. My bruises and bumps only hurt when I touched them or looked at them. Tylenol 3, I hoped, would get me high enough to fall asleep soundly that night. I recorded it all, without any spelling help.

"Wow. Come here," they said to each other. "Her handwriting and spelling are *perfect.*" To me they said, "You are really smart for your age." I was sixteen. How smart do you have to be to spell *hair tie*? They gave it all back to me except the pills. They told me, "We make you write down everything you came here with so you can't say that anything that isn't yours is yours and vice versa. It's just a precaution. We're not saying you're a thief." I understood where I was then.

I didn't have anything worth stealing—none of the Victoria's Secret Love Spell perfume that I basically drenched myself in every morning or the wardrobe I'd dedicated years to perfecting. Or the ten, fifteen dollars I usually had from my parents. But by that point my parents hadn't been giving me an allowance. I didn't even have a toothbrush or clean underwear. I didn't like what I was wearing that day, November 10th. If I'd known I would be taken away, I would have worn something nicer.

They brought me to a room just down the hall from the main office. The room was bleak, cement floors and plain wooden furniture. One bunk bed and a twin-size frame. Dull white sheets and a window that would set off an alarm whenever it was opened. It faced out to a traffic light. I stared at all the cars driving back and forth. I wondered how their lives were, if they were anything like mine. I imagined my boyfriend's white car, like the horse with a prince, coming to save me. He didn't believe in God, so I was positive he wasn't praying for me. But I'm sure he had to have been thinking about me. After all, he was the reason I was there. He was the first person I told. He and my best girlfriend, Samm, told my school counselor. The counselor called me at my sister's house. My parents said they were going to take me out of that place, home-school me. I could not live like that. I answered the counselor's questions, told her what happened with just "yes" and "no." She called the police. And here I am. The officers promised that it was only temporary, until the story was straight. I thought I was going to be gone for a couple of hours. And then I was handed sheets.

The woman quickly told me that I could take a nap if I wanted, that I wouldn't have a roommate, and that dinner was at six. She shut the door. I lied down on the bottom bunk and curled my legs up to my chest. And I cried. I cried really hard for a very long time.

When I finally got up it was dinnertime. I felt like a zombie in a nightmare that wasn't even mine. I missed the week before all of it had happened. I missed the week before that and the week before that. If I just closed my eyes I would wake up as a five-year-old in Mom and Dad's bed. I opened my eyes, because all I could hear were girls talking loudly over each other. I went to where they were. I stared at the food in front of me, I watched everyone begin to eat. I thought for a second about not eating, about just starving myself because there really was no point. My life was over. Instead, I picked up my fork and I listened to these immature girls and their conversations. One girl asked me why I was there, and when I told her she laughed. "I don't see any bruises." They're fading, I said. "Lie!" she said. "Tell them you were lying. Go home. You don't want to be in The System. You won't be happy. It's not worth it." It's too late, I said. "Well, you screwed up," she said. I didn't care what she thought. She knew nothing about me.

Out of ten other girls, only one was there for the same reason as me. The others had stolen cars, sold pounds of marijuana out of a school locker, beaten up a best friend for having sex with her man, taken credit cards from parents, or committed a combination of a few crimes, like prostitution, hitting teachers, failing drug tests. Some had been there for six months, others a few days. I felt sorry for all of them because I knew my family would be calling soon. Their families could not have cared about them the way my family cared about me. And then I remembered where I was. Maybe my family didn't even love me anymore. Time was going by so slow.

The girls were all rough and tough. They liked to cuss and pierce each other's eyebrows with safety pins. They talked dirty about boys and gossiped about people as soon as they left the room.

"Gurl, where did you get those earrings?"

"These? Just Wal-Mart. I wasn't sure about them. You really think they're nice?"

"Hell yeah. You should let me borrow them sometime."

"Maybe."

The girl with the earrings walked away and the other girl started laughing. So did everyone else. I really didn't think it was funny. I went to my room after that.

I lay in my bed, thinking about how much they said they hated their parents. They were lying. They had to be. Hours were turning into days and my head was hurting. They must cry for their mothers.

Regret must fill them during their five-minute timed showers. Their horrible mistakes screamed insults in their brains as soon as their roommates fell asleep, when they wished they were alone or pretended to be asleep while flashlights shined on them in the middle of the night. They must have missed their parents while the adults at TLC were taking and giving meaningless points away. They had to feel like that. They had to feel like trash and want to change their ways, pull back time so they could have never made that first mistake, told that first lie. They had to have wanted it so much. Maybe none of them felt like that. But I did.

I hung out with the black girls, who there were more of, because the white girls liked to fight. But most everybody tried to get along, because no one wanted to lose points. If you got points you were rewarded with something, getting the first shower or being allowed to stay up an extra hour. I mostly stuck to myself. I read *The Hobbit* in a couple of days. And they let me watch a lot of dumb old movies on VHS, romantic comedies that were entertaining but not worth remembering. I wasn't allowed to drink milk at every meal, and that is probably what bothered me the most.

Only the special cases like me weren't allowed to attend the school that was held in the basement with the boys from the building next to us. It was another precaution. I wasn't allowed to go outside or use the telephone. They were afraid that someone—they never specified who—might come and hurt me. I knew who they were talking about.

I kept re-reading the letter I'd written to my family the first night I was there and never sent. I apologized for what I had done. It was my entire fault I was there. My dad could have controlled himself, but he'd been controlling himself for a very long two years. I was a delinquent just like the rest of them. I had never been arrested, I'd never been in a cop car or handcuffed. But I was a liar. I told all kinds of lies—white lies, unnecessary lies, hurtful lies—and I hid everything. I was a complete stranger to my family. I would laugh in my sister,

Olivia's face—and push my brother away. "I'm not going to change!
I'm going to do whatever I want. If you loved me, you would stop trying to control me."

Olivia's birthday is November 11th. That was the first and only
year of my life that I couldn't call and wish her a happy birthday or
tell her I loved her. I couldn't apologize. I imagined all of them together, everyone on the couch in my big family room with the comfi-
est quilts around their legs. They were crying over me. It made me
sick. There would be no cake and no song for my sister.

At least that's what I imagined. I was waiting and waiting for someone to tell me that everything had been cleared up. That my family
was going to have to go to counseling and Dad would have to go to
anger management. Just a few more days. Maybe even a few more
hours.

I hadn't talked to anyone I knew since I'd left. I already missed
hugs and kisses. I just wanted to be forgiven. On my third day at TLC,
I went to court. My caseworker and I got there before my family did.
I was sitting on a bench when my mom came in. Her eyes were red
and puffy; she looked tired and angry. She looked like she had been
betrayed. I saw her and she saw me, but she didn't say anything, she
just looked away. I didn't understand. I felt different, I felt sorry. I was
pleading with her without saying anything and she ignored me. I cry
more than most people. I was too upset to cry. I'd thought she would
run to me, hold me, hug me, ask questions. I don't know why I'd
thought that, and I feel stupid now even writing it.

She paced and tapped her foot, holding her purse on her shoulder.
I watched my three big brothers walk in, my sister with my three-
month-old niece and two-year-old nephew. None of them said anything to me. I never thought my family would leave me, but at that
moment I felt sure of it, utterly abandoned. I blamed myself completely. I was getting what I deserved. Just like my dad said I would.
No matter how small the second was, no one should ever feel like
that about their family.

I started crying and I stood up. Olivia told Aidan, my nephew, to give me a hug. I was so thankful that he did. I held him for a long time. My dad wasn't there, and I was glad he wasn't there. I'm sure he was just sitting at home, watching TV. Ever since the night that had really determined the next year, I'd been having the same nightmare. Seeing him in real life was not something I really wanted.

I had never been in a courtroom before, but it was exactly how I would have pictured it. The lady judge was up high, the woman next to her typing away. Two tables for the state and me, a desk behind for The System, and a table for a computer. There were pews behind the tables where my family sat. I was next to a man I'd never met, who introduced himself and shook my hand while I was dazed. It all went by so fast, and the tears that were streaming down my face didn't feel wet. I was going home. I stared at the floor and listened as the judge said, "Ann Littlewood will be put in foster care until further notice. We will meet again December 15th. I will see you then." Just wake up, Annie.

I heard my mom ask the judge if they could give up their parental rights. I look back on that moment as one of the only times I truly wished I were dead. It felt literally as if my heart burst. There was pain in my chest and in my legs. My head began to throb. I didn't want this to happen. Why couldn't she see that? I didn't know that this could happen. This is not happening.

My brothers were crying, and my sister had already left the room. I got up and tried to walk toward the doors. I just wanted to leave. I just wanted to wake up. I felt David grab me, and I started screaming and crying and hugging him so hard. He apologized and told me it would be OK. "Mom didn't mean what she said. She's just angry." I didn't care. She said it, she meant it, and I don't care! "We're all here, Annie, aren't we? We want you back. We're going to get you back." Maybe I don't want to come back, David! Maybe I'm happy and better off being away from all of you. "You don't mean that. You're just upset, which you should be. I can't believe you did this, Annie. You messed up big this time." They asked us to leave the courtroom because another family was coming in to get torn to pieces.

We all left fighting. Or maybe I left fighting. Mom saying she read my diary and now she knows how much I hated her. How much I wanted to leave, how many drugs I used, what I did after the surprise 16th birthday party she and Olivia had thrown for me.

When I got back to TLC I lay down on the couch in the living area, which we weren't supposed to lie down on. I didn't care, and today they weren't about to tell me to get up. I was leaving that night for a foster home. They saw my bloodshot eyes, and I did not speak to anyone. I watched TV show after TV show. They kept telling me my ride was coming at 6 o'clock, 7 o'clock, 8 o'clock, 9 o'clock, 10 o'clock, and finally 11 o'clock. I grabbed my black garbage bag full of donated clothes and *The Hobbit* I was going to steal.

I got in a van with a man who wasn't my foster parent and a girl who was sitting in the front seat. I wasn't tired and she felt like talking, so I let her talk. She was interesting just because she was so different from me. My family was upper-middle class, religious. I had married parents with college degrees. Her story was not like mine, but she acted as if she was better than me. I thought that was funny because I never thought I was better than anyone. She was sixteen, too, but she treated me as if I were years younger. She was a coke-head and had gotten pregnant by her twenty-four-year-old boyfriend. She had had an abortion, and then she got pregnant again and decided to keep it. The baby miscarried; she wasn't all that bothered by this. Then she'd gotten in a fight with her mother, who'd kicked her out again. She said her boyfriend was in rehab and once he got out he was going to adopt her. She complained that her mom had forgotten her cell phone charger and only packed shorts. "It's 40 degrees outside and she gives me shorts? I swear she's an idiot."

When I finally got to the house I'd be staying at for the next eight months, I was still positive I'd only be there for a few days. It was around 12:30 by then, so late. The girl I was riding with opened the door and lit up a cigarette. "Good luck, kid."

I carried my garbage bag up to the door with the man who'd been driving. He knocked. Within a couple of minutes, the dark house lit up and a black man in a bathrobe opened the door. He had glasses that were maybe a little too small for his face because he looked over them at us. He was tall and needed to shave. It took him a second to register why we were standing at his door, but when he did, he smiled. "Why hello! I wasn't sure if you'd be coming tonight or not."

Ghost Stories

~~~~~~

I want to tell true ghost stories. When we were younger, my brother and I had contests, but everything came out fake and ghoulish, Poeian tales of hearts beating in the floor or escaped madmen with hooks for hands, nothing more. My mother, however unknowingly, will always be the winner of these contests. She told me real horror stories from her life in Korea, rife with scarier ghosts than I ever imagined. She and her friends used to play in a field, and when it got churned up for planting, the farmers found bones. The neighborhood kids kicked around skulls, tapped ribs to create xylophonic music. I can see my mother, Nanyee, standing a little back, hesitant to explore the remains but deadly curious. Her uncle was a physician and kept aborted babies in jars in his office, one for each of the nine months. She'd stand in front of the shelves, staring as the sun made the fetuses glow, tiny bodies rotating slowly in preservative, leaving a trail of oil and dust.

When Nanyee walked through the outskirts of Seoul, she saw dogs tied to trees in the courtyards of family homes, some starving and some dead. Stolen from their owners, the dogs were being saved for food, either a delicacy or a last resort. Nanyee's dog, Happy, was given to their maid as a gift. He got stewed. When the maid offered the family a leg, Nanyee's brother Isaac (Seung-hyun) punched her in the face. My mother's family owned many pets, and I've never been sure as to why it was hers that was given away. She said it was because Happy, until his cooking, was old and howled through the night. But the distrust in her voice tells me we're of the same opinion:

The dog was hers and not one of her three brothers' and therefore expendable.

When my family moved from a tiny apartment to a proper suburban house, complete with backyard and stone walls, my parents gave me a Ridgeback puppy. I don't remember asking for one, but perhaps it's because Happy was Nanyee's best friend. She also kept pet rabbits, never understanding that they, too, were meant for the table.

But I don't want to give the wrong impression, saying my mother had pets and a maid. Her family was poor, though there're always those who are poorer. Nanyee remembers the first time she saw a toilet. She had rich cousins, and she'd go into their bathroom and hit the handle, watching the water get sucked down into the tiny black cavern. As an untended toddler my mother just went outside on an ash pile, with the chickens ganging up on her, sharp beaks level with her crouched eyes.

Some stories Nanyee told me about Korea aren't horror stories at all, but funny, touching—making me disdain my life in America. Unlike Nanyee, when I was little I wasn't allowed to wander by myself, not even in the burbs and especially not in the nearest city, Boston. I wasn't ever given money and told to disappear, to entertain myself. I dream of buying steaming noodle soup from a grimy vendor, eating the fish-paste balls while skating on nearby frozen streams and rivers. I never did anything alone when I was young, although I craved solitude and space—tough in a country that stresses socialization and material clutter. In grocery stores I'd wander away to different aisles, inevitably paged over the intercom, and in Macy's I'd climb into the center of circular clothing racks and hide from my mother. Nanyee remembers her first department store, in Seoul, as an overwhelmingly pristine convenience. She used her allowance to buy a precious jade ring, and on her second visit she purchased little silver boxes to hold tiny secrets and joys. When I was young I'd make her show them to me, held in a silk bag in a special drawer in her desk, and I would glare at the delicate pearl and turquoise inlays. I am always tempted to steal them.

Nanyee once got onto a bus in Seoul, the cheapest public transportation. She sat there alone, staring across the aisle at an old man in his seat. When she moved to get off the bus, he grabbed her crotch. She told me this casually, slightly embarrassed, when I was probably five or six. At the time I felt more anger toward my mother than toward the old man. I could not understand why she'd want to tell a story in which she's victimized and appears weak. I knew that if it had been me on the bus I would have attacked the dirty old man. I would have screamed, I would have kicked, I would have been the epitome of self-righteous rage.

I realize this story—both her story and my response—is why Nanyee never left me alone when I was young. I see her protection, but she doesn't understand how different we are. It's not bred into me to be meek or quiet. I immediately feel the anger of being wronged. I wait for it and then use it in my attacks, cataloging the hypocrisies of those around me, perhaps overly eager to expose them. At age six I ran around our house screaming "I hate you" at whoever upset me, smashing my feet into the walls until our photographs fell. I was a brat but forthright in my belief that other people have no right to encroach upon my body or my personality. I've picked over this particular ghost story of Nanyee's. I've made her turn on the metal stairs and spit in the old man's face, backhand him so that his head goes crashing into a window or the metal bar of the seat. I feel a heat even now, angry more at the opportunity lost than the innocence taken.

Nanyee has a large photo album from Korea, black-and-white images of her and her school friends, rows of girls organized by age and height, wearing the same Mary Janes, knee-length black wool skirts, and bobbed hair to control lice. My mother is always smiling, although everyone else keeps a straight face, the blank look of posed photographs. Here is Nanyee dwarfed in front of her cement middle school, Nanyee conquering a seaweed-strewn rock on a school trip to the coast. I look at my mother's photographs and am in awe of her permanence. Her face has not changed; everything is the same except her skin. What used to be soft and creamy is now tanned, wrinkled, spotted. I think she is beautiful, but recently my grandmother has started to send her skin care products from Los Angeles, acid peels and fat-rich cream.

I can see doubt poisoning my mother. The photo album carries her past Korea into her first years in the United States: South Carolina, age fifteen, the late seventies. Her smile disappears for a while and, once she's left them, she looks more like the uniformed brethren from her school, serious and afraid. Nanyee leans against a car in the trailer park where she lived, sunlight on her bell-bottoms. Though her bright orange shirt says "Kiss me!" her eyes are half-closed and concerned.

I haven't discussed these stories and photographs with my mother in over ten years, since whenever I first realized that secrecy can be easier than communication. Nanyee and I talk about her work—she's a physician—or my school, but we, or maybe just I, avoid actual discussion. She doesn't like reliving the past, and I'm a little resentful that she's barred me from Korea, giving me small stories to replace what I do not know: the language and her (my) family. I still furtively flip through the album, wondering about her constant cheeriness and why there are no baby photographs until she is three or four.

Much of what my mother has told me bothers me, and yet I cannot and do not want to forget the stories. They're so foreign and yet so familiar. Wholly Americanized, I apply an Orientalist perspective to my mother's childhood, setting up the space between Korea and America as an unbridgeable divide. This is wrong, maybe racist, of me, as my mother is neither a traditional Korean woman nor I an average American teenager. I started her storytelling. For years, I constantly questioned Nanyee—until I lost the strength to continue the burden of kicked skulls, dead dogs, dirty old men, babies in a jar. I realize Korea is a constant wound in my mother. The stories are a step toward reconciliation.

However, when I take out each memory and turn it around in my head, I find it incomplete or, worse yet, false. Whose bones lay fallow in that field, how did her uncle get nine monthly spaced fetuses, and what happened to the family left behind in Korea? I don't actually have the courage to ask these questions. I'm not sure I could handle the answers. I consider my own body, how as a girl I was taught to say a strong American "no" and be enraged. My most pressing question is if there were other people on the bus with her, leaving downtown Seoul. The wondering only leads to disaster. I get angrier and angrier as I picture passengers averting their eyes, a disgusting quiet filling the bus after my mother leaves.

Nanyee's photographs have become as mute as most people on a bus, as me, unwilling to speak, and I slip the book back among the other albums. Although Nanyee never gave me a clear warning, I instinctively know I should guard her stories, and add to them. I should wait until I have a little child of my own, always a girl, who I can whisper into and fill with ghosts.

What Can Be Learned at School

The Best Kind of Popular

I used to be a small-town girl. I used to go to a middle school in Granger, Indiana. At the beginning of sixth grade, I thought I had a decent amount of friends. I was content with my social status and really only worried about getting to class on time and wearing a smile, hoping I could brighten someone's day. My grades were pretty easy to remember: I got straight A's the whole year. My favorite subject was Language Arts. I loved writing stories, and I didn't even mind editing. I never really paid much attention to what people thought of me or what the latest gossip was. It just wasn't what I was interested in.

Between semesters that school year, my family decided to take a little trip to California, where my mom's fiancé was currently residing and she was going to look at law schools. We didn't know what town we were going to live in until we saw the house. I immediately fell in love with the stucco exterior; stucco seemed much more *glamorous* than aluminum siding. That's my room, I decided, as I gazed at the grand front window on the second floor. My room in Indiana had two windows, but five windows back there couldn't compare to the one right in front of me. "And this is where I'll walk down and meet my date for prom," I said more than once, directing my mom's attention toward the spiral staircase. I even threw in a few examples of how I'd walk. We ended up buying the house.

I was actually moving across the country! Soon I was going to be a California girl. I was going to live in the state everyone longed to live in. Surely nothing could go wrong.

Well, the truth is, something did as soon as I realized what I was getting into: I was going to have to leave my dad and stepmom, my brother, my friends, and the school and teachers I loved. I wouldn't be surrounded by the Notre Dame fans who overtook the town every Saturday. I put off telling most of my friends that I was leaving, but I just had to tell Clara, who'd moved *to* Granger from a city only an hour from where I was going to live. "California is great! You'll have a blast!" her family encouraged.

As the day approached, I began imagining myself being the sweet girl from an agricultural state who the popular California kids would think was so nice and cute that they just had to have her in their crowd. The unsettling thing was that I'd never considered wanting to be popular before. In Granger, a lot of people didn't know me, and I was OK with that. I wanted my personal life, well, personal. I didn't want the whole entire grade finding out about how my boyfriend dumped me (not that I ever had a boyfriend in the first place). These scenarios started to worry me. I was afraid I was going to turn into a stuck-up, too-cool-for-school girl.

Toward the end of that summer, my mom, my stepdad, my brother, his friend, my cat, and I drove cross-country for five days to our new home. The first thing I wanted to do when I got there was hang out at the church, where I knew I'd be able to find good friends with even better morals. My first church friend, Courtney, was so welcoming and fun to be around that I was 100-percent Emily with her.

My dreams began to change. I'm not saying that I never think of what my life would be like had I talked to the group of girls in one corner, who were covered in fashion labels, instead of the two who'd been sitting away from the rest of us and just seemed so easygoing and relaxed. That's how I met Brittany and Danielle, who are identical twins and now two of my closest friends. They'd been just sitting there, in their own part of the lunch spot, talking quietly, and I went to join them. I loved that they didn't like being in the center of things. Back then I couldn't always tell Brittany and Danielle apart, but they never got upset about it. There's something special about these two, and now I love sitting in my California backyard with my low-key friends.

One weekend, several months after we'd moved, I went back to Indiana and was chatting with friends when the social ladder of our old school came up. One of them said, "Emily, you were popular last year."

I replied, "Ha! Trust me, no one important liked or even knew me."

"Yes, you were popular," she insisted.

Then my other friend added, "Everyone talked about you . . . in a good way."

I was surprised. I was shocked. I was excited. But then I remembered: I didn't *want* to be popular. I didn't want my life broadcast on students' blogs. Suddenly I was scared. Scared that everyone knew my secret crush, that everyone knew what I got on my standardized tests—which was, for me, very private data.

As soon as I got back to California, I told my mom, who said something I will always remember and tell my kids. She said, "Emily, that is the best kind of popular. When you don't know that you're popular, you don't bask in it. Then you can just be yourself. You realize that people like you for who you are."

I've heard many wise words in my life. If I can tell you which ones to take to heart, though, they would be my mom's. Don't try to be popular. Don't try to be cool. Just be you, and you won't even have to try.

A Retelling of the Black-Letter Days, the Red-Letter Days, and the Fine Line That Ties Them Together

~~~~~~

I'm looking back into a hodgepodge that I might call my life until now. A few days in particular. Gloomy ones. You've heard of black-letter days and red-letter days, right? Good. So you won't think I sound like too much of a loon going on and on about them then.

Assigning colors to days is just one of those things a kinder-gartener doesn't give much time or thought to. But I wasn't your usual girl. I might have been called a little bit of an outcast. Being one gave me more time to think.

I'd found out about the days in a book I read when I was six, and I knew it had to be true. It always worked like this: On some days everything was dark, and that was because someone had sent you a black letter in the mail. You just didn't know about it. Other days were nice and bright, meaning someone had sent a pretty red letter instead.

I never came across any letters like the ones I'd read about—though it was not for lack of trying. I'd gone so far as to pick up the mail, every day, as soon as I got back from kindergarten, first grade, second. I grew up in a house with my extended family: It was my mother and me, my aunt and uncle, and my grandmother and grand-father. All of the adults received their mail in the same place, and I made it my task to sort it daily. I'd run up to the mailbox by the road and right back while my aunt watched. After a while, she saw my frustrated face there, as I sorted through the stacks of letters and arranged them in eleven little piles so I would know whose room to put them in. She noticed my eyes going wide whenever I saw a snippet of color on an envelope.

"Que estas haciendo con eso, Lorito?" she asked me. What are you doing with that?

"Estoy buscando cartas rojas." I told her, in so many words.

She smiled, her pretty face lighting up. My one tool as a mystic disappeared then. My aunt explained to me that the red and black letters were one of those things that exist only symbolically.

Sure enough, there it was in the encyclopedia from my dad's library. The red letters originated in medieval churches, red letters on the calendar to announce solemn-eyed ceremonies, the feast days of our Catholic Church. They weren't magical, just *dates of holidays*. That didn't mean I stopped believing in them, though. Black days would always make life worse. Red days would make it better. Sometimes it depended on how I looked at things which day was which.

The earliest black-letter day I can remember might have easily gone unnoticed as a typical third-grade winter's day. I'm not even sure why it felt like a black-letter one to me, but it did.

Nothing was really different. I was on time. I had my brown hair combed straight and flat on my head. I was wearing my usual plain white shirt, my navy mom pants. My scruffy square loafers squeaked loudly on the floor, still wet from the dirty snow-and-salt mess outdoors. The squeaking to announce myself was unwelcome, redundant: I was the tallest girl in the grade, as tall as both of the tallest boys. I looked *manly*. Weight was a non-issue in the family, at least where kids were concerned. You were given food and you ate it so you would grow. I might have captained the wrestling team if there was one. You know—you had to be heavy, not the least bit delicate. I fit the bill perfectly. Except I wasn't a boy. I was a girl. An oversize, clumsy, mannish girl.

I saw the world in colors. *Doesn't everyone?* you must be thinking. Sure, the lockers along the walls kept their dull gray hues, the green chalkboard. Our narrow desks remained as amber as ever. It wasn't the appearance of things. It was just like, some days the air felt heavier with tension, and I was on tenterhooks. That was the unusual and inconvenient thing about me then. Personalities could sting my mind in just the way a too-bright, hideous shirt could. Personalities made me claustrophobic.

This feeling ambushed me as I looked over the knot of students around my desk. During class, I could usually forget all about the feeling of being out of place. I mean, there wasn't much difference between reading a textbook in a crowded room and reading your father's encyclopedia, or *Much Ado About Nothing*, sitting on the floor of your bedroom, right? If only it were that simple. A few things cut my comfort to the quick.

The loudest members of the motley crew I had to sit near were squabbling—right around my desk, and right when I wanted to work on my favorite subject. There were too many colors, too many people near me.

Our science teacher had been trusting enough to step out to talk to the principal, leaving us alone to complete our worksheets. Forty-point value, nearly as much as a test. And what did the students do? They chatted. Most of it was about siblings, or 'N Sync, or whatever was in vogue. Empty things, really. Not until the period was nearly over would they all become friends of mine. The type who smiled and showed their gums and politely asked, "Laura, since you know all this stuff, could you tell me what this answer is? You're so smart. Please?" I wasn't chatting, I would not chat later. I could not put up with either circumstance.

But it was hard to shut myself off when there were people sitting and talking right behind my head. I could hear a girl, with a name something like Alisandra, bragging about her prospective future. "I'll, you know, like make sure he's cute. He's gonna look *exactly* like Nelly." She was average looking, not really anything unusual by herself, but her hair was meticulously styled and her outfits much tighter than school regulations specified. Her friends liked her; the rest of us tried to ignore her. I saw her as bright pink, a color I despised. She wore it all the time. Pink hoop earrings, pink scrunchie, horribly annoying pink pencil with feathers on it. I *hated* that pencil. She didn't think of that as she waved it dreadfully near my nose to illustrate a point. She was the model of popularity—the girl who didn't care about anything. "He'll play football and rap. We'll get this, like, mansion and my room will be hot pink with these fluffy feathered pillows and just so much stuff." She clapped her manicured fingers together with the wrong color glee.

I was doing OK at blocking her out. Five short-answer questions and the vocabulary and I'd be done. Then a third party joined the conversation. Christopher, the loud boy with the violently tailored moods and the jeering laugh. He wasn't quite like her. He was worse, darker, harder to ignore. I loathed him more than I ever could loathe Alisandra because I'd actually *liked* Christopher once upon a time. He'd always been confident and charismatic. But back before popularity was in our vocabulary, he'd also been nice to everybody. I saw the current version of him as red, but the cruel shade of it—the dark, brooding color of those pointed race cars. He smirked as he listened, making clinking noises on the table with the silver chain he always wore. Bling, the boys called it.

Whatever *that* was. The music, the style, the language. They were all white, these kids, but the only music they listened to was hip-hop or rap. I lived in a nice brick house, with Handel and Bach floating from the CD player. What I learned of trends was from that classroom, on days like this one. I didn't really learn, per se. I caught trends like I caught colds, disliked them as much as the flu. I hated them about as much as I hated Christopher when he spoke like this. He talked about how he was going to go to war and blow things up. He then proceeded to make all the sound effects of the artillery, and a few more besides. I might have made some sort of face.

"What about Laura?" he asked Alisandra then, as if I couldn't hear.

"She probably doesn't understand what we're talking about. Dreams, futures. We've got plans. She'll stay here with the books and teach, right? Like one of them nun teachers."

I completely ignored them.

Christopher snapped his fingers. "She think she's too good for us or something?"

"You know she never answers anyone other than the teacher," Alisandra said. "And her friends are, like, so *gay*."

Friends? The only person I really knew was a boy called Ted. Ted had trouble reading and a mile-wide shy smile. He was a friend, the only friend. He was about half my size. And of course Christopher had no reservations about striking him. Just like that—a pinch, a slap on the face. It had happened more than once, out of sight. Did Christopher think that was what was going to make him a strong person? Blowing things up? Hitting people?

That word *gay* was just meant to be hurtful and derogatory, like the other words—*geek, teacher's pet*. I heard those words a lot, and they didn't bother me. I had a 4.0 average for as long as I could remember. This was not, in any way, a bad thing. It was a *necessity*. The one thing I could always trust, my backup.

"Oooh. I think she's deaf. Or dumb." Christopher kept on with it.

Alisandra giggled, because that's what she does.

Recklessly, I decided I'd had enough of them both. I spoke quietly, so only the two of them could hear. "The day you pass an exam is the day I listen to you. I somehow doubt you have any clue as to how anybody's mind works. Especially mine."

Alisandra laughed and chewed on her fingernail again.

Christopher just glared at me from across the empty desk. He quieted down and turned away as the teacher walked back into the room, but I'd caught sight of his look. *This is war*, it said.

It was only half a year more. I told myself that I could handle it. Perhaps somewhere in the future I'd get a new seat.

A year passed, red days with the black, and then another. I could hear little bits of gossip, insignificant "lub lub lubs," like rain on windows I'd shut tight. I won a still-life drawing contest. I listened to corny jokes Ted made up and nearly split my sides laughing.

We were in fifth grade and we were in gym, playing soccer. What made it start as a black-letter day was that Alisandra and Christopher were on my team. At least goalie was my favorite position, and this time the teacher had put me there. Big was good for goalie. She'd just looked me up and down. "Lowe, you! Get to the goal."

I had girlfriends now, all three of them on the other team: dark-skinned, slim Georgiana, who had strong basketball hands too big for painting up with polish; sensible Annie, the new girl who the popular girls fawned over until they got tired of trying to make her dress like they did; my closest pal, friendly blonde Meg, who wouldn't even listen to kids who spread rumors. We'd kind of grouped together over projects and desks. We were in the same science class this year.

I grinned and waved across the field. Sweat trickled down my cheek. I wiped it away with the back of my hand, which I dried on my sweatpants, not the jersey. I wouldn't have touched that with a ten-foot pole. I still remember the grimy red material. It smelled vaguely of sweat and something unrecognizable from the last person.

The boys fiercely battled in the outfield, as if they were playing in the national league. They put that much effort into it. There was Christopher, running like there was fire on his heels instead of a bigger boy. Thankfully, I was far away from all the action. But I watched closely, just to be ready if the ball got away from them and I had to keep it away from our goal.

Then I got distracted for a moment, and I missed the collision. All I saw was the taller guy whirling about and catching himself with a hand on the asphalt, then Christopher toppling and crashing, the ball all caught up under his feet. After a few seconds, almost everyone ran over to him. Partially it must have been seeing him fall, but a great deal of it was hearing him. It was the strangest thing I'd ever heard. Christopher was screaming and crying like my five-year-old cousin had when he'd cut his hand on a piece of glass.

It was a lousy thing to happen to anyone, I thought. I could almost feel what it must have been like to fall on this surface, to be Christopher. Sharp needles of pain overlying bruises and the heavy impact of them. I knew this because of the eight-inch scar on my elbow. *Poor kid,* I thought. I stopped myself. This was Christopher.

I walked over, peered down at him. He sounded like he was dying, and I didn't see a trace of the Christopher I'd always seen. He didn't get up. He stayed curled in fetal position, no blood anywhere except for a gush from his mouth. He was holding something white in his palm. The gym teacher finally figured out that he'd chipped a tooth. For those few minutes, I hung around, though I had no clue what to do. I knew I wasn't going to carry Christopher, all wailing, to the nurse's office, although I probably could've. I remember thinking that he even *looked* like my little cousin. Our stocky gym teacher decided to take him to the nurse and send him home. He was gone the rest of the day.

When Christopher came back, his sneer was restored. Every one of his friends welcomed him as if nothing had happened. But I never saw him as red again. The thought made me nervous after that, in some strange way related to the sight of dirty jerseys and blood so close to the brain.

I could talk on and on about how I learned to see both of the bullies in my class and everyone else as a collection of colors and layers. Every dimension of their selves came out of problems and triumphs that I don't know the cause of or understand. I grew to notice other people's black- and red-letter days. The girl that shared my locker slammed it. I saw the crumpled test in her fist and the fight with her sister on her face. The tall kid behind me refused to look at the teacher when something at home had kept him there the day before, and I knew. Maybe not the particulars. But I knew the look. I knew what people had to go through every day. I wondered why a great deal of them remained the same.

There was a terribly loopy, messy scrawl on the last page of my fifth-grade yearbook. It said, I think, "Have a good summer. Read good books. Christopher." My eyes watered when I read it, and I can't even describe what it is I felt. I shoved that book away under a pile of faded nature guides and all my class pictures.

That school year was the last for those kids and me. My aunt read about a charter homeschool, where I could take more than one year's curriculum at a time. It was nearly a relief.

The next time I saw kids my age, I looked like a completely different person. At twelve, my long hair had become an annoyance, so I clipped it short. By thirteen, I'd discovered that I liked to run long distances to get rid of frustration. When I wanted to smash my fist into the side of a tree, I ran instead. I ran fast so that nothing, not even thoughts, could catch me. *One mile . . . two miles . . . six miles . . .* Running helped me deal with my first attacks of teen angst, the loneliness that nothing except action could quite peg or take away. I found I was able to skate for twenty miles to build my resistance. I did sit-ups and crunches with weights piled on my stomach, along with tae bo, aerobics, Pilates, and anything else I was able to learn.

Those habits had long since gotten rid of ten pounds of extra baggage. And then some more vanished on me. Time began to work its magic. My nickname became Skinny. I did a double-take the first time my aunt called me that.

I found that I liked to work out to rock music—nearly anything and everything with decent lyrics and energy, including the most serious of eighties pop songs. Bon Jovi reaffirmed me with "It's My Life." Lifehouse tempted me to pick up the old guitar that had gathered dust in a corner. Dido's music gave me something more to agree with my cousin on. I also finally started to focus on my faith as a Christian. I closed my eyes and felt. I looked for Jesus in the people around me. My bible held its place on my desk, and I'd read two, three chapters at a time. It almost felt like a conversation to me.

By ninth grade, I'd become more of an individual, less of a stereotype.

Don't get me wrong. There were no numbers I called, no other kids I talked to. I still wasn't the most sociable type you'd ever meet.

After some time of this, I convinced myself I needed a change. I needed words, conversation. I needed to see what else was out there, find out if I could handle it. Then I got a letter in the mail: a white envelope with my name, not a snippet of color on it. A simple message, a simple invitation. I jumped at the chance to join our church's youth group.

The day came. I woke at an ungodly hour to get myself ready. I wasn't used to being around teenagers. What did they wear, anyhow? I couldn't find the right thing. Fixing myself up was somewhat of a chore—the heels, the jeans, and the black shirt. I'd been on the verge of wearing a T-shirt and sneakers, but then I looked in a mirror and I thought, perhaps they would be there. I might as well look impervious.

"You look pretty," my mom told me on the way there. She smiled sleepily, smoothed my hair, and for a moment I wondered why I was doing this.

I had the feeling she understood. I leaned over, kissed her on the cheek, and stepped out of the car.

I don't believe in the existence of black-letter days anymore, I told myself. I paused outside the door. I could feel the old vague cold that crept over me when I was ready to freak out. I hadn't changed at all.

The door opened and the sight of so many people, people roughly my own age, was a little overwhelming. There was a seat at the back of the room, next to another girl who looked as out of place as I felt.

She sat straight up, a lone spot of dark among reds and greens. I asked her if I could sit, and when she nodded, I took the seat next to her.

I didn't see anyone in preppy clothes, no faces like Alisandra's or Christopher's. I did see two boys I'd studied with back in fifth grade. I smiled to myself. They were former members of the nerd pack, and I hardly recognized them at all now. They were vastly taller than I was.

I found out that I could actually introduce myself to the girl next to me without sounding stupid. "I'm Amy," she said. "I'm a freshman, and I'm kind of nervous."

"That makes two of us then."

She played saxophone, and in public high schools, she told me, cliques could create war zones. In her school, a fight broke out about every two hours. Band members were heckled.

Amy dressed the way I usually did: the dark T-shirt, the jeans, the canvas sneakers. After a while, with donuts and seltzer in plastic cups, the group settled down to watch *Patch Adams*. I'd heard of it, but we still didn't rent many movies at home. It was funny at times, absurd and embarrassing at others. And I'd nearly forgotten the ick factor that came when people swore. Overall, it was a comedy that didn't quite fit. It had tragedy mixed in, tears and side-splitting laughter. So that's what I talked about when it finished. That, the symbolism of butterflies and freedom, giving and receiving, the atmosphere in hospitals. The way you could never predict just how cruelty might repay good, but it was enough that you did good anyway.

I kept on shooting things out, a mile a minute. I felt like I wasn't only addressing my local priest and a roomful of kids I'd just met about a movie. I felt like I was addressing ghosts of the past, thoughts that had no shape or form until I said them.

I almost felt sorry Christopher and Alisandra weren't there. I would have wanted to tell them, "Thanks," and look at them closely to try to see what they were thinking. I'm not sure how it would go, and I am really sure of very little. At fifteen, it's still kind of tough to see that people can't be compressed into one color all the time. They shift and change, letter days or not, many layers of many colors. It's confusing, mind-boggling, harder than ever to understand. Until you really know someone, you'll be forever second-guessing words, looks, intentions, what might or might not be in your mail when you get home. But until then you try. And that is enough.

Elizabeth Case, 16

Hey You, Freshman with the Face!

~~~~~~

I guess it was a little bigger than I'd expected. I mean, I wanted something new, but knowing all of five people in a school of 2,050 was a little daunting. I spent my first lunch alone. Loser. I watched this guy, an asshole senior, come up to a bunch of girls sitting to my left and offer them some candy. Starbursts, M&M's. Who would be stupid enough to actually take it? None of them were.

I had the most fun in English class. I'd been lucky enough to get one of the most sought-after teachers, known for his philosophical discussions and unusual classroom style. We played this crazy game where you spun around in circles whenever your name was called out. I've always been terrible with names, but by the end of the period I'd gotten most of them down. This one guy, though, Tyler, just could *not* get Michele's name. He'd come to her and freeze up every time. Even after our teacher made him repeat her name like ten times, he blanked.

I didn't have a third period. It was supposed to be Spanish 3, but the system, or the counselors, didn't understand that a freshman could take advanced classes. Most of the other students didn't even know I was a frosh (I didn't advertise) until finals. I was in chemistry honors, too. Woohoo. That's what I get for having come from a private school.

I'd spent ten years there, junior kindergarten to eighth grade. My whole life. There were a couple of kids who'd been there as long as I had. None of us really talked much anymore. Well, you couldn't really avoid contact with anyone when your grade consisted of 130 kids who were more like relatives you don't live with than classmates. Part of the reason I left—and yes, it was my choice to leave—was the social factor. I mean, I couldn't really imagine dating a guy who I'd seen wearing Pokémon boxers. And I just wanted to get away, to meet new people, to explore something. I wanted to reinvent myself, and I couldn't do that at my old school. I still visit occasionally, though not as much as I should. I don't know. I guess I just got caught up in the sleep-deprived, slightly boring world of a high school freshman.

The first few months were hard. I spent a couple of weeks tagging along with Sarah, who used to live across the street. I didn't really have much in common with her friends, but they were nice enough and it beat sitting alone. Then I moved on to Callie, who was the ex–best friend who still thinks she's your best friend. But she'd changed a lot since we'd been inseparable. And that crowd didn't work out so well either. They were all so . . . happy. All smiles and makeup and hair curlers. Fake and cliché, so a partially antisocial wannabe rocker girl didn't really fit in. All I listened to was indie and alternative—no Jay-Z or Justin Timberlake coming out of my headphones. I wore black *and* I enjoyed school. Blasphemy.

By this time my schedule had been sorted out, and I wasn't in the same English class. I had a much more reserved teacher. Not reserved as in orthodox-strict. More like she was just shy; it was her first year teaching, and she had trouble exerting any sort of control over the class. That's where I met Alaska. I went out to lunch with her and her crew, and I was hooked. They were so laid-back and, to put it bluntly, awesome. Awesome and hysterical. No drama. Everyone was friends—just cool with each other. There were nine of us, kind of: Alaska, Dylan, Johnny, Julian, Tony, Michele, Chris, Kevin. Niev was sometimes a part of it, too. But Chris and Kevin weren't around a lot, and Niev only ate his vegetarian meals on the hill with us every once in a while. Ah, the hill. We used to spend breaks—lunches, before school, anytime not in class—on that lump of dirt. We've moved on now, first to the bleachers, then to the overhang between the two chemistry classrooms. But the hill will always be the place I remember. I watched Logan a lot from there.

I think I first saw Logan when I was with my mom, trying to fix my schedule. He was wearing these hideous rainbow pinstriped pants. Well, that's what I remember, anyway—and that he had a pair of skates in his bag. I practically jumped out of my shoes, because absolutely nobody I knew skated. Nobody. But here was someone, a cute, cool-looking someone, who was not only a part of the culture but carrying around evidence of it as well. "Oh my god! Mom! Someone else skates!!!" I did that shouting-but-whispering thing. I didn't see Logan again until Spanish. About a week later, that's where I first let on to Logan that I knew, vaguely, about the skating scene. He was wearing a Senate shirt and I admitted to recognizing it.

I still don't think he knows I skate. Not that I do it much anymore. I made excuses during the fall and winter—basketball and volleyball were too demanding and finals consumed my brain and left it soupy. But the truth is, I feel like such a dork, like such a poser trying to skate at the park. I'm not that good. OK, I pretty much suck. I can do all of four grinds and that's about the extent of my talent. I did land a 360 once. That was pretty cool.

Plus, I'm too lazy to get out of bed and ask my parents to drive me to the Sunnyvale skate park. It's nothing compared to Vans. But Vans is gone now, closed down, turned into another clothing superstore.

So, I dreamed of my skater-boy Logan. Callie dreamed of Nick, and sometimes of Julian. Alaska made out with Dylan. Alaska started going out with Dylan. Julian, who is still undeniably in love with Alaska, hung out with us less and less as their relationship progressed. Then Callie fell for Julian, who sort of fell back for her. And then their, like, four-day relationship caused all sorts of drama and controversy over the holiday break because Johnny said that Julian was going to play Callie. Things got way out of hand and proportion. Adding to the insanity were Johnny and Michele. I don't remember if it was before or after break, but Johnny and Michele kind of liked each other. Except she didn't want to go out with him. It was complicated.

I started slacking off on my schoolwork, which for me meant B's instead of A's. A side effect of both my private-school education and my personality was that I had to be the best, do the best. If I didn't, no matter the circumstances, I beat myself up. I'm still trying to get back on track. Still, sometimes I feel like I've lost all motivation. At my old school, everybody was encouraged to do really well. There was an intellectual atmosphere. Awards were handed out, and one of my proudest moments was being chosen as the year's top expository writer. At this school, there's no support for that sort of thing. Though the change has made me realize how cloistered I'd been. Hell, Mexican and black kids made up no more than 3 percent of my old school. Not that I didn't have a great time there. I got a fantastic education, and I found a couple of best friends. (Here's my shout-out to Diana, one of the greatest girls in the Milky Way. We really need to get together and make those music videos.)

Until I started high school, I'd never completely realized how broad and all-encompassing this world is or how much life can change in a year. In the twelve months since I wrote this, I traveled out of the country for the first time and fell head over heels in love with England. And I'm no longer obsessed with Logan. I called him once over the summer, in what had to be the most awkward, pause-filled, four-sentence phone conversation anyone's ever had. Initially, he didn't even remember who I was. I've moved on, a couple of times, and he's faded into a rather good-looking, write- or laugh-about-it-now memory. I suppose every girl is allowed one of those per life phase. I took my first AP class and am about to leave on my first college tour. I turned sixteen, and now my parents pay way too much for car insurance. I found out my grandmother is dying of lung cancer and am going to visit her in New York this summer.

Yeah. A lot can happen in twelve months.

Sara Harari, 16

Life Goes up a Wall

~~~~~~~

I got home from school and felt like tearing all my hair out. I couldn't understand his complete mule-headedness! Of all people, *he* had to end up in my sophomore World History, the one class where we discuss ethics. Every time he walks into the room, every time I look up at the teacher and see him out of the corner of my eye, every time he speaks, I can't help fantasizing about punching him in the face and breaking his nose cleanly in two. Disfigured for life, he will be forced to see the error of his ways. I eagerly await the day that I, the pacifist of the class, will be able to beat up this stupid, stupid football player. Maybe flaming liberals like me who support women's rights, world peace, and wind turbines just weren't meant to get along with sexist, war-obsessed, gas-guzzling, raging conservatives like him.

On principle, I don't discriminate against entire groups of people based on a few. Football players may be an exception. The three of them in my history class think that the entire school revolves around them. It doesn't.

Todd is the worst of the bunch. He believes that we should kill all Muslims because "Those scum are going to bomb us all before the year is out." And the annihilation he proposes wouldn't be genocide as, let me quote him here, "It would be awesome."

At the beginning of the year, my school decided to have a Diversity Day. There was ribbon dancing, break dancing, and Armenian dancing, panel discussions about gay rights, and lectures from minority group leaders. That day I walked past Todd, who was loudly complaining, "I can't believe we have to do this stuff. It's so dumb. Who cares if fags are getting beat up in New York City?"

My god, just being in a room with that boy drives me up the wall.

A few weeks ago, I was working on an in-class project on imperialism, dutifully researching America's bloody takeover of the Philippines in the early 1900s. Todd sauntered up to me and asked, "Is it true that Harris and Paul were caught *doing* it in the library bathroom?"

Now, Harris and Paul happen to be, in my opinion, two of the hottest guys in our grade. Both are tall, sandy blonds, charming and intelligent. They also happen to be dating. And Harris is my best friend, which may slightly prejudice me. Paul had told me that this *particular* rumor—there have been others, many others—had been started at a school dance after he tried, unsuccessfully, to beat up one of Todd's cronies when the football player called Harris a fag.

Let's just say that I felt like a ticking bomb. I had never been this mad in my entire life. Life seemed to slow down, like in one of those *Matrix* rip-off movies when they prepare to decapitate an enemy. Then it hit me. Taking Todd's head off means suspension. Suspension would mean lots of work to catch up on, plus some *very* angry parents. I sighed. Not worth it. I turned back to the Battle of Tirad Pass, in which, my textbook told me, the Americans "heroically" killed or wounded fifty-two of the sixty opposing Filipinos. I took a few deep breaths and started taking notes.

"Come on, Sara. It's true, isn't it?" Todd's voice penetrated my shell of studiousness. I gritted my teeth and turned back to my work. "So you're telling me that it *did* happen, right?"

Stealing a glance to make sure the teacher was out of earshot, I turned to face him. "One, Harris is my best friend. Two—"

Todd rode right over me. "Today, in the cafeteria, I almost couldn't finish my lunch in peace—"

"What a pity," I interrupted, shooting a withering glance at his broad frame.

"Because," he continued, "I looked up and saw these two *people* draped over each other." He said *people* like the two he referred to weren't really humans but some type of leprous apes not talked about in polite conversation. "It was *them*." As if he could have possibly been talking about anyone but Harris and Paul. "And then," he paused dramatically, "they *kissed*."

I rolled my eyes. "Really? Do you want to hear something even worse? The other day I was walking across the quad, and I saw—I saw—my god, I almost can't say it out loud! I saw a girl run up to her boyfriend and—and give him a kiss, right on the lips!" I blinked at Todd.

It took a minute for him to process. Maybe I'm being unfair. I'm sure he can actually form sentences without thinking too long on them first. He's just not smart enough to think up good comebacks. A beat. Then I noticed a maniacal gleam in his eyes.

"I think gays should be tarred and feathered."

I got up out of my chair, trembling, and stalked out of the room. Down the hall, in the bathroom, I found it very hard not to break the mirror.

Gym at Riverton

~~~~~~~~~

I started going to a school called Riverton, in a really white area of
the Bronx, in seventh grade. Before that I was going to a school I
liked, on 17th Street in Manhattan, but my mom thought it was
pulling me in a bad direction. She said, "You need fields and open-
ness." Riverton had fields, so I went there. Turns out the worst parts
of my Riverton experience were probably spent on the fields. Except
for maybe the parts spent in the gym, like school dances. I once danced
there with a kid named James Pinky. He had a perfect bowl cut.

At Riverton there were mandatory gym uniforms that were revolt-
ing and uncomfortable. Mine got washed maybe once a semester.
The sweatpants had nipple-high waistbands; the crotch started at
your knees. They were tight and scrunched around the calves, then
baggy in the thighs and butt so that you looked like a blown-up rub-
ber glove waddling around trying to kick things. Gym was like war. I
was forced to battle all these suburban beasts. Half the kids there
were from Riverdale or Westchester, so they were athletes since
birth. Greta Stein was an example. Her motto was "Blood makes the
turf grow—kill, kill, kill!!!!" Each time she touched grass she became
an animal or a Viking. She actually gnashed her teeth at people, and
she would grunt heavily. She could punt a soccer ball and make it explode. Whenever I was around her, I wished for a metal shield or
sword. My biceps are seven inches around when flexed; this is
smaller than some people's wrists. I'm retardedly uncoordinated, or
maybe just unmotivated when it comes to sports, so I would try to be
as neutral as possible in gym games. I'd stand on the side like a

stump. Some days we played flag football, which was really obscene-looking. You had to wear a belt with streamers hanging over your butt, and the tagging was like butt grabbing instead of just tapping. You had to yank the belt off the person's waist. The gym teacher was a creep who wasn't ashamed to talk about people's torsos.

The swim coach, Kunkel, looked like a hammerhead shark. He always shouted, "Dunne, look alive!" His voice was insanely deep. It was like talking to a truck. Swimming at Riverton was a whole new level of torture, like a private-school hazing ritual. They made you swim every single day for two weeks in a pool you could tell was sweaty. It was coed. I was really pale and scrawny. It was freezing, and when you got out you had to look at all the other pasty, weird kids in bathing suits and also be looked at in yours. In ninth grade I looked like Gollum. Not much has changed, really, but in ninth grade it was more like fetal Gollum. Swimming at school was the most awkward thing I've ever done. Obviously there were girls who liked it, liked to be in bathing suits in front of everyone. It made me want to pee in the pool to screw them over.

Moira was my sole ally at Riverton. She had brown hair, and her left eyebrow swirled upward at the end, like an eyebrow cowlick. Instead of running, she trotted, because she had a passion for horses. One day she led me to a secret bathroom she had discovered in a secluded wing of campus. It had a pleasant windowsill for sitting, and Moira and I soon became a pair. Hiding was our main activity, and no one ever looked for us, which is lucky for them because had they found us, we would have shunned them in a traumatizing way.

When swimming time came around, Moira told Coach Kunkel she was hydrophobic, to the point where she pukes. He was either brainless enough or nice enough to believe her and let her skip. I wasn't as suave as Moira, so I had to face my foes alone. I imagined her lying in some grass, in a comfortable turtleneck and long pants, being dry. This angered me. I would do the eighteen required laps as fast as possible in order to get out of the pool and into clothing.

Coach Kunkel must have mistaken my haste and horror for talent. "Dunne, you're a shark! Join the team," he'd say, and I would get really awkward and mumble "no thanks." Then he would start blathering how my torso was a prime swim-team torso. I knew this meant it was disproportionate to my legs. I was a long slimy fish with little stubby flipper legs. I was scared of diving since it clogged my ears. When we had to try fancy flip turns I rammed my head into the pool wall. But that didn't stop Coach Kunkel. Soon his hassling went beyond the pool area. He'd see me in the halls and boom, "Dunne the shark!" and I would turn red and flip out. Then he called my mom and told her about me needing to get on the team. She was all for it. She valued team mentality. I didn't join the swim team.

Like swimming, CPR class was mandatory. It was taught by Coach Gratch, who was as fierce as her name sounded. In CPR we gave mouth-to-mouth to mannequins, life-size limbless torsos with heads. Some of them were black and some of them were white, except for a few that had black heads paired with white bodies or vice versa. Riverton was constantly talking about the importance of diversity in education.

When you pushed on the mannequins' stomachs, they made clicking noises. Coach Gratch told us that in a real-life procedure, two or three ribs usually break—but you have to ignore that and keep going to save the person's life. CPR was a fun class. But when the certification exam finally came around, it took me two tries to pass. I'm still not sure what I did wrong the first time, but whatever it was, I know it was embarrassing because it involved making out with a mannequin in front of my entire grade.

Lisa Chau, 18

Stuck in Traffic

~~~~~~~

Have you ever had one of those days when everything drives you crazy? A day when you just want to go crawl in a hole and never come out? My average day at school is enough to make me want to live in a hole for the rest of my life. From the second I step out of my house to the moment I get home, the insanity of high school could put me in the nut house.

Everything's OK until I get there. I own the coolest car in the entire world: a RAV4. My maroon, tape-playing, door-freezing Fuck-Mobile takes me on a joyride every time I turn the key in the ignition. But wait, hold on. I know what your dirty mind is thinking. Let me clarify the origin of my car's name: In a very tiny nutshell, it used to be my older sister's. Before you go assuming things about her now, fact is, the car broke down in a parking lot somewhere a year or two ago, so she left it there overnight. And someone, who obviously did not have anything else to do, decided to key the word *FUCK* on the car in overwhelmingly large capital letters. From then on my friends thought it would be funny to refer to it as the . . . yeah. Now back to my story.

When the air was colder and the roads were icier, I'd have to leave my house ten minutes earlier than normal to scrape the snow and ice off of my poor little car. Except I could never get to the scraper. Why? Let's just say that my car decided to glue itself shut every winter morning. (Michigan weather can do this.) The locks were definitely frozen. I don't know why, but the only thing that would ever open was the trunk door. So I'd end up climbing in from the trunk all the way up to the driver's seat. Then I'd turn on my car, kick the driver's side door open, get out, close my trunk door, run back in the car, realize that my door was now frozen OPEN, run back to my house to get some sort of string, fall on my butt because I slipped on the ice, and finally strap my door closed. By then, I'd end up so late that I didn't remember or bother to clear off my car. Instead, I usually cracked my window open and drove to school with my head poking out.

To make my mornings even better, by the time I would get to school, the closest doors to the parking lot would be locked. I'd then have to speed walk around the entire school, out of fear of running and falling again, and sulkily charge into class infinitely late.

I hate walking in the halls. My objective for every five-minute passing time between classes is to not touch a single soul. But there are students who carry their whole lives in their backpacks, turn just a little bit to talk to their friends, and end up knocking me into fifty other people. The worst is when people stop in their tracks and attempt to do a U-turn. I just want to repeatedly smack them on the head with my calculus book, and then after that, smack them again with my physics one.

Then I have to deal with class. What can I say about class? I don't hate it, but I don't love it either. I always fall asleep, and I don't know whether it's because I'm bored, or just . . . bored. I just can't stay awake. Especially when the teachers' lessons include PowerPoints, overheads, and movies; they're like sleeping pills. We all sleep with our lights off at home, so it's only human that we sleep when the lights are off at school, too. It's not really the students' fault for drifting off; it's in our nature to sleep in dark places.

But then there are times when I'm actually awake during school. I know, surprising. What could keep me from sleeping? People who wake me up. I distinctly remember this one time I fell asleep in Global Studies. A friend woke me by pounding his fists on my desk, and I thank him to this day for doing it at the exact moment crap came shooting out of this guy's mouth, splattering chunks of I-don't-even-know-what on the ground ten feet away from me. But the worse possible thing to wake up to is puke. Not to mention that day was blazingly hot, so all the unidentifiable throw-up was diffusing in the room and into the hallway. Which brings me to another point— classroom temperatures are ridiculous. Classrooms are always so flippin' hot or cold, but never in between. My attention goes to my freezing hands and toes, my sweaty back, or the upchuck on the floor, and I become too preoccupied to fall asleep, let alone concentrate on schoolwork.

There's one event of the day that should be the most joyous of them all—lunchtime. I'm not going to lie; I like lunch. I love food. But going to lunch just doesn't satisfy me as much as you would think. For one thing, the lines are long. Really long. There are students who literally jet out of their classrooms as soon as the bell rings, and run like the wind all the way to the cafeteria just to get their food a little faster. But being a senior this year, I am frankly too lazy to run to lunch every day.

Since I gave up on running, it takes me fifteen minutes to order the school's infamous chicken Caesar wrap. I am then forced to inhale it in order to get to my next class on time. It's a pretty sight to see, my three best friends and me (we're dainty pom-pom girls) shoving food down our faces. Sometimes I get out of line and just grab something from the à la carte line, even though I always need a hot lunch to fill my stomach. Why would I skip out on hot lunch? Cutters. I hate cutters! They should be put in jail. Cutters are fooling innocent students and keeping hungry people from the food that they stood in line for! I should confront them one day, but I'm too nice. No, I lied. I'm afraid they're going to eat me. But one day, I'm going to pinpoint a regular cutter and cut in front of him. That should make him angry. But then I suppose I would be a cutter, too, and would have to hate myself, and that's not cool . . . Since fourth hour, which is my lunch hour, is the only time the bathrooms by the cafeteria are open, I usually go to the bathroom during lunch. The other ones, with the missing doors by the classrooms, kind of creep me out. Why no doors? My best guess is that it has to do with the fire in the boys' bathroom last year. Someone decided it would be funny to start a bonfire in the wastebasket. This probably led to the removal of the bathroom doors; if there were ever a fire now, the administrators would be able to see it right away. My guess is as good as yours.

Anyhow, if I had my way I would drive home and use my own bathroom. Why? There's always a bit of, let's say, moisture, on the toilet seat. It's kind of repulsive. After wiping it off with a wad of paper and then covering the seat with ten strips of tissue, it's almost not worth going anymore. But then you really have to, so you finally sit down, or hover, whatever your preference is. Then you do your business. When it's time to flush, what do you see? Feminine products thrown behind the toilet. It's as if there were a party thrown in the bathroom by Always and Tampax, and they forgot to clean up.

After lunch, my day is typical. I hike through the hallways. I fall asleep. I wake up to some guy puking all over the floor. I go to the bathroom and check to see if there's a fire in the wastebasket. You know, the usual.

But there's one more thing I cannot escape. Lanyards. Our administration thought that our school would be a safer place if the students wore IDs. They even thought ahead and put these IDs on lanyards that release when pulled on. I like to snap the breakaway part during class and to bite my ID. It's a habit now. Although the lanyards were introduced with good intentions, they really made the situation worse. First of all, none of the teachers check to see if we're wearing our actual IDs. My friends and I switch all the time. Being one of the only Asian girls in my high school, you'd think someone would notice me wearing an Arab guy's ID. So much for safety or even identification. And students pull on each other's lanyards for mere entertainment, saying, "Hey look, I'm choking you!" Exact words, I promise. High schoolers are really dumb sometimes. When I first got my lanyard, it didn't break away. People were choking me like crazy. When I finally broke it in, I was relieved that I would no longer have to worry about dying during school. Point is, I don't think students would have thought to choke each other in the first place were it not for the whole breakaway lanyard idea.

After all the craziness, the bell finally rings, making me want to jump for joy and run blindly out of the building. But I can't. I have to weave my way through the hallway, go out into the parking lot (where there's usually a crowd of people watching a really lame fight), and wait for the real traffic to subside.

Packing

~~~~~~

I'm trying to breathe.

The bathroom light's dim and I'm staring at the mirror. My mouth's twisted at the corners in an ugly grimace. I'd laugh at how I look, but it's not funny. My eyes sting.

It's April, I'm fifteen, and my parents tell me we're moving in July. "San Diego will be wonderful," my mother says in Korean, as if she expects me to grab that sentence like a present, squeeze it tightly.

I stare at her, shock coiling tight on my tongue. I sputter, I spit, "I don't want to go!"

"What do you mean, you don't *want* to?" she snaps. Her stare knifes into me.

"I DON'T WANT TO!" my voice explodes. I'm being a howling brat. But the matter at hand is viciously weighty, life-altering. My sister is five, chubby-cheeked, and totally resilient: She'll forget in no time. She hasn't even started first grade yet. But my world's cracked out of orbit. It's blurry at the edges and worse when I blink.

"There's nothing to *cry* about," my mother says, the word rounded in Korean, *oorruh*, not the hard dip and grin of *cry* in English. She laughs in a quiet breath. She thinks I'm being ridiculous.

Now I'm in my bathroom, thrusting my hands in the tap water, trying to scrub the red from my face. I don't want to leave Barstow. It will be the first move in four years. Four years is a long time to stay in one place for me—enough that I thought I wouldn't have to leave another school behind.

I define my life by the schools I've gone to. It's the only way I can remember how many times I've moved. I've lived in more than eight cities, usually only one or two years each, most dotting the breadth of southern California: Los Angeles's graffiti-stained streets to Riverside's sweet suburban orange groves to Pasadena, home of the Rose Parade. And once, for only six months, in Dayton, Ohio, crisply folded in snow and bordered by woods. I'd started fourth grade in September with everyone else in California, then had to move that winter and finish off the school year in Ohio.

I've learned how to pack my life neatly into cardboard boxes. The easiest part is books; they come in standard shapes and stack, fitting cleanly. Unpacking them is just as gratifying: They slide onto shelves and fill blanks with bright spines. Cookware is harder and has to be bound in paper. The most awkward are the things that people who move less frequently don't even bother taking with them, like hangers. My mother never assigns me the difficult tasks, because I'd let wires and wooden skeletons tangle; in her hands, they unknot and spring free once they've arrived at their new home. But there are always things I lose, no matter how hard I try. The worst thing is the people. Somewhere there must be a how-to book on letting teenage friendships go: Step one, announce you're leaving. Step two, not-so-bittersweet gatherings, all softened by vehement promises to keep in touch. Step three, move away. Step four, write and write, and realize that you can't possibly record your life in these envelopes. Still, I eagerly pick new kinds of stationery, collect e-mail addresses.

"Dear Deborah, How are you? I am fine. Remember that one time you gave me that sticker, well I got one for you this time. Also, I got a new dog!!! I miss you. Write back!!! Love,"

They all go something like this. It's not sad, not really, because my life goes on, too, but it's troubling. They'll get older, they'll get dogs, they'll grow out of their shoe sizes and change clothing styles, and will they remember me? Does it matter, either way? I only remember faint, vaguely rosy details of each city. This is six months of Ohio:

Drew was hilarious and grinned a lot, tan skin, a round face, hair shaved so his scalp showed. "You used to be quiet, now you're so loud!" he'd said at the end of the year. Beth: rectangular-rimmed thick glasses, mousy hair in unruly waves, pointed nose, pale. My favorite friend, because she was as quiet as I was, at least on the surface. I think I made her cry once with my bossiness. We must have made up, like kids do, "sorry" and "it's OK," apologies in the form of orange popsicles. This is troubling, too: my friends forever frozen as they were when I left them, even though I know they've moved on.

People get replaced on both sides. It's my fault, too. Somehow everything ends up being cut apart like packing tape. Or maybe that's not the right analogy, not always; maybe it's more like a hunk of cheese, grated away until it's gone. You nick the skin on a knuckle. To my parents, not seeing someone for months, even for a few years, they're still friends. But to me, a friend must stay constant; we must thrive. If we grow apart, it's lost because people change, especially if you're fifteen. There are too many things that matter: different favorite color, new crush, new car. Suddenly you don't know that person anymore.

My friend Zul, from fifth and sixth grade, Riverside, sent me a letter a few years ago with a photo: her as a cheerleader, fierce, grinning, proud, with cheerful teeth and dark hair pulled tight from her face into a smart ponytail. Did I suspect she would become a cheerleader? Sure, of course she would. Not the ditzy giggling type, but a warrior, assured and capable. But it's not enough because people will never tell you the exact details that make up their life, just things that occur to them. I know because I do it, too.

"I have some of your pictures," she writes. I'd locked on to Japanese animation obsessively, and I used to copy pictures off of trading-card stickers, thinking I was so good at drawing. Round Sailor Moon eyes, with adorably pointy noses and small mouths. "I hope you still draw." I do still draw, but I've moved on, realized that I wasn't so good after all. I'm now obsessed with drawing profiles, the nose and the edges of the lips, the forehead, the eyelash from the invisible side of the face. I don't bother to tell her this, and that letter is one of the last times I'll hear from her.

My father is an ordained minister of the United Methodist Church, which means our family relocates whenever the bishop assigns him to another congregation. I'm a P.K., a Preacher's Kid, which is strange to announce at a new school because it has loaded connotations. Oh, goody two-shoes most people think and immediately censor their R-rated swearing, as if I'll call down the Almighty Wrath of God to scorch the soles of their feet.

I never thought I'd get used to Barstow—that little tourist stop on the way to Las Vegas, in California's Mojave Desert, dry and mercilessly hot. Miles of dusty sand, brush, and rock cramp it from all corners. It's literally in the middle of nowhere. But I did get used to it, somehow. I got used to 110 degrees in late May and driving forty miles to reach the next city.

I made it past the painful first day of school, the nerve-wracking routine of invading a place where everyone else has jostled shoulders and built up kingdoms of nicknames. I'd done it so often that I know how to square myself. I find an open spot at the lonely end of a lunch table and eat quietly, waiting for someone to talk to me. This is why I've always been a nose-burier in books. I can distract myself and make friends effortlessly—war-painted animals, doomsday viruses, kid heroes.

Lunch that day was abrasive, I remember: A Mexican girl in front of me in line shoved her face near mine and demanded, "You China?" I wanted to cross it out in midair, in bright red ink: ~~China~~. Chinese. I wasn't a country by myself.

"No," I said, "I'm Korean." Would she really care to know that I'd never been to South Korea or that I'd been born in California? I was American, just as she was, but Barstow was a smaller community than what I'd been used to. There were so few Asian kids that we were distinct and instantly recognizable. "CHING CHONG CHING!" some boys screamed once when my dad picked me up after school, nothing I hadn't heard before. In the last class of my first day, I befriended a girl, Annie, with curly strawberry blonde hair and a bright grin. She was a P.K., too, and knew about moving because her dad was a U.S. Army chaplain. They moved her to Japan the next year, and for a while I got her letters in equally curly red handwriting and sent letters back until they stopped.

Here they call it Promotion when you graduate middle school. It passed quickly, and high school wasn't so scary either. By ninth grade, I had a group of friends, Denise being the closest—long curly hair, braces, petite but well curvy, hazel eyes under contacts. (These last two details show that we were supposed to have moved on to makeup and boys.) She's smart and sharply competent; she accepts that I'm quiet yet sees that I'm loud inside sometimes. Denise is my complement: more outgoing, knows how to dance, can poke boys in the shoulder and earn a grin. Our other friends' ways are more crass. They take pride in being punky: hot-pink hair, black eyeliner, lip piercings, metal-studded bracelets, bondage pants with too many zippers. Secretly I like their MTV fashion sense. They also take pride in getting bruises after skateboard crashes. Curse words peel freely off their lips in the teenage exhale, becoming noun, adjective, and verb. Barstow is a kiln for oddity and rebellion because it's up to our generation to break the dusty monotony.

I don't get into heavy conversations with these other friends, I don't reveal my secrets. I've been labeled "the smart Asian girl," demurely quiet, even if my head roils with bloody knuckles and sharp teeth. "She never talks," says one of my friends when we're hanging out next to the freeway bridge, watching the others ride their skateboards and howl down a steep ramp. I wait for people to come to me. It's really my fault that the layers of silence have stacked up.

And Barstow isn't exactly fun, most of the time—our "mall" is tiny and half shut down. With no other choices, Wal-Mart is where everyone shops; K-Mart's gone out of business. My family drives three hours to reach the Korean supermarket in Roland Heights.

It's my sophomore year of high school. It's too *late* to move now.

I've never had the security of, say, the band niche, where the orchestra will accept you based on your musical instrument, or possessed a day-one charisma like so many boys I know. They kick their insecurities away and replace them with raucous quips and can tell the world to piss off. Nobody likes the girl who can answer every question, but they like the boy who makes class more interesting.

Near the end of this year I'd found yet another friend, Nadine, who's similar to me in many ways: She's strong in her Christian faith, she has an avid adoration of anime and a sense of humor that includes irony and literary wordplay. She questions things around her, lunges down the valedictorian track, and viciously loves to play *Tomb Raider*. Nadine and I could have been closer, best friends maybe. But now I'll have to leave her, too.

"The schools are much better," my mother says of San Diego, as if the promise of academia is enough. "The new church needs your father. It's very small." I don't care how great it will be: I'm graduating in two years.

I couldn't remember if I'd ever truly protested a move like this. My mother probably hadn't expected it. We never fight about moving because I will lose. Her words were sharp. "Do you think it was easy for me?" she demanded. I knew what was coming next: her immigration and assimilation difficulties, the language barrier. "It was hard. It's still hard." She doesn't have to tell me how she hates the way her thick accent makes her sound in English, unsure and hesitant, when the woman I know can be ferocious, sharper-tongued than anyone else. She was saying to me, get over it. You'll survive.

But I ran from it and slammed the door—even though I know. I know that whatever staggering inconvenience this is to me, I have no choice. I drag an arm roughly across my face. Some part of me says maybe there's a reason we're moving. Maybe God wants this for us. Maybe it'll be better there.

I take another breath.

There are possibilities: a bigger library, a new selection of classes, bright lights hitting off dark water, frequent trips to the aquarium. Maybe I'll even be able to go to a concert. There's no chance of any band I like touring here. My parents had visited the city, my school: perfect weather, "like being on vacation," my mother had said, gesticulating officiously. The beach, the malls, the bookstores, and green everywhere. No stubbly plains but concrete stretches of lazy palm trees, with metal monoliths downtown.

I think of the changes. I think of the constants. I think of what stays with me—my family. They have taught me never to take things for granted, to be perpetually thankful, to pick out the bright pieces. My father recalls a time when he was a child in Korea. He had to eat fish and imagine the salt because they couldn't afford it. Now we have a huge kilogram bottle of salt that I use far too liberally and cost less than a bottle of water. My father, who has the steadiest patience and an eager enthusiasm and grins he's so unafraid to give to new people. He tempers my mother's fast boiling points and roars with real laughter. My mother, not the nagging Asian matriarch, but an artist with a critical eye, with hands that can cool burns and deftly chop and can sculpt pieces that should be displayed in a museum but instead rest cutely on our fireplace mantle. My sister, five and as zesty as a can of soda wildly shaken, who I am secretly fiercely proud of. They've helped shape who I am: to value *people*, always, to read books, do your best, be happy, we love you.

And with each move there is more and more comfort in the intangible, the digital. I've found that the Internet isn't stuffed full of seedy sixty-year-old perverts but people like me—who live wherever, doesn't matter—posting adamantly about favorite bands, books, movies, arguing video game nuances. I'm not going to lose these friends: If they change, I'll change with them.

I looked up a few childhood names on Facebook some time ago. I immediately found profiles that I recognized, but I didn't message them. I just grinned to myself in a wave of warmth, wondering how they were doing, how much they'd changed, what they were into now. Then I closed the window.

I won't ever be completely ready to move. But coping with all these changes will help me face the adult world head-on. I'll continue to adapt, to grow, to learn. I just have to trust that. I close my eyes and tell myself, in another bathroom that soon won't be mine, it'll be OK. I flick off the light.

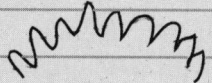

Friendships: Gone Well, Gone Poorly, Just Gone

Lies We Have Told

I dreamt about Kate last night. She was twelve years old, golden
hair streaming down her face while she cried. Not just cried, but
bawled. I don't remember why but it was probably my fault. It still
seems like it was always my fault.

Kate and I weren't the same person. We had different interests
and we didn't even spend that much time together. But the time we
did spend together was crazy. We were thirteen, and when we were
with each other, we knew no limits. There was one time we went on a
hike for hours, and sometime halfway through we picked up Irish ac-
cents. I don't remember who started talking that way, I just remember stubbornly refusing to be the first to drop it. There was another
time we dressed up as the Riders of Rohan—you know, the horsemen
from *Lord of the Rings*—after watching all of the extra scenes and
learning about their fighting tactics. We wore our costumes to the
opening-night show, buying our popcorn in jodhpurs and all. It was
just like us that we couldn't stop at a sane place.

Eventually, though, Kate and I drifted apart, because we are just
too different. She doesn't understand why I care about things like
grades and speech team, and I don't understand why she ignores the
teachers and skulks around at home after school. Even though we no
longer sit together at lunch and can go for weeks without saying a
single hello to each other, we still retain a sense of guttural loyalty.
She keeps a key to my house for times when she needs a place
to crash, no questions asked. When her mother goes manic, or her

sister goes depressive, I'll walk into my room and she'll be sprawled on the bed reading Dorothy Parker. I'm always surprised, and it's always awkward. But I let her know every time that if it helps, if it calms her down, then of course she can come over.

So when she calls me at three in the morning on a Tuesday in February, weeks since I've seen or heard from her, I sneak out of my house without a second thought. We meet at the elementary school playground between us.

It's sleeting, my clogs are entirely inadequate footwear, and my fleece leaves me shivering. I know why she called me. The school network of gossip had broadcast that she'd tried to kill herself by taking ten Advil. Ten Advil? I'm furious with her. Why can't she just do it properly? I know this isn't the reaction you're supposed to have about a friend's suicide attempt. But I'm sick of her depression, sick of her manipulation, and my normally charitable disposition has been warped. Have I not taught her how to do research? She just doesn't listen. She's sloppy. Then I realize exactly how horrible I sound, and I curl up sullenly on the frozen picnic table. I see her coming now. And when I see her, I am sad for her. Still furious, but so much sadder. She's practically flying through the winter air, tall and thin. Her pale skin has flushed with the cold or from running. I don't move near her; she'll come.

I'm on top of the picnic table and she sits on the bottom part, so I'm looking down on her a bit. "Are you OK?"

She says, "I went to the hospital because I—"

"Took ten Advil. I know." Her face changes to slightly confused, like now she doesn't know what game we're playing. But honestly, neither do I. She's altered the rules on me. We weren't supposed to become the teenagers who "have problems." So seeing her now, depressed, broken, all I can think is that she's betrayed me. And I am very, very angry. "Why? Why did you do it?"

She looks like this wasn't where she was planning to start. But it's an OK opening, so she shoves up her sleeve. Scars line her arm.

They aren't all that neat—Kate's never been tidy. She looks at me and she says, "That's why."

I get her point—she's depressed, she's cutting herself. What is she using to do it? Her scars are too deep to be a steak knife and too short to be a cooking knife. I grab her wrist, harshly. "You're using the knife I gave you, aren't you? The Swiss Army knife we carved pens with? The pens we used to write letters to the actors. *That* knife?" I look her straight in the eye, furious, and she nods and looks away.

Kate has finally begun to grasp the depth of my mood and she tenses. She knows I like my information in order, preferably high-lighted and bullet-pointed. So she starts talking. "If you want to know why, people try to commit suicide when they're getting better. When they're beginning to come out of a depression. Because they have more energy. So they can actually carry out their plans." Christ she sounds flat. I'm sure she memorized that from some doctor.

But she's got me focused again, just like she wanted. "So why are you depressed?" This might not be the best question, but it has to be asked.

Kate lectures about how it's chemical, how drugs can treat it, and all the bullshit we hear at school but we know isn't true. In the end the drugs aren't going to help her. They might be making her feel better now. They might be acting as a straitjacket—because without them she would try to kill herself again and again until she got it right. But to say they'll make her better? They won't, and neither of us thinks they will.

I don't know why I'm not quite satisfied, but something hasn't been said. Kate must have known that I was already aware of her de-pression, likely her suicide attempt, even if I hadn't talked to her in weeks. She could have held this conversation over the phone. So I sit there and look at her. I ask very quietly, "What else?"

She gets up. She takes a step away from me. She turns around and finally glances back toward the picnic table. She takes a deep breath, squares her shoulders, and looks me in the eye. "I'm bisexual," she says, no preamble.

I close my eyes. I am at home. I see the golden round wooden dinner table. I smell couscous and salmon and salad. I hear my brother practically bouncing with enthusiasm telling us about his psych class. They've learned about the Kinsey scale, and he thinks it's the greatest idea since last week's Jungian dreams.

But when I open my eyes, I'm back with Kate and the world is an uglier place. I realize that she doesn't want to hear what a bunch of old-fart psychologists think. I rub my eyes to bide for time and try to find something to say that doesn't seem too corny. "Oh. I never knew." I'm working hard through my memory here. She has a boyfriend, David. "What did David say?"

Kate scowls. "He says it's fine with him." She hasn't liked him in a while, I think, but couldn't quite bring herself to dump him.

Then, out of the blue, she looks at me imploringly. "Will you be my friend?"

I haven't been Kate's friend, really, since I was fourteen, and she hasn't been mine. Am I supposed to lie? This is a depressed girl who cuts herself. This is a girl who takes ten Advil because she might want to end her life but isn't certain. This is a girl who is very, very scared of her sexuality. This is a girl I pity. This is a girl I want to help. But to be friends with? I'm scared to be friends with her, and I hate myself for thinking it. I hate that I'm too weak to do something, that I can't make her better. So I do the next best thing I can think of. I lie.

I look at her and I smile and I tell her, "Of course."

And she believes me, because right now she'll believe anyone who says they want to be her friend. And because this is the only time she's ever seen me lie.

The truth is, for three years, I was there. Sixth grade to the middle of ninth, I listened when she needed to talk. I encouraged her to make friends, to join clubs: GSA, mini-golf, Spanish. I met her boyfriends and girlfriends. But the truth is also that I wasn't there. I never talked. I never mentioned my family or my friends or my life at all. I never gave. I never loaned her CDs or clothes or confidences.

The last time I saw Kate she was crossing a street, the day before I left town. I turned my head and pretended not to notice her doing the same thing. These are the daily lies that she and I have lived. And the biggest lie of all is that I am here. What kind of a friend am I?

Sarah Harrison, 17

Tampoons

‾‾‾‾‾‾‾‾‾

It starts in fourth grade. I stand in the hallway outside of the girls' bathroom.

I inform my friend, giggling, that there are "tampoons" in there. But I sound too thrilled.

She wrinkles her careful nose, shakes her head. There's something about her that makes me feel sloppy and always will. Today she's not generous.

"Don't you mean *tampons*," she says, not gently.

What. Yeah, oops.

But I'm not embarrassed. Not yet. Oh, the realization of a word mispronounced and the accompanying bile always rose from my stomach a little too late, even at that age. Tampons, Tampons, Tampons. The first proof for me that a little knowledge could be converted to power?

Well . . . don't you want to go look?

No.

I'm so eager to please her. She's so pretty. Her hair is shiny, so straight and dark. I once reached out with one hand, enchanted, wanting to touch it. But I controlled myself.

Fifteen minutes later, the entire fourth grade has been arranged in rows in the auditorium. We pretend to be quiet. A man on stage talks; he is not magically charming. She sits three seats down, talking to somebody. And when I look at her the others part; she's far away, between rows of corn. Her hair falls forward, shielding her face with haughty silk curtains, automatic. Now she's whispering, she of more wisdom than a ten-year-old should possess, *This looks suspicious.* She turns and looks at me. She's honest since her hair has shifted to the side, and her face is terrible. It makes me know I wasn't afraid of just nothing. "We'd better stop," she says to the other girl, looking right at me.

Then it *is* too late. I know that I have made a ridiculous mistake. I'm turning into one of *those* women. Those women who don't know. Those women who are always a little bit out of control, those wince-inducing women who take up the entire room. They talk too loudly, they boom at you. They lean into your face and spit, their laugh is grating. Their complexions are too red, and their skin is the surface of an orange—large, uneven pores stretched tightly over faces. Thick and soft white arms in a sleeveless blouse look worse from behind. At the age of ten, I have been given a cosmic advantage: I know that the worst part of the body isn't anything laughed about in hallways and nothing in a bathroom. Never in the corner of the yard hanging around the head of crying Jack, whose pants are around his ankles. The worst part is the line an unfit arm makes with the back, from the back. It's not a line but a curve away from the head, creating the impression that there has been an overflow. Food turns to cud in these mouths. This is a woman who clutches the stem of her wineglass too tightly—the cool, icy neck choking under sausage fingers—until the goblet breaks off into her hand.

"Oops," she would say, getting up to help. "Oh god, I'm sorry! I'm such a klutz." Hahaha.

Then the hostess, the graceful hostess, leans over with something in her hand that's a little bit too classy to be a rag and wipes the wine away.

"Oh," she would say, fingers shying away from the wetness on the cloth. "That's OK, it's part of your charm, isn't it?" Hahaha.

And I'll want to thank her for making me feel better, and I'll want to reach out with one arm and slap her. But I will control myself. I afford her what she refuses me. I can look through thick wine and see her the way she wishes to be seen.

Big Shoes

~~~~~~

On June 27, 2006, I got up relatively late, and because I wasn't working, lounged around in my pajamas until I had to get ready for my friend Felicia to come over. Felicia, my sister, and I watched a documentary, *Mad Hot Ballroom,* and then, since it was beautiful and sunny out, we got dressed up and went out in the yard to do a photo shoot. All normal things we do on a normal day. Hours later, when I came back from dropping Felicia at her house, that's when things began to shift.

"We really need to talk . . ." Whenever these words had come from my mother it always meant bad news, and it was even worse when she waited until my friend was gone to tell me. The last time was when my grandfather died, and I immediately wondered who in my family could have passed away. My grandmother? Who was sick, who was old? I braced myself, but I now know I couldn't have prepared or guessed.

Sarah Bradford was one of those people who, once you met her, treated you like you were her true friend. If she knew your name you were important enough to say hello to, catch up with. This is unusual in high school. I never would have admitted it to anyone, but I really wished I could be more like her. It was hard for me to grasp how she could throw aside all inhibitions and just walk up to someone, whoever they were, and start a conversation. I've always been on the shy side and very concerned with what I was saying, worrying that people were judging me. Sarah had the ability to just talk. This was only intensified when she was on stage, for a dance recital or school musical. She could project charisma and charm and sing from her heart.

Sarah was also one of the best dancers ever. That's how we met, through dance class. Sometimes she would come in, all smiling, and tell me the smallest details of her life—about the new sneakers she'd bought and how they weren't fitting because she had a bunion from dancing on pointe for so long and the ridiculous ways she was trying to wear them in—but she was even better at listening. And, in a scene where conversation about food is almost always about dieting, Sarah would cheerfully, no hang-ups, bring sandwiches into the studio and talk about how much ice cream she'd had with her friends while watching a movie. Any comment that could be taken as ditzy (it happened) was disregarded, because Sarah's ditzy behavior wasn't fake; it was endearing.

By the time Sarah graduated from high school she'd become the best jazz dancer in her class and was given a solo. She'd come off stage out of breath, most of the makeup on her face in pools. Yet the last thing anyone would think about her was that she was sweaty and tired, and it didn't matter to her that she had to reapply her makeup or change into her next costume without a rest. I had to really work in order to become a good dancer and everything that comes with it; Sarah just seemed able to do it.

What I know now is only what I've been told and read in the newspaper. Early on the morning of June 27th, it had been raining relatively hard before Sarah set out for her part-time job. The roads were really slippery. About a mile from home, she lost control of her car. It was just one of those freak things; she hydroplaned and skidded off the road. The car stopped when it made contact with a tree, and because she'd forgotten to put on her seatbelt—like every young person does every once in a while—Sarah was thrown from the vehicle. She died on impact.

How was it possible that a girl only four years older than me was dead? What was so wrong with the universe that Sarah's parents would outlive their daughter? It didn't make sense and, nearly a year later, it still doesn't. I've experienced two deaths since Sarah's, and neither affected me like this. When someone dies young, all you can do is keep asking why.

Sarah was always smiling or working her hardest to make other people smile. I measure my grief over her as bad days and not-so-bad days. Some days everything I do reminds me of her. Dancing is difficult. And my friends don't really understand the loss I feel because none of them were part of the family of our dance studio. In the worst moments, I try to remember that she's smiling down on me and begging me to smile with her. The grass is green around her headstone and the shadow from the tree shimmies on the ground as the wind shifts the leaves. I stand there and bury my hands deep into my pockets, hoping that I don't cry too hard. I can hear the speed and music and danger of the cars driving by. I realize that Sarah had what any person really wants during their lifetime: family and friends who loved her more than she could ever possibly imagine. I look up at the sky and put a smile on my face, "Hey, Sarah, promise me one thing? Teach those angels how to dance, will you?"

An Orchid, If That Is What It Is

〜〜〜〜

I smell gin and tonic, corn syrup blood, and lavender air freshener. Ruffled chips, sour cream dip, the sterile scent of Frick museum art classes. I see the pastel, boutique colors of leggings and their matching shirts, cursive across my friend Ava's flat chest in French. Ava, my best friend when I was nine, nine years ago, nine my favorite number, the month I was born, the number of times I would count to with my finger fortune teller. Ava who lived across the park, sheltered by wooden floors and locked wine cellars, Ava now in the middle of nowhere. Everyone forgets about her when listing who left, classmates lost along the way. I remember silently and hope that no one will ask for another pinky promise, or, to this day, "Of course we know you didn't. But did you?"

My best friend Ava's giggle makes up for her mother's shaded voice, sunglasses burying her smoky red eyes, quenched only by popped corks. Ava's voice is like a balloon filled with helium, floating gently around my head. My mother watches Ava's mother French braid Ava's obedient hair. My mother says now that she never liked the way Joyce laughed or the way she wore her sunglasses inside. Ava's mother always had her hand on my mother's shoulder, but on pick-up from a play date, they would talk standing up and only in the foyer. Ava's mother said *foyer* the French way. Both mothers were committed to our story that they were friends. Once my mother got stuck, alone in their elevator, on Halloween. Ava's mother, safe in her grand foyer, laughed morbidly and said, "This is outrageous." Ava's mother stood, legs crossed like she was sitting. Her voice was all panic and perfume, and my mother always sighed, a sigh that said, *I will be your neighbor. I will follow through.*

Ava was the back of a brunette's head, fine strands of brown that grew and grew because her mother thought all cuts were open to infection. My friend Ava's hair always ended in a light green bow, a kite. And just as a kite has a way of spiraling down, so did Ava.

When I walk past her building, I wonder if the doormen still remember not to let me in. That mural of the meadow on Ava's wall, the four-poster bed, the washing machine. Her Beanie Babies had the same fake flower scent her room had.

Ava always had party favors without the parties, those shiny red packages you pull for the spark, not what's inside. Every holiday was celebrated, every activity played, every toy tested, perfection. She said *orange* in a Californian way, one of the ordinary words I made her repeat over and over—so juicy and fresh and special. I wanted to learn to say it her way; it was better. Ava poured forth laughter like blood, pooling around her ankles like the woman in the shower in the same horror movie her mother took us to so many times at midnight on Fridays and sometimes Thursdays. Her mother secretly craved to be that woman, naked and bloody, the victim. I watched, knowing each second that it would give me nightmares. But I said I liked it, and Ava nodded, too. Her mother did not make the connection between shivers of cold and shivers of fright. She just buttoned her daughter deeper into a cashmere cardigan because movie theaters are always ten degrees colder.

My friend Ava never liked the Spice Girls. She liked dogs more than cats but was a member of my third-grade cult, Cat Honory. She ate turkey sandwiches with too much mayonnaise. Ava's grandmother taught me to peel carrots; she ate Jell-O with gin and had Rapunzelline white hair whose ends I wanted to pull out of her clip and climb up. Ava was an anthology, a fairy-tale tradition. She was ageless because I had known her forever and only for a year.

I considered confession, writing a letter. I have a draft in my notebook, but it reads in a way I could share with my mother: "I'm sorry, but what did I do wrong?" I could never send it, and I didn't, but now I look at it and ask myself the same. What am I sorry for? What did I do wrong?

Ava loved to play hide-and-seek; she loved to eat sushi. She taught me that wasabi and a lot of other things sting, that the pretty green Play-Doh the color of her bow would tie my throat in little knots and suck the cartilage from my nose. I never touched it. I drew a wobbly line between the wasabi and the rice, and I would not allow my chopsticks to cross. Now when I order sushi with my best friend, stick my chopstick in and plop the poison on my tongue, I realize my taste buds have gone numb.

It's easier to continue a lie than to admit—I used to set out dates at night when I would come forth, when no one would care anymore. I wish I had known that secrets get stronger over time. In physics now I wonder whether it has something to do with force times distance. My arms, like Ava's, are weak; we never could do back bends. Ava lent me Stila lip gloss. Ava loved Stila lip gloss. She loved white gloves and ballroom dancing, black patent leather shoes, Purell, pearls, pocketbooks, and pleated skirts. Sea Monkeys, American Girl dolls, *Little Women*, horror movies. Ava loved Christmas ornaments, one-minute chocolate-chip cookies. My friend Ava loved almost everything; her mother said so, too. Her mother was the only thing Ava did not love.

Ava's mother's cotton-ball hair was dirty and sometimes fluttered off, strewn with colorless lint, so dappled that I couldn't tell whether the gray was covering the white or the white the gray. It was Sunday and spring—months after the fall—when my mother pointed to the cherry blossoms. I walked beside her and felt a smile fall onto her face, a little sideways. We watched Ava walk down Park Avenue with her mother, holding hands. As we approached, I saw my mother and hers make eye contact. They turned away from us, one after the other in quick succession. My mother said nothing until we got home, and still not to me. I was on my way to the kitchen and she sat on a wicker chair pulled close to the phone. "Unbelievable . . . as if Elizabeth was the victim . . . as if my child was evil. Poor Ava."

It's hard for me to line up my memories of my friend Ava in order. I cross town to walk by her building and wonder whether they sold the apartment. I walk through the school and the museums, places that had once existed only when we were together. The year of Ava was the year I read *The Phantom Tollbooth*, the year I wore dangling earrings for the first time, the year I decided I would be an actress. Now those decisions, those experiences are minor parts of who I have become, but Ava, she is always there. There's no pride in keeping my secret but in telling it, a story more than a confession—to write the last thing you would want on paper. I wanted to see how the story felt on my tongue and how it scattered. I thought the days with Ava and the way it ended on the stairs was the transition, the metaphor. But it is my life since. And it is still too soon to tell the truth in a straightforward way.

My days with Ava were not separate days; they were an abstract always, reflected in the light that would stay on in her building across the park. I would imagine it, because my best friend Ava would not sleep over. Chronologically one cannot see the extremes of our friendship or the accumulation of motives, because it was not time that transformed me. We wore the same soft lavender sweaters and the same cherry-red lipstick that was really ChapStick. I still sometimes wonder why Ava would not spend the night. Whether it was her mother forbidding her or her own discomfort. I think I should have seen the signs that this sisterhood was to Ava like artificial sweetener, to me like sugar. If Ava was allergic to cats because I had one, allergic to dish soap because that was what dripped onto her palms when she could barely reach my kitchen sink. If she was afraid to sleep over because she was allergic to me, then she was not innocent.

But I suspect that it was Ava's mother who, disgusted, waited for the right moment to accuse me—it didn't much matter of what. Her mother did not fake innocence; she was dirty. Her mother was responsible for the flutter of Ava's lashes, the pucker of her cheeks, the curl of her bangs, the lilt of her knees, the perfect child. Did she want to ensure that her only daughter, who resembled her estranged husband—broad cheeks, red around the eyes, vein-fair lids, dimpled chin—would be faithful to her needs?

Perhaps it was in watching Joyce French braid Ava's hair and clasp on her bow that I desired to remove it. But I was not so young and not so ignorant. I saw that Joyce would never let me pry something so crafted from her hands without consequence. I tried anyway. Maybe it was because at nine years old I could not let go of such a dream of having Ava the way I wanted her. We would cross the streets alone, Ava and I, and sleep at my house with Nick at Nite. I saw in her more potential, more character than her mother allowed. And as I watched her eyes hollow out, I wanted to save her.

I had called Ava—to whom I was attached, in love with, inseparable—on Easter morning: "What are you wearing? How is your hair? Can we be sisters?" Joyce rang the bells of her daughter's name, "Ava," with a mocking sort of charity, like the Santa Claus outside Bloomingdale's begging for some change, an opportunist to say the least. It was Ava, her daughter, who she loved so much she sent her husband away to Iceland "on business." It was her only child who could even get away with being chubby. Ava, my best friend, who I would push down the stairs and wanted for all my life to be free. And, according to her mother, Ava who I poisoned with chocolates and wanted to be. There I was, in front of her mother's two-thirds-gin gin and tonic, sticking my hand in her bag of chips, dipping an Easter egg in her food coloring. I plucked off Ava's bow and unbraided her hair.

The day after, Joyce, chivalrous and neighborly, sent us an Easter card and a plant. I forget the name but the flowers were unforgettable: large spoons with paisley points protruding sharp from each center, fans that seemed plastic and unwilling to close. Unreliable, they altered from a creamy color in the light of afternoon to a piercing white at night. I never saw them in the morning. These flowers stood by the tray of my father's pens beside my parents' bed, matching their sheets. I cannot think of anything in nature that is this color, but these flowers were not natural in any way. They were flamboyant, distracting, oppressive to the wallpaper, and sarcastically optimistic. They sat, self-sufficient and not calling for water, exotically inhuman in their needs. They made me uncomfortable, so I could not pull my eyes away from their sticky pupils. They lasted, like ghosts draped in a color too off-white for clouds or snow or Ava's pale skin.

The flowers smelled stronger than the surface soil after a forest fire. Their scent was lightning sharp and my mother couldn't find it: Was it gas from the stove? Mold in the bathroom cabinet? I followed her as she traced paths around the house, sniffing the air and producing no culprit. It scared me, but not because I thought our apartment was burning. I pulled my mother through to their bedroom and placed her vein-veiled hands on the flower pot. She knew it, the sharp smell, the pose. "An odd selection, not to my taste, too strong." It was there, a personification of my friend Ava's mother, choking us.

The moments before the push were all truth-or-dare whispers and mischief giggles, not an actual game but a moment alone with a friend on a landing. We'd tiptoed down to music, swinging arms and recorders back and forth like double Dutch. Ava leapt hyenalike from step to step, braid riveting in the flickering staircase lights. There is no way to look back and love my friend Ava as I did without hating me. "Walk in front of me, Ava, and close your eyes." I pushed weakly, and that was enough. Ava fell. She fell down each of the eight steps and I followed, the same steps I still have to take each day, even though I try to avoid that floor. I wonder if Ava fears me now and how much of it she felt. I wonder if she might not even remember.

It was in that moment on the stairs that Ava and I became mortal. Ava never looked more human than when her fingers gripped the steps and skidded past the last black sparkling edge. I wanted to let go of my friend Ava's hand and I did. I longed to be the one to push her and I did. She stuck on each step and I pushed her and she cried. My friend Ava did not trust me or her mother, but most of all, she did not trust silence. So before she fell she laughed and laughed and eventually she listened. She lost all balance, became a kite bounding wildly through the air. She reached the trees and then I laughed. She was free.

All that propelled my best friend Ava down those steps—one, two, three, four, five, six, seven, eight—at that moment repelled me. My fingernails buried little secrets in my other hand, the lies I told my mother, my teacher, her mother. "Is something the matter?" the teacher's voice, pulling us into the learning specialist's room. "Ava, did Elizabeth do something to hurt you?" She shook her head violently and bit the ends of her braid. "Elizabeth?" He asked me the same question. "Yes, yes," I said, "yes!" I still see that teacher. I pick up a nine-year-old I babysit from his classroom: "Hello Elizabeth." I blush.

I didn't know then that what I did could have been forgiven. Age nine and I felt like a murderer. It's only now, after assessing my motives, after reading *Macbeth* and *Crime and Punishment* and wondering what it means to step over the line, to have blood on one's hands. Purell and white gloves. The lies that I even tried to tell Ava. First, "Are you OK? This is our secret." Then, "What's wrong? Are you mad at me?" Later, "This is unfair."

I did not let my friend fall. I pushed her and I lied. Regret mixed with victory. Lies corrupted my sanity, and I wanted to defend my parents, my teacher, my friends who stood by me.

Ava was pinned to her mother. I imagined her breathless under sheets, forced to stay awake and watch horror movies. That's why, after I had pushed my friend Ava, she did not complain.

When I gave Ava and her mother chocolate, as an apology that still proclaimed my innocence, Joyce returned them to me and called the cherry center poison. She strangled my name through the phone my mother held. "Obsessive compulsive" she'd called me, my mother said. Those words flowered in the pit of my chest, large and cruel. I didn't know what they meant. Now I know it was psychology she was using, calling me irrational and fixated. On what, I still wonder—did she fear my fascination with her daughter or herself? Did she fear letting me too close, that I would know too much?

"She has nerve," my mother said. "She has gall. I never liked her, don't trust her. I wouldn't let you go there again if you wanted to."

"Why did you scream?" I pleaded with her. "Now Ava will never be my friend. You're the cruel one!"

"You didn't hear the other end of the conversation, Elizabeth. I won't let her say about you what's true about her."

I hated that my mother tried to defend me when I was guilty. I began to sleep on my back under the covers so she couldn't kiss the nape of my neck, "ninety-nine kisses," or scratch my back with love.

Ava's mother was stealthy. She knew how to obtain a sure confession the day she stroked my arm, leaned into my breath, "You were just being playful, Elizabeth, right, sweetie? Just playful pushing, like girls do." If that was the way, if saying yes would take Ava's eyes off of me, I would do it, and I did.

"Yes, it was just a joke," I said. And it was true but it was not all true. I was not a playful pusher. But my cruelty bonded mother to daughter and buried me in their past. Who in the world knows the truth now? Who forgives, who ignores, who remembers? I had to push Ava down the stairs to pull away her mother's hands, and so I let her mother's hands push me out of my best friend Ava's life.

Ava's head bobbed out like a kite stuttering on the wind, stuck through the roof of trees on the outskirt of a meadow. I have never seen a meadow like that, but they always say it's a meadow like that that leaves one most vulnerable in a thunderstorm. Green pastures spread out with the swoosh of dandelion powder, the sway of wildflowers, the open sky. Lightning pins storm cloud to carousel, electrical circuits breaking out with rearing white and golden horses, white and golden daisies. Ava's white skin, my golden touch. I wanted to take it back: the lies, the greed, the gold.

In a meadow natural and swirling with life, lightning can dance across the ballroom, a ballerina with white gloves. The best thing one can do is curl into a ball and kneel, pray, or pretend he is not there. But also in a meadow, even lightning just falls to ashes and disappears. And that is what's scary.

Just weeks ago, I left my apartment with a friend. The elevator door opened onto Joyce Monroe standing with my mother. "That scared me!" I say, then, "How *are* you?"

Joyce's hand is already on my mother's shoulder. My mother giddily explains that she'd run into Joyce shopping on Madison Avenue.

"What a small world," my mother repeats every time Joyce speaks.

"I don't remember the city being this hot!" Joyce says.

"Yes," I say, not caring. "How's Ava?"

"She's writing, like your mother tells me you are. Now I know why you *had* to be best friends." My mother laughs charmingly, infatuated with chance, surprise, fate. "Do you have her e-mail address, Elizabeth? Ava misses you."

"I don't know," I answer, certain Ava hasn't said a thing about me but glad for a moment that she's far away and somewhere other than in this lobby with our mothers. I look hard at mine and quickly at Joyce, feeling betrayed, fallen, and somehow forgiven.

Crushes Sweet and
Excruciating, Sex, and
a Love That Ends in
Desert Rehab

Jocelyn Pearce, 15

The Match

~~~~~~

You were tall, cute, and athletic. You had dark hair and dark eyes, and perfect skin that was tan even in the middle of winter. You always seemed to be surrounded by people, always a group of smart and good-looking teenagers all as smart and good-looking as you. You always had a pretty, popular girlfriend. You were in honors classes. You were on the soccer team. You were one of those people who had everything.

I doubt I was alone in having a crush on you, or in learning the hard way the real meaning of the word.

Here you were no exception: To people like you, I was invisible. When I spoke, you didn't hear me, even when I stood less than three feet away. When I made eye contact and smiled—following the advice of my ninth-grade health teacher and ashamed of myself for doing so—you looked right through me. Every time.

Except once you said that you liked an essay I'd written for English about how I wanted to travel the world someday. I treasured that moment. It was ridiculously precious to me. Another time you greeted me in the hallway. It was such a shock. As always, I'd taken a long way to class just to see you; I was willing to be late. It was worth it. "Hey," you'd said. I loved your voice so much I forgot to speak. Those were rare occurrences, though. I can count on one hand the number of times you noticed me in the years I thought I was in love with you.

Every time you didn't see or hear me, I learned again that whoever thought up the word *crush* didn't call it that arbitrarily.

Crushes hurt. Every day, my heart was crushed under your size-11 shoes.

When I discovered you were on the soccer team, I went to a game. I dragged a friend along with me, claiming only a sudden interest in a sport I'd never watched before. You and I belonged to such different social circles that I didn't want even my closest friends to find out I'd foolishly aim so high. You sat in the cafeteria at a table full of people who are worshipped. I sat in the library, two flights of stairs and several long halls away.

You didn't notice me at your game either, three rows up in the bleachers and shivering in the forty-degree weather. But I barely cared. That night, I fell in love with the sport. I realized that soccer is the most popular game in the world for a reason. It's the suspense, the fast pace, the team dynamic, sure—but other sports, basketball or hockey, they have that. I don't know why, for me, that ball being kicked around a field struck me as so much more exciting than one being tossed through a hoop, but it did. It still does. I can shut my eyes and see the winning goal (not yours, you lost) from that match. I still hold my breath in anticipation.

Several weeks later, I sat on a bench outside school, waiting for my ride. Only a few people remained, hanging out in front of the building. You were one of those few people. Two wooden benches covered in graffiti sat between us.

I'd pretended, as I'd walked by, not to notice you. I couldn't help myself, though, and before long I found myself staring. You turned. You caught me. I jerked my head around and looked straight ahead at the passing cars on the street below. My face was bright red. You *knew*. I was mortified.

I realized something then: It didn't matter. I'd said a number of stupid things in front of you and embarrassed myself more times than I cared to remember. So what. Who hasn't done something dumb in front of a crush? Every crush in the history of civilization must have been painful. The thought was strangely liberating. Could I perhaps have been *lucky* in that you almost never registered my existence? If you didn't notice any of the good things about me, you didn't notice any of the bad either. As soon as the last bell rang and you headed to soccer practice, you probably forgot about the moments I'd dwelled on for weeks.

In a way, even after all of the pain, I came out ahead in our one-sided relationship. When I watch soccer on the Spanish channel (the only one I get with any matches less significant than the World Cup), I feel the same thrill I got from that first game, or I'll kick a ball around with friends, and it's all thanks to you.

You, I'm as over you as I can be. I make a beeline to Biology now, get there in plenty of time. I'm sure you haven't noticed not noticing me in the hall. Still, my breath always catches when I see you. No matter how many crushes I have on how many different guys, no matter how many I'm over, you're one I won't easily forget. But I'm not sorry you crushed my heart. It was an unexpected blessing, and soccer really is the greatest sport in the world.

Decent Guy on the Planet

~~~~~~~

I f there were an award for the girl who was sure she'd never get a boyfriend, I would have won, hands down. Last September was a good month, mostly. I started my freshman year at high school and was pursuing modeling (which later went downhill, but that's another story). I should stop there: Yeah, I look enough like a model, disproving a lot of what you think about the girls who always have boyfriends. I'm a five-foot-seven beauty, and most people tell me I'm pretty. But I've *always* been thin, and I've *always* had high cheekbones and light blue eyes. It's old news to me. And it's news of no consequence to a girl—even a girl who's the type to be paid to look pretty— when she's convinced there's not a decent guy on the planet who will like her.

So, last September, I was forever single but made sure that I had a ton of fun with other things, like off-campus lunches. Overpriced croissants and lattes within walking distance became a social ritual, and my friends were the best. My friends *are* the best, and full of school spirit. Hang out with us for two seconds, and you'll either walk away confused or start laughing your head off. But aside from daily excursions with my group of friends, aside from good grades and appropriate attitude, I couldn't deny it: I wanted a boyfriend.

I'm a shy girl, surprisingly quiet when I'm not around people I know well—girls or boys, men or women, even a slightly rude cashier can scare me into silence. With friends, though, I'm my normal loud, spazzy self. I can make people laugh by imitating teachers, random adults, and just the general public. But I also like nothing more than to spend an entire Saturday up in my bright yellow room, reading novels alongside my cat, Grover, with my Marilyn Monroe poster smiling down on us.

I wanted a boyfriend mostly because I'd never had one. I'd seen my friends go through guys, and it seemed like something I shouldn't miss out on. I also had this habit of developing crushes on good guy friends—which was never exactly ideal because they were unaware of my true feelings. And they had a habit, also not ideal, of falling for a close friend of mine just as I was getting up the courage to confess.

After my friend McKenzie got Ray, though, things changed. She'd had boyfriends before, but this one was really cool—a junior who everyone knew she'd liked since sixth grade. They were neighbors, family friends and all! She came to school one Monday morning, smiling and giggling, squealing, "Oh my god! I'm going out with Ray!"

I was so happy for her, but at the same time, I asked myself why I still didn't have a boyfriend. McKenzie even shared my shyness when it came to talking to potential candidates. While Ray definitely had a certain quality about him that was considered attractive by many girls, it was more the getting-the-guy-you-want idea that I liked about their situation.

That day comes back to me every now and then—McKenzie's expression when Ray hugged her, claiming her as his girlfriend in front of everyone—but now I see it in a bittersweet light, since he dumped her two weeks later. I have since decided that Ray is an idiot, because no sane guy would break up with someone so beautiful, sweet, and laugh-out-loud crazy.

I had a good little crush going myself at the time. My friend Jake was really cool. He was hilarious, tall, and nice to everyone. I enjoyed hanging out with him, but, true to form, I wanted more. He was the first guy I could actually think of asking out. And if McKenzie could get her guy, then I could, too, right?

Fast-forward a couple of weeks, and I'm walking toward the stairs to Algebra after lunch Jake has class on the second floor, mine's on the third. (Knowing a crush's basic schedule is just something that happens over time.) I tell my friend to go ahead up, while I wait for Jake at the base of the stairs.

As we walked from the first floor to the second, I asked him out, in the weirdest brain-numbed state. It must have hidden my hyperventilating and general spazziness. He blushed. He said yes. Then we arrived and parted at the second floor. My fear of never-ending singleness had suddenly been stopped, but it was so surreal that it took me a few days to think about anything other than the amazing feat I'd accomplished.

It's been a month and a half, and my and Jake's relationship isn't perfect. But I'm so glad I conquered my fear and asked him out. He's just as cool as I thought he was, maybe better after I saw the comedy play he wrote and starred in for two nights at our school. I know we won't last forever, but he's a perfect first boyfriend for me. And in the future I won't be as scared out of my mind to ask a guy out—which is good, because I plan to do it again. Until then, I have Jake.

Cribs

~~~~~~~

Grinding is the most basic form of dance, requiring no skill or co-ordination. Multiple kids can rub against each other in a grinding chain, although I suppose that's very middle school. Grinding is sexual yet harmless. It takes you to a different place. Suddenly all you can hear is the music—the techno, the rap, the reggae—and all you can feel is the breath on your neck of the person you are with. You know everyone is watching you, you attached to your guy. You hope to god they don't pay attention and that they do.

Your friends come over and whisper, "He's a cutie" into your ear, followed by his friends who say, loudly, "She's hot!" Looking forward to the phone calls after the party ("Who was that boy you were on tonight?"), you focus back on him.

"You're a good dancer."

"Thanks."

You feel the rush of it all, the human part, as the bass fades and you can no longer hear the lyrics: *Work that, let me see you drip sweat. I'm really, really hot.* It's a natural high, but sometimes a guilty one because of how much your parents would disapprove. Your mother had said, "Inches apart! You shouldn't give up your body like that." You can't even think what your older brother would come out with, but you know you would be ripped away from the guy. Still, *that was sexy.*

I had a Super Sweet Sixteen party with one hundred of my "clos-est" friends. This included boys I didn't know well—most of the var-sity hockey team's juniors and seniors, along with some football players—who'd been invited without my permission by desperate girls. *Great*, I thought, *this is going to be a nightmare*. The nerves shot through my body, electric like the pink and blue streamers I'd rushed to drape around the room. Some events person at the tennis club had wrapped Christmas lights around the banisters next to the stairs, filling the off-hours jockey space with festivity. What were my parents going to think about the kids who'd show up wasted? The ones who'll bring alcohol and share it? I could imagine cleaning up after drunks with my upset mother.

"Oh Eliza, will there be dirty dancing? Sorry, will there be *grinding*?" she'd asked me the day before. Of course there would be, and of course she was going to be disturbed by it. I always laughed at her use of "dirty dancing." How obsolete. "My goodness," she'd said, quite seriously, "I hope you don't do that, Eliza."

Waiting for the guests to arrive, I paced around the club. *Gorgeous*, I thought. But my black leggings clung to my shaking legs. The DJ couldn't find an electrical outlet in the whole place, and I was hysterical. "It's about time," I said, viciously, when it was finally discovered. My two best friends got there, the only people in the world who fully understand me. "Everyone is stressed at their own party," they assured me. "Don't be worried, Lyze, you'll be fine."

I smiled, but I still felt pretty nervous. I just wanted my parents and the other chaperones (mostly my friends' parents) out of the picture so they wouldn't bother me about the way we dance. My party had to be the coolest Sweet Sixteen this whole year. I wanted to have fun. I wanted every hockey player to say hi to me at school. I wanted to be remembered. I wanted to hear someone say, "Eliza Appleton is a legend."

More and more kids showed up, and I became increasingly worried. Recently at my school there'd been a dance that got so out of control the police came and shut it down at 9:30. Condensation seemed to drip from the ceiling there as people danced, drank, did drugs, and basically sexually assaulted each other. What if the law broke up my birthday party?

Various scenarios were giving me a headache, and I realized it was better not thinking about things I couldn't control. I tried to remain calm: Grinding is not illegal. Then the music played faster and grew more interesting. Suddenly, many girls were dancing like sluts. I, of course, did not, because my parents were watching, and chaperones were everywhere. Boys grabbed barely dressed girls and groped them as they moved in sync. My best friend's father leaned over and whispered to me, "If that three-hundred-pound football player doesn't get off of that little sophomore, I will punch him."

Bang! It hit the parents hard: What would all the sexual dancing lead to? Had they asked me, I'd have told them that it wouldn't lead to anything. Dancing can be thought of as an art, as expression, perhaps even as make-believe sex. Make-believe. The most exciting thing about grinding is being able to tell your friends afterward that you danced with ten different guys. That you're an excellent grinder and know many ways to do it. Grinding is about feeling good. It isn't harmful, nor is it serious. So why do grown-ups freak out about it so much?

I find parents to be truly funny. I'm sure they were wild and crazy—smoking weed, doing drugs, having sex—when they were our age, a lot more than dancing. I learned in my history class that 2,500 years ago, the ancient Greeks worried that their children would come to no good, that they wouldn't work, or marry. I guess human nature, or at least parents' human nature, hasn't changed over the centuries. I can understand parents being concerned, because of physical and emotional dangers, if their child is having sex. But why are they so worked up about grinding? Is it because they fear other parents will judge them to be too lenient? Some parents (not mine) want to appear cool to the kids, and a few even to the other adults. Some are plain old strict, fearing our fun will lead to trouble. They scare us by telling us not to get too close to boys, not to dance like that—but then how will *we* look cool to the kids? How are we supposed to gain experience? How will we learn when to say no, and when not to? It seems to me as though adults are afraid of our sexuality and give us no credit for having good sense and self-control. Some kids may need to be restrained, but most of us know when to stop.

Sex education at my school is geared toward making every physical connection between a man and a woman into a disease. No kissing boys, you'll get mono. No having sex, or you will get chlamydia, syphilis, and AIDS. In one class we had to come up with every slang word for the reproductive organs, including *pussy, beaver, stick, wood*, and sixty more. I wanted to ask what the point is of learning these terms if we're not supposed to use them. Condoms are more than 99 percent effective, but the teachers at my school always say the best way to avoid getting pregnant and STDs is to be abstinent. I guess that's true. But while grinding I'm still abstaining, right?

I think that if toddlers were taught about the world the way we're taught about sex in school, they would never leave their cribs. I know it's important to be informed about the risks that go with sex, but shouldn't we also learn about it in a positive way? At a dance when I was a freshman, one of the chaperones felt she had to have a word with several girls about grinding. "It's like you're giving the boys a lap dance," she said. "They're just using you to rub up against them. What's in it for you? It's demeaning and very inappropriate. It's like sex with clothes on." The adult missed the point: The *good* part is that grinding is sex with clothes on. And we girls like it, too. Girls are allowed to enjoy sex as much as boys do, right? I suppose the consequences of sex are potentially worse for girls than for boys—but then doesn't that make grinding the great equalizer? Venereal diseases are not transmitted through pants!

A week or so after my party, while my father was still talking about the secret drinking and the "dirty dancing" every night on the phone with his friends—turns out he's a bigger gossip than I am—I found myself lost, dancing with a boy at another Sweet Sixteen. As I moved with him to the low beat, I couldn't have been more sold on the beauty of grinding. Until I looked next to me to find a senior boy all over a sophomore girl, grabbing her in all sorts of places her parents would be unhappy about. My mom had once asked me if I danced "like a whore." *Certainly not like that*, I thought. Dancing like a whore is one thing; acting like a whore is something totally different. I winced with some disgust, but then smiled as I sunk back into the rhythm of dancing and realized *thank God* my parents don't follow me around to parties.

The Sun's Shining Hotter

～～～～

There's an elephant in the sky. And a typewriter? No, Nevada. Everything's blue and white and green and big. Pieces of the sun kiss my skin and project colors through my eyelids. Nothing is moving but the light breeze, flirting with a few stray leaves and lost acorns. My chest rises and falls with a lazy sense of warmth, the air whispering *sssspriiiinnnggg*. Feels like exhaling over a cup of tea, where every burst of breath makes ripples and you get a poof of hot air back at you.

Absolutely no sound.

"What're you doing?"

The sound of me screaming. "God! What does it look like I'm doing?!"

"Looks like you're lying down in the middle of your driveway, dead or asleep."

I stand up and twirl my hair, like I do when I'm uncomfortable. Or pissed off. A most unimagined disturbance in my at-one-with-nature moment, approximately two feet taller than he was when I last saw him, is looking down at me. The same blond hair, the same sly mouth that turns into a grin just as often as his mother screams from the back window about whatever reckless, boyish thing he's done today. The neighborhood kid who never used to fail to hit me with a Nerf ball the second I least expected it. The little boy who I pretended to be married to in fourth grade, until he called me a monkey and I divorced him. The one whose mother put him in private school so he wouldn't continue to terrorize the lower-class population with mocking use of their street slang. That's his thing: For someone who grew up in a house the same size as my own, he sure thought himself superior to the rest of us. The kids of our cul-de-sac hadn't seen or heard from him since the transfer—but no one ever forgot him. That's his other thing, I suppose.

Now here he is, looking at me and my crazy, I-don't-really-care-right-now after-school clothes.

"And I thought you were dumb," I say.

"So did I," he says, smiling like Jimmy Fallon. "So did I. So ya come here often?"

"You get expelled often?"

"They don't expel kids from prep school. They just hire a therapist."

"Bastards!" I say sarcastically. "What kind of hell have you given them?"

"Well, it's only my first semester."

I nod. One semester? Has he really grown up so much in that time, or have I just not been watching? I mentally kick myself. You hate this kid, remember? "And right now? Did you come just to drive me crazy?"

"Tempting," he says. "No, actually, I followed you home."

I roll my eyes. "You did not."

"Lodged myself in a bush. Nice place. Might come in handy."

"Shut up."

Silence.

"OK, don't shut up. Why'd you come and scare the crap out of me?"

"Oh man. If I would have known you had to go to the bathroom, then . . ."

I start to walk toward my house, officially bored. Stupid boy.

"Wait," he says, grabbing my shoulder. I turn around, stare at his hand, and grimace. He tilts his head in the direction of mine until our heads are a little too close for comfort. He slowly parts his lips, and says, "You have a leaf in your hair."

"Oh."

He unravels a piece of leaf from a curl, lifts it to my vision, and smirks.

The sun's shining hotter. Inside me this time.

Boy One

〰〰〰〰

Boys. I can say that boys are dangerous creatures. They are. They stick around and follow you until you figure out that they like you. They get closer, and then they get distant—or they do both at the same time. There was that day I ran out of class, when I felt so alone and destroyed by my classmates, and you grabbed me and (oddly enough) asked if you could beat up the guy who'd started it. For me, you'd wanted to hurt someone. Then once you'd made it clear how you felt, you realized it scared you, that you weren't ready. Me, I don't think I could ever trust someone like that. Like you.

It sounds kinda lame, but I hold on to Josh Hartnett, my complete celebrity heartthrob obsession, because I know he will never hurt me. Because he doesn't even know me! I try and I try to let that real guy in, but I'm just not ready—and that's when I realize that my life is screwed up.

That's when I realize I've lost all hope, that if I can't trust a nice guy who actually wants to love me and hold me and take care of me, something is wrong with me. I'm a failure. I have no one to talk to and no one who will take me away from my miserable life. And I'm not just saying this because I'm upset or pissed. But honestly, who can I blame? It's no wonder I've never even had a crush on anyone. I have never been able to accept that I might actually need that person in my life who will erase the ones I can't bear to stand.

I'm alone and it's my fault. I can admit that. It's everything I've done—pushed away plenty of boys and taken crap from the others. So for my guy out there, whoever you are, please be patient or slap me back to reality and take me away from my misery. Just don't wait forever. I don't have forever.

Samantha Lewin, 17

Finding Myself in Utah

〜〜〜〜

I woke up as slowly as I could that sunny morning. I kept my eyes tightly shut, holding on to the moments I didn't have to spend in reality. I waited, but my eyelids weren't heavy anymore and red light had aready replaced the darkness I craved. I opened up my eyes.

Fuck . . . I'm still here.

These were the first words that came to mind and they continued to echo inside my head. I scanned my surroundings. I was alone in the middle of the desert, far away from my home in New York. That hit me slowly, like poison in the blood. No more glittering concrete under the polluted city sky. No more cluttered apartment safely four stories off the ground. And no more comfort beneath my black satin sheets. I was in the middle of fucking nowhere. I was out of place from the dirt in the air, the dead shrubbery on the desert floor, and the cloudless sky. I pulled my legs out from under my nylon sleeping bag. The tarp wrapped tightly around me crinkled. I struggled not to make too much noise. I flexed my feet, just to make sure they were mine. Thick white gym socks had replaced my four-inch black platforms. No more refuge in adolescent Goth attire. I wondered if I could find a way to rock the Wal-Mart clothes they'd imposed on me.

"Good morning," a voice, female, all business, called from behind a homemade shelter.

I looked down, hoping there might be a chance that I'd never have to say another word. I pointed my toes, studying them.

"Would you like your shoes?" the voice said. A pair of heavy black boots fell from the sky.

They'd been brand new just days ago but were already covered in dirt. I stared at the empty holes; there used to be laces. I wanted to ask but I still didn't want to speak.

"Do you remember what we talked about yesterday?"

I shot her an empty stare, quickly avoiding her gaze. Instead I focused on the amber hair pulled back in a low, sweaty ponytail and then on her glowing forehead. The all-American freckles didn't suit her; they almost made her appear sweet, when really everything from her voice to her posture was cold and harsh. She glared at me condescendingly, and suddenly I remembered.

It all hit me like a movie stuck on rewind. I see the darkness, the car, the office. I feel the wind beating on my bare arms and the chill of the airport climate. I hear my own screams and cries. I look down at the black laceless boots on the cracked red dirt.

"Yesterday? Remember?" she repeated, as if I didn't speak English.

I studied her filthy red hair, her freckled and burned cheeks, her protruding chipmunk teeth. *Brigitte*, I remembered.

Yesterday I'd been dropped off, at another location in this vast and empty place. The driver had opened the car door for me; it didn't open from the inside.

"It's all just a dream," I'd told her, clinging to my only picture of Will.

The driver looked into my eyes and sighed. "Well, I hope you wake up soon."

I sat on the ground and found a nearby stick to draw with. *Will*, I'd inscribed in the dirt before a worn-out hiking boot trampled my message.

Someone bent down to look at my face, but I wouldn't look up.

"Nice to meet you, Samantha. I'm Brigitte. I'm going to help you out during your stay here." I looked up and saw her thin, chapped lips curled into a forced smile. My tears fell harder and faster.

The driver stood and watched from two yards away. She leaned against the black car, undisturbed by the sun and undisturbed by my tears. Suddenly she seemed to remember something and walked toward me, bending her body low to meet mine. "They're not going to let you keep this picture here, but I'll give it to your therapist to hang on to for you."

I let go without a word and turned my head as the last mode of transportation headed toward civilization left without me. I was far away from my world, a world that consisted of freedom and fallacies. A world I missed so much it burned. But I knew. Here there were no cell phones. No makeup, no music, no parties on rooftops. Just miles and miles of dirt.

I broke the silence. "I don't belong here."

Brigitte nodded, and I proceeded to tell her that I was just a girl who'd made some mistakes, just a girl who'd paid the price.

"Please, get me out of here," I begged.

Her eyes told me that she'd heard this before, that I was just another broken person. Her eyes told me that I was in the right place.

"Answer me," she snaps. "Do you remember what we talked about?" Her stare is just as cold as it was yesterday.

"Where am I?" I ask, ignoring her question.

She looks impatient. "Emily!" she yells over her shoulder.

She grabs my arm and drags me along on her quest to find someone else to deal with me. She grumbles that she has to walk me to wherever this Emily is, because on suicide watch you can't walk by yourself. I try to keep up but my feet drag and kick in the dirt, my laceless boots slipping off.

"Emily, here. Samantha. It's your turn, and don't use that knife around her." Brigitte leaves me with another stranger.

"Don't mind her, she just likes to keep things in order," Emily says.

We watch Brigitte march off.

"You should eat something." Emily sounds genuine. "You had a long hike yesterday, your body needs nutrition."

I did?

I wipe the sweat off my brow as last night seeps into my memory. I remember climbing a hill for miles in the pitch black. My eyes were fuzzy, and all I could see was haze. But I remember the pain and the sweat on my shoulders, a collection of camping tools strapped to my back for hours. Those forty-five pounds of equipment were useless to me. I had everything I needed to survive back home in the little black bag I carried. God, it went everywhere with me. My friends called it the magic bag, and it was for us. My cell phone, my wallet, my drugs, my makeup, my cigarettes—my life, greeting me with the odor of crushed lipstick and stale tobacco. I could still conjure that smell, even through the awful hike. When I'd touched my hair, it felt hard and matted with dirt and rain.

I touch my hair now. It's still hard and matted. This confirms to me that the desert is my new reality. My thick, straightened, newly dyed blue, black, and purple hair is a twisted mess, a burden on my head.

I look at Emily. She is young and beautiful with soft features. Her golden hair is tied back with a ratty bandanna. She has dirt and grime all over her neck, cheek, and hands. She's using a knife to carve a spoon, despite Brigitte's direct orders. Her disregard for the rules intrigues me, and I wonder if there's a badass hiding behind her gentle green eyes.

"Where am I?" I speak for the first time in the desert.

Her expression is sympathetic but still: "You're in a wilderness program in Utah."

"Wilderness," I see my father mouth.

"Sam, how would you like to go to a wilderness program?" he says and grins.

I hate his grin. I hate all his faces.

"What the fuck is a wilderness program?"

It doesn't exist, I tell myself. *I hate it when my dad makes shit up.*

I walk into the bathroom numbed, unbothered by my father's suggestion. I climb on top of the sink and reach into my magic bag.

I hear whispers, faintly. My dad talks, then my mom.

"Only one option" echoes off the white porcelain tiles.

I block it out and focus on the face in front of me. I recognize the girl in the medicine cabinet mirror. I don't like it. I don't like her.

More lipstick. Redder. Brighter.

"Out of control," I hear, even fainter.

Quiet, no one said that.

I hear my mom crying.

More eyeliner. Blacker, thicker.

Don't worry. This isn't real, I tell myself. Only it isn't me. It's the stranger with the dark black eyes and the bright red lips. There's something clearly missing in her, rows of holes.

"I don't know how to break it to her, but she is going to Utah."

I definitely heard that.

"That's not going to happen!" I scream and drop my mascara.

I hop off the sink and storm across the hall to my parents' bedroom.

"I'm going to run away."

My parents look stunned but their eyes are still kind. *Why can't they hate me?*

"Where are you going?" is all they can ask as they notice I am in full costume.

"Out."

I leave them and go to unlock the front door, not for the first time today. But there's a new bolt screwed in tightly and tauntingly a foot over my head. I reach to unbolt it and notice it's immobilized by a key lock. *Are you fucking serious?*

"Fuck you!" I scream. "I need to go out."

I bang my head against the door, and my parents come rushing in.

"I need to go out," I say, kicking the door again and again.

Big, wet tears come pouring out along with all the excuses: "It's the first day the cops are gone, Bonnie's waiting for me, she needs me . . . Please? I won't go out Friday and I'll be back in a couple of hours."

My mother looks at my father with sad eyes. You can tell she feels sorry for me. She's always been on my side.

"No!" my father says, looking surprised that he'd said it.

My heart beats fast. Can I not manipulate my way out of this? Am I not in control? *Impossible*. I reach for a cigarette.

"I need to go out," I cry again, this time using the cigarette as my excuse. I am out of ideas. "Ten minutes," I beg.

My parents are surprised to see me holding a cigarette, because I never smoke in front of them. Maybe that was enough for them to believe I didn't do it. They always opted for denial when they could. But no one says a word. The bolt and lock are still there.

My blood is boiling. I march to the kitchen and light my cigarette on the stove. The fact that I'm a prisoner in my own home makes me want to burst out of my skin. My heart races as I watch the walls close in. I sit on the black granite kitchen counter, violently inhaling my cigarette.

My mom comes over.

Say something. Hate me. Anything.

She fills a paper cup with water. She takes a sip and stares at me.

Hate me. Why can't you hate me?

"What are you smoking?" She hands me her water. I ash in it.

"Newport, want some?" My mother was a smoker for twenty-five years.

"Oh no, I can't smoke. If I smoke I won't stop."

Since when are we making polite conversation?

My father walks in.

"Here, have some." I point the filter toward his face. He inhales deep, like a freshman learning how. But still he manages, and his eyes tell me he's proud that he knows how to smoke a cigarette. He smiles and I smile and my anger is all a joke. It's all a joke. It has to be.

"What's wrong?" Emily coaxes me gently enough.

So I tell her, I tell her everything I just saw.

"Wow." She looks shocked.

She must be new.

"When was this?" she asks.

I think. If I came here yesterday, then today must be Friday. "Wednesday. Two days ago."

Yesterday I was in New York. Today I'm in the Utah desert. I should have known. I should have let myself believe. I just didn't want to. So here I am.

"You should eat something." She's trying to help me.

"Not yet," I say, because I still need her company.

I lie down and rest my aching head. I play with my now bare belly button and feel my naked wrists brush against my hips. My naked wrists . . . my bracelets. Yesterday my arms were covered in jelly bracelets from elbow to wrist.

The lady with the black hair tells me that I need to take them off.

"No." *No way.*

She tries another approach. "Don't worry, we'll send them back to your parents."

My look tells her not to bother.

"No one else has bracelets out in the field," she reasons.

The field? What the fuck is that supposed to mean? I see girls and tents, but I have no idea what to expect.

"If you don't take them off yourself, we will have to do it for you."

A threat? I can't handle it. I'm too weak. She watches me as I take off two hundred some-odd jelly bracelets one by one, color by color. A piece of me dies each time I place another carefully in her plastic bag. I cry hardest as I come to the one he gave me, an ugly ping-pong table green.

The lady with the black hair never takes her eyes off me. She just watches as she orders me to free myself from the black clothes tightly smothering my body. I have nothing to hide behind. No costume, no bracelets, no piercings. Not even a stitch of clothes. She hands me the wilderness uniform. The shirt—plain, oversize, red— and the khaki shorts. I can't stop the tears.

ong?"

I sit up to look at Emily.

"Nothing, I just miss my bracelets." I can't imagine how materialistic she must think I am.

"Why?" She seems willing to give me that, that they were special.

I try to explain. My bracelets were the only gifts my friends and I exchanged. They were my only witness to all that happened. They were my photo album, my memory bank. But most of all, they were proof to me that I am part of something, that I belong somewhere. And now?

"Do you know what they'll do to you in Spofford?" Detective Santos tries to break me. "Do you know what they'll do to your pretty little face?"

You disgust me. "Yes," I say. My expression matches his, only mine has thick, black mascara-filled tears.

I wait in his office as he takes Bonnie into the next room. I hear her screams, loud and painful.

This isn't real. This isn't real. I watch the beige walls and hunger for something vivid. I play with my bracelets. Red, orange, yellow . . .

"Don't fiddle with those," my father tells me. "They're going to think you don't care." He smiles reassuringly. He must not think this is real either.

I stand and walk around the room only to find Will's picture: He is a wanted man. I take it and it becomes my picture of him.

I hear Bonnie scream again. She comes into the room with Detective Santos. I hug her.

"Don't fucking lie," she says and pushes me away. I want some kind of explanation. But I'm left open-armed and abandoned.

It's my turn. And I cry. "I don't know where he is, I swear." It's a half-truth, but Detective Santos has no reason to believe me. Bonnie already told him the whole truth. I failed my test, and I am caught.

My father whispers things to Santos that I cannot hear, and instead of Spofford, I find myself in Utah. And for some reason I couldn't see it coming, I wouldn't let myself. I guess I opted for denial, too. But I see it now, loud and clear.

Emily is done carving her spoon. I am sobbing. She begins to sand down the splintered edges.

"Don't worry, it's always hard the first couple of days," she says. "You'll start to have fun."

I nod, still teary. I don't believe her because I can't yet see how anything could be more fun than the life I'd been living.

"What about you?" I'm so awkward.

"What about me?" she helps.

"Why are you here?"

She laughs. "I work here."

I feel stupid. "I know," I say stubbornly. "I mean, do you go to college or anything?"

She does. She tells me all the realizations she's come to, being the brilliant college girl that she is. She tells me how secure and sure of herself she is. How she is a true speaker.

Lucky her.

She has a boyfriend. Joe. Joe knows her better than she knows herself, apparently. Joe likes her from the inside out. It all sounds like a far-fetched fairy tale to me, but I believe every word. I don't want to. I want to believe that there's no such thing as true happiness. I want to believe that I was after the only thing that came close.

"I had a picture of him, but I couldn't bring it out to the field," she says.

I know the feeling.

I can imagine her photo. It must be adorable. They're hugging and laughing together under an apple tree. A nearby friend must have captured the total bliss of Emily and Joe, a candid photo of the perfect moment in their perfect lives.

I can see my photo of him. It's a younger, more distorted image. It insulted me to see someone I held so dear, and so highly above myself, in poor black-and-white photocopy. I admired and adored him. There was so much I was jealous of. He came from a broken home and carried the power of perseverance. He commanded attention and found admiration wherever he looked. Maybe what intrigued me the most was that he was hidden by makeup, cloaked in black, and no one could truly see him. He was the exact opposite of vulnerable, and I was the dictionary definition of it. But this is lost in the *Wanted* photocopy. It doesn't do him justice. I am staring into the dull microbits that are supposed to be his eyes.

His eyes, what do they look like? My boots are strappy black sandals again and standing on Central Park grass. I look up. He's staring right through me, his pupils dilated to the greatest degree. He has pulsing green cat eyes.

"Will? What's up?"

No response.

He has an intoxicated grin on from ear to ear. He moves through the grass mischievously but with grace as he balances on his usual black platforms. A skateboard lies in the sun only a yard away. He picks it up, though it is not his.

"Will!" I'm impatient now, like a spoiled child. I am aware of what he's capable of and yet I don't comprehend it at all. "Who are you going to beat up?"

He looks at me, his pupils a flowery mess. His wrists glow and the colors of his bracelets melt and mix in my compromised vision. Everything seems especially bright to me. He takes his index finger and presses it gently against his lips.

"Shhhhh," he silently orders.

He crouches low and keeps moving, still sporting his conniving grin.

This has nothing to do with me, I tell myself. I walk toward the rock, the edge of our usual hangout. I want to leave. I am surrounded by people I recognize but not by people I know.

One of them turns me around, and the world goes silent.

Silent except for a fast and hard smack sharply against a skull. I don't know how to register what I see: a body lying on the ground, a lifeless wreck.

This isn't real. This isn't real.

This isn't over.

I stand in shock. I am still. Behind me I hear rapid footsteps and trampled grass. Sirens. Police lights reflect in circles across my eyes. I know I'm in trouble when the officers get out of their cars: "Nobody move!"

Still, how bad can this really be? I have no idea.

I stand face to face with the police.

"I didn't see anything" is the first thing that comes to mind, so it's the first thing I say.

And with those words I am free. Free to reunite with him, the criminal. Free to sleep together on city rooftops.

Free until further questioning revealed that I was a liar and I got sent to this godforsaken place.

"I don't belong here!" I shout at Emily as if my anger is proof.

She stays calm. "Where do you belong?"

Goddammit, another one of those thinking questions.

"Here, I have a present for you." She hands me the final product of what took hours to carve and sand: a single, perfectly polished wooden spoon.

"I can't take this," I say, as if I don't want it.

"Trust me, you're going to need it."

"I will?"

She smiles. "Everyone has to make one, it's the only way to eat."

"Then I'll make one myself. It's fine, really."

"You can't make one yourself. At least not yet."

"Why?"

"You're on suicide watch, remember?"

She says that like I know the rules or something. I find myself getting frustrated all over again. "And what does that mean exactly?"

"No one explained this to you?"

"No."

"It means no tools, no alone time, and no laces."

I looked at my boots, quieting myself. "Why no laces?"

"Because you can kill yourself with shoelaces."

I guess that makes sense. Only one problem . . . "Why would I try to kill myself?"

"I don't know, why don't you tell me?" Her kindness annoys me because I don't understand it.

"Tell you what?" I ask.

"Why did you try to kill yourself the night before you came here?"

I did?

There I am on the kitchen counter, surrounded by my mother and the smell of the gas stove and burning tobacco.

My mind freezes as I see my dad exhale a smoky grin.

What happens next?

I push myself to remember, but the rest doesn't come as easily to me.

I look at the cigarette in my hand. I know it's missing a small portion of tobacco that now rests in my father's lungs. All he can do is laugh and smile and expect the same in return.

Don't you get it? This isn't an act. This isn't funny. You really do have a fucked-up daughter.

I feel more enraged then ever. I refuse to let my father connect with me. I refuse to share a moment with him. I run into my room and slam the door. I throw everything and nothing into a small black duffel bag, convinced that I will be running away today. I fold up Will's picture and put it in my pocket. I trash my room. I knock over everything, looking and packing and thinking.

How can I escape? This is my quest. And I'm trying to find a way out by terrorizing my room.

I think about the pills. God, I have so many pills, oblong blue ones, skinny white ones, fat white ones, orange, red . . .

Black rivers come down hard as I can just hear my brother saying, "Why do you let her get away with this shit?"

I've been asking myself that same question.

I'm kneeling on the floor next to my overturned desk drawer. Piles of clothes lie all around me. My crisp white furniture stands innocently in the mess. I glare at my abandoned Victorian dollhouses. *Everyone is just so fucking disappointed.*

I swallow the skinny white pills, fat white pills, and round white ones, hoping that soon I will be free.

Everything gets fuzzier. I search for something I can hold on to—anything that feels real. I find a black Sharpie and so I write. I make perfect scribbles on the floor. I have no sense of start and stop. My thought process runs much more quickly than ink and arm can follow. Nothing feels real. Not my mind, not my body, not the marker.

I lie in bed, wandering in and out of consciousness.

"Sam, can you come out here for a second?"

How does a second turn into eleven months?

"Sure." I stuff the Sharpie in my pocket and open the door with a skip in my step, happy that reality feels more distant to me now.

I'm greeted by my parents and by two unknown towering bodies. More cops, I assume.

My mother begins, "Sam, we enrolled you in a program . . ."

A wave of disbelief washes over me as the facts begin to add up. Then I just break down. My knees collapse and I fall forward. One arm grasps the wall while the other holds my hair back. I push my limp body into my bathroom, right there. I bolt *my* door shut.

I face the door and hold it closed. I try to panic but I can't process, I can't find it in me to think things through.

"Sam, please come out here." My mother's voice.

"What did you do, Mom? What the fuck did you do?"

"Come out here. We just want to talk to you," says a stranger. He's done this before and won.

I can't stop my heart from beating. I am so afraid. "Go home! We don't need this," I plead.

"I'd love to, Sam, but we have a plane to catch."

My hands are wrapped tightly around the doorknob. "I'm not going anywhere."

"We'll take you in handcuffs if we have to."

I try to match his aggression. "You think I give a fuck?"

"Sam . . . come on," my father tries. He's the one who starts to shake the doorknob.

I want to just let go and cry but I force myself to hold on.

My father starts to remove the hinges.

"Don't touch the fucking door!" I try my hardest to yell and scream and scare them away. But I can still hear the clanking of the cold metal.

"I have a knife in here, I'll kill myself if you don't stop."

This was the thing that stopped them from breaking down the door. The only weapons they had now were their voices, and I was not about to be persuaded.

I turn my back to the door. It's supporting all my weight because I can't remember how to stand. The background noises become faint mumbles as I concentrate on straightening my drugged body. I manage to focus my mind for a split second and see myself in the mirror. I look tangled and limitless, and the only part of me that looks like it works is my fist wrapped tightly around the doorknob.

I watch myself ask, "Am I leaving tonight?"

I hear one of the strangers. "Open the door and we'll talk."

I unlock and then slowly push open the door. Before I can even read their faces, the two thugs grab each of my arms.

"It's time to go," they say.

All I have with me is that single black Sharpie and a photocopy of Will. I don't look back. I don't even say good-bye. I just close my eyes and convince myself that I'm dreaming.

I open my eyes to a star-filled sky and a cold wooden spoon in my hand. Not a single tree, rock, or shrub has moved.

"I didn't really try to kill myself," I tell Emily, sincerely.

She nods. She always gets that answer.

We sit in silence together, and I close my eyes, embracing the late-night desert breeze. It relaxes me. I almost like it.

Emily's voice moves in the coolness. "It's getting late," she says.

I agree, not because I'm physically tired. I'm just tired of thinking.

We walk two yards back to the staff shelter together, her hand grasping my bare arm and me sliding across the desert field in my boots. She doesn't have to say another word; I understand I have to sleep with staff. I'm on suicide watch.

I crouch under the plastic army-green tarp, where Brigitte is already sound asleep. Emily and I take off our shoes and lie down on either side of her. I'm still fully clothed but I hardly notice. I'm ready to pass out. Well, almost. For some reason, I am unsatisfied with ending the night like this. I feel in debt to Emily and I am overwhelmed with the desire to show someone some gratitude.

"Emily?" I say softly.

"Yeah?" she whispers back.

"Thanks for the spoon."

Anything
Extracurricular:
The Beach, the Horse,
the Bee, the Lousy
First Job, the Stellar
Future Career, etc.

Mini Mountain

~~~~~~

Everyone claims they will always remember their first love. Whether or not this is true, I don't know. But I can assure you that I will always remember mine—though my first love was essentially a rock—and the reasons that it found me I don't know, and I'm not sure I ever will.

It was day four or five of an outdoor adventures summer camp. Living in Seattle, every city kid has to participate in one of these at least once—when your parents decide it's time for you to appreciate how close you are to the forests, mountains, and rivers. We had introductions day, river-exploration day, and hike-to-the-waterfall day. Then it was climbing day. The counselors had towed a twenty-five-foot plastic climbing wall out to a field that would be our training ground. I was nine years old and with the red-haired girl who would be my best friend for that week. We stood below, looking up at the daunting wall full of big, sweaty, plastic holds. We watched most of the boys awkwardly pull themselves up the harder parts, craving approval and praise from the crowd. Most of the girls stuck with the intermediate wall, climbing about three-fourths of the way up and falling down. As much as I hadn't wanted it to, my turn came. Realizing I'd never get away with keeping my feet on the ground, I decided to push myself. I chose the easy route and sped right up it. With a surprise shot of confidence, I tried the intermediate wall and found the same success. In camp terms, I was now the quiet little blonde girl who's a pretty good climber.

All I remember about the start of the next day is just how huge and completely submerged in nature that outdoor rock we went to seemed. The idea was that the rock itself was all you had to help yourself get up it. And all there was to catch you if you fell was the rope that the counselor attached to chains at the top just minutes before. Somehow I made it up again and again. Just two years later, I would find myself with friends at the base of the very same boulder, as the climber putting the rope through the chains at the top. And I would realize that that rock hadn't been very big at all.

I would have forgotten all about rock climbing at the end of camp—I was more obsessed with seeing my friends again and getting back to normal fourth-grade activities. But, taking a tip from one of my counselors, my mom started looking for a nearby climbing gym for me. By the time I'd completely forgotten about the summer, she'd found a place that offered kids' classes. I signed up for the soonest one I could get into.

That's how I ended up sitting in the loft of Stone Gardens with thirteen other girls and boys between the ages of nine and eighteen. There was the climbing version of the popular, pretty girls—clearly Tara and Anja, who were near my age but had some sort of higher quality about them—and I told myself I wanted to be in their group one day. There were the kids who were old enough that they could afford to be nice and helpful to everyone else. There was the no-clue-what-I'm-doing group, kids who'd been in the class for a while but weren't really catching on (or weren't really there to climb). And there were the regulars, who were already, or on the verge of becoming, hooked on the sport. Our leader was J. or Jay, depending on how professional he felt that day. J. was the big brother I'd never have, with his regular pranking and wet willies, and the rare treat of a crazy yet true story that we hoped for every week.

Months passed, and I went from using whatever holds I could reach to climbing increasingly difficult routes with holds specified in various colors of duct tape. In just a few months, I had worked from climbing a carefree 5.6 to a skillful 5.9 grade, no problem. It took me from being just another drop-in kid to having a reputation and someone who wanted to partner with me each week. I was soon given a nickname by J.: Mini Mountain. Having a nickname in this class was a major honor; having a J.-invented one was even bigger. Soon it was shortened to just "Mini!" as Tara and Anja, who I was now in with socially, would call out. I was rapidly moving up to their level.

But outside of class, which was only a couple of hours a week, the obsession had yet to strike. Then the second-biggest event of my fifth-grade career occurred: J. decided that his time as class ringleader was over. After a few weeks of replacement teachers, one finally stuck, and Winslow became the new J. Winslow was still fun but had a bit more of a serious element than J. He decided to introduce an Advance Junior Program, for which he handpicked students he thought were in need of a bigger challenge. He invited me, along with seven other climbers, to join the new class. Surprisingly, Anja and Tara weren't included, for reasons I still don't know. (They were asked to join six months later.) Honestly, it's not something we ever talk about. It's a common thought, but it's never come between us.

The class was the best thing that ever happened to me. Climbingwise, the most important thing we were going to learn in AJP was how to lead climb, meaning setting up the rope, and before we were considered old enough, fourteen, by gym rules to do so. But the bigger breakthrough was that in this small community, Mini blossomed, loud and crazy and popular. Mini always voiced her opinions, and friends, teachers, and anyone who worked at the gym forgot who quiet Kirsten—who gave no objections and no one really knew much about—was. People would introduce and remember me as Mini, the girl with the huge personality and climbing confidence. I would find myself counting down the days until the two-hour Monday night class, wanting to be Mini for as much of my life as I possibly could.

At eleven, I stopped going to AJP and became the second-youngest member of the junior climbing team, working toward regional and national competitions. I really liked being a part of it, but the commute meant my mom had to pick me and my sister up from school at 3:30 or earlier and get me to the gym at 4:20. After practice,

I wouldn't get home until 7:50 at night—tired, hungry, dirty, and with a full load of homework to do. My parents loved the idea of me climbing, but they didn't love all the late-night activities that came with it or the idea of such serious competitions at my age. I decided to leave the junior team and go back to AJP.

When I turned thirteen, my life was temporarily messed up. My parents got a divorce. They sold our spacious house on Mercer Island, and my mom, sister, and I moved into a small house in Seattle. But I didn't care about the size or location of the house at all. It was exactly what I wanted it to be: just blocks away from my gym. And we happened to move just in time for me to train for the 2006 junior team tryouts.

As I was preparing to leave AJP again, I really started to notice the variety of people in the class, and was amazed at how we all managed to be friends somehow. In school, none of us—ages nine to eighteen, girls and boys, punks and preppies—would have been in the same social group. We would have all likely ignored each other based on incorrect stereotypes. But climbing had brought us all together and erased the holds the rest of the world had on us.

By the time I joined back up with the junior team, a lot of my friends had either moved away or gone to other teams. But I had Anja with me. (Tara would have been there, but she was busy with religious classes at her church.) Through September, our coaches Sydney and Shawn dedicated themselves to preparing us for the upcoming American Bouldering Series, with the ultimate goal of making it to the nationals to compete for a position on the U.S. climbing team. Unfortunately, I missed several competitions in this series due to distance and lack of transportation, so I wasn't prepared to compete in regionals. I wasn't disappointed though. I'd worked hard, figured out a lot, and I knew what I needed to do. I aim to make the state's top-ten ranked climbers under eighteen, soon.

I've met some of the most amazing and interesting people through climbing. They accept me for who I am and help me figure out who that is. At a climbing gym, you can't help but forget about labels. You can see the girl covered in tattoos and look at her and think she's cool, and at the same time, see the big buff jock guy and think he's cool, too. You see the stronger climbers doing the hard stuff, and advising the newbies on how to get that route they could do in their sleep. People aren't afraid to ask for help, or to fall down several times.

I've changed so much since the first day I stepped onto a wall. Four years later, you couldn't even recognize me next to that shy, uncertain camper sitting on the bus to the boulder alone. Now you can find me at the gym with my team, every Tuesday and Thursday from four to seven. You would see me, the outgoing blonde girl, running around, climbing and laughing and surrounded by friends and jokes and a nickname. I am Mini, and this is big.

Kelly Otterness, 14

Lately

~~~~~~~

My horse is buried in my backyard, between two bushes and beneath the cracking Montana dirt. My mom says that someday Montana will just blow away, because each year an inch of soil turns to sand and catches in the wind. I wonder how many inches it will be before patches of Lately's mane show red above the ground. Who will find her in their backyard, as they plant roses that won't grow in the soil turned to dust?

I had stood there, behind the house and past the first row of windbreaker trees, with a fistful of weeds—the greenest thing I could find—offering them up to Lately. She snorted, would have pawed the ground in indignation but for her hoof. The skin around it was swollen red and purple, the flesh exposed and raw. The vet told us her tendon had been cut, her leg mangled by barbed wire in some corner of the pasture. She would not heal.

She protested the gift of brittle leaves even as she stood dying. It would have been the last thing I ever gave her, so maybe it was better that she didn't accept. Her final memory of me was not a dry, grainy taste in her mouth. It was my hand on her nose and neck and suddenly entwined in her mane, then gone—a little girl running back into the house before the shot between the folds of her skin and the darkness beneath the earth. At last her leg would heal, as the sinews broke down in the dirt and nothing more than bone remained. There would be no trace of a ripped tendon or the tiny hole in the skin where the needle had been or the little girl's soft fingers in her dark red mane.

Our friend Suzanne said that sometimes a horse does not fall quietly, sometimes they stiffen and fall backward, the tail breaks—and then the rest of the adults stopped her before my ears were polluted by the mistakes of the world. But I would remember, and thank whatever controlled the bodies of dead horses that Lately had landed softly in her grave dug by orange machines.

Eight years old and she was twenty-something (twenty-three?) and there were not enough years in between for us. I would never grow enough to understand that she was not a very big horse. When I fell off of her into the dirt one summer's day, she stopped and waited for me. She was so tall from my place on the ground, with her red-brown coat spotting white with freckles that come with age and sun and long legs and a white stripe (was there?) running down her face. A soft muzzle that snorted when I reached to hold her in my hands.

Lately loved the train that ran by the big red barn just down the road; she could hear it before it appeared from the horizon. Her ears pricked—and we'd stop and wait for the rushing monster that moved so slowly in our eyes but faster than ever she could run.

And when the train goes by, as the years go by, I see her running past it, a spirit with more power than any metal beast. Maggie, who has moved away and who is not a friend but simply someone who has shared too many memories to be just an acquaintance, used to say that when the train came through, the clouds formed a horse and we knew Lately was there. Even though sometimes there are no clouds in the sky and the train rumbles past me, I like to think of my horse like this, in the way of old memories shared with people with whom I have no future.

Erika Kwee, 16

East

~~~~~~~~

My trip to China is a secret. Not a secret in the dictionary definition way, because my parents had to arrange for my airfare and housing and especially for going on the program in the first place. But it's a secret in the way that no one outside of our small group knows what we really got out of it. We went for the virtuous purposes of language immersion, cultural exchange, and community service, in preparation to be volunteers for the 2008 Olympics in Beijing. But I think we all learned something a little less tangible, a little more real-life that July.

Though the months of preparations for the trip were pretty much filled with logistics, I couldn't help but think a bit in romantic terms about this being my first trip to China. China, a land rich with heritage, a land where my great-grandparents and ancestors lived. A place where I might do a little bit of that self-discovery that everyone was always talking about, finding my roots and such.

See, the program sounds much more impressive than it actually was. But honestly, I think it was also much more fun that way. Although we had three hours of Chinese class most days, in the span of twenty-four hours it was barely anything. We learned mostly by osmosis—making nervous conversation with the Hong Kong hairdresser as he did who-knows-what to my hair was probably more valuable than an hour of vocabulary exercises. The big stuff, otherwise known as *teenage life happening*, took place in our free time. There was backstabbing, betrayal, hysterical sobbing and hysterical embarrassment, broken hearts, rejection, jealousy, twenty-four-hour bffs (best friends, not so forever), pettiness, gossip—all within a ring of about eight campers. Actually, it was all very educational. I learned that even though we were in China, American teenage drama was alive and well.

I learned that the most sweet-faced, sweet-voiced, seemingly most sweet person you could ever hope to meet can be a totally different person around boys. And you just can't keep forgiving her for that.

I learned that surprising talents lie under somewhat deceptive exteriors, and that you should definitely get an autograph when you come across people with these qualities, because one day they will surely be famous.

I learned that everyone loves a girl who never gets upset but that very, very, *very* few members of the human population possess this genetic makeup.

I learned that you can seriously injure yourself from laughing.

I learned that you can also get seriously injured by an irate merchant who is completely offended by your low offer for her obviously high-quality products, and that when she starts shrieking at you in Chinese (which, even though you're supposed to be learning, you don't understand a word of), you should just walk away rather quickly.

I learned that being paired with a roommate who likes to get up in the morning and is willing to gently wake you at precisely the time you need to go get ready is a godsend.

I learned that when you're all messed up because of some bad news from home and are sobbing on the floor in the bathroom, and your friend—in a well-meaning but misguided gesture—attempts to lock you in there with her until you tell her what's wrong, you should not wrestle with her and finally break out of the suffocating room into the hallway. For you will surely bump into that twenty-three-year-old (so cute!) guy who lives on the eleventh floor of the dorm you're staying in. This is a big one.

I learned that in the grand scheme of things, a month is insignificant.

It is also everything. The memories have become fuzzy around the edges, as all of them do, glorified in my mind in a process that began the moment we stepped onto the plane home, away from the messy success of finding ourselves.

When my parents asked, "How was the trip?" I only mumbled, "Good," not really knowing what to say. It's hard to put a month's worth of experiences into an honest answer, and I've never been a good one for communicating with my mom and dad anyway. For a while, I'd yet to come up with a satisfactory response—to the point where my parents decided that maybe the trip hadn't been educational enough and maybe I shouldn't go back for the Olympics next year. Thankfully, they changed their minds, and I just recently returned from another incredible summer in China. All that I could not convey to them is the secret that everyone who went on that first trip holds, what we really learned, though maybe I've wrung too much meaning out of it. Anyway, it makes me happy.

Lucy Bennett, 17

The Hamptons

〰〰〰

W hat you hear about the Hamptons is usually about some sup-
posedly great thing, like Diddy's White Party, or the newest
trendy boutique, or the tons of celebrities who pretend not to want to
be seen on its beaches or in its clubs. But even though there's the occasional celebrity sighting, in reality the Hamptons are nothing like
people imagine.

For me, summer starts when I'm packing up my bags, jumping in
the car with my family, and taking the two-hour drive from Brooklyn
out to Bridgehampton. Barbecues in the backyard, playing tea party
in the pool with my little brother, walking up to the candy kitchen
and buying the biggest ice cream cone we can find. Somehow everything feels lighter there, like we're living on a watermelon-, firefly-,
hydrangea-filled cloud.

Three years ago my grandmother bought a house right down the
road from ours, giving us a place to stay when my parents rent ours
out—which they do for high season every year. My grandmother's
place is smaller but sweet, with a beautiful backyard. Being a retired
art dealer, she keeps the house littered with odd pieces, pieces that
sometimes can't even be classified as art. My mom loves to mention
how she and her siblings had to tiptoe around their childhood apartment for fear of ruining some supposed *objet*, like "the crumpled-up
piece of paper" that sat on a table.

The weirdest piece of art in my grandmother's Hamptons house
lives under a glass coffee table in the living room: It's a translucent
lime-green statue of a naked obese woman, her butt sitting on her

heels and her arms stretched out in front of her. She's about the size of a loaf of bread, and she is smiling as if she has just won the lottery. I've named her May and we have become fast friends. I can always count on her pudgy green face smiling up at me from under the table, reminding me not to take things too seriously. When no one is watching I like to crouch down to her level and run my hands over her back and feel the smooth, solid body under my fingertips.

Nights at Granny's are never without a lovingly prepared dinner, and we all sit down and eat together. (In the daytime, it's every man for himself in the food department.) Her huge stainless-steel refrigerator holds only a tin of cookies, Grey Goose vodka, olives, and some sort of cheese—unlike our refrigerator, same style but usually filled with ice pops, cubed pineapple, and leftover pizza.

By six o'clock, with newly purchased ingredients in tow, you can always find my slender five-foot-eight grandmother, draped in slinky black pants and a white T-shirt—Granny uniform, she wears nothing else—standing next to the sink, her back facing the world. Gaultier perfume and the crisp, fresh parsley she's chopping mix together and create a sweet yet chlorophyll-like smell. A bright yellow pot, filled with a reddish-brown mush that always tastes so much better than it looks, sits bubbling on the stove (also huge, also stainless) waiting to be stirred, like a shoe before the foot. My grandmother turns and drops the parsley into the pot but can't get all of the green flakes off of her gold ring–covered hands—wrinkled from too much time in the Bridgehampton sun.

Noticing the parsley, my grandmother wipes manicured fingers on the canvas apron that protects her black pants. Hands clean, she pulls at her short and thin curly brown hair so it poufs up like that of an Upper East Side poodle.

If, in my seventeen years of life, I have learned one thing about the enigma that is my grandmother, it's that she has a deep fear of being alone, and that's why she always makes dinner. Why not have everyone over for a big lunch? Why not make pancakes in the morning? Why not skip dinner and fake it with snacks at a movie? Because that would mean being alone at night in the dark. When the sun is out, people are around town, shopping, swimming, eating—no one is ever really alone during the day. So every evening, my mom, brother, father, cousin, and I file into the kitchen, nibble at the almonds and wait for the stirring, chopping, and tasting to be over. Then we can eat and ultimately save my grandmother from the night.

Our conversations are almost as consistent as our dinners. I manage to say something shocking and inappropriate, which makes water come out of my little brother's nose. My mom and my grandmother without fail get into an argument, and my dad is always excused early to go fix something at my grandmother's request. The meal usually ends with Mom and Granny stealing bones off everyone else's plates, which they greedily suck, and Talia, my cousin, slamming her glass down in offense to some earlier comment my somewhat tactless grandmother had made.

Staying at my grandmother's also means staying with Talia (or Tye-ya as Granny, whose years in New York have made her incapable of pronouncing *l*'s, says it). Though she's five years older than I am, and we see each other rarely over the rest of the year—she goes to college at Hamilton, upstate—Talia's one of the high points of the season. If it's summer, then we are always together. Like peanut butter and jelly, Batman and Robin, Mary-Kate and Ashley, one is not as good without the other. There are two floors in my grandmother's house. The ground floor, where my parents, brother, and Granny sleep, is filled with classical music, novels by Kafka, and CNN. But past the fifteen stairs leading to the attic is mine and Talia's, period. It's a whole other world, a world my grandmother barely ever enters (except for the occasional shouted up "Are you cold? Do you need more towels?"). A world where we can do and say what we want, where clothing covers the floor and MTV plays all day—a perfect world.

We wake up at twelve, tan until three, shop in East Hampton from three to six, and then you know about dinner. After dinner we force my dad—a mixture of Bruce Willis and Uncle Fester, a man who all my friends are scared to death of but who in reality is the nicest, most generous man you will ever meet—to take us to Carvel for sundaes and then to rent a movie. Hot fudge and 80s chick flicks are perfect, like a cool breeze on a scorching day.

The Hamptons is a late-night swim with my cousin and brother and trying not to make a lot of noise so my parents won't wake up. The Hamptons is sneaking sips from my dad's wineglass while dancing around the lawn trying to catch fireflies. The Hamptons is sitting out in the sun with a good book and huge bowl of guacamole. The Hamptons is summer.

Jaclyn Humphrey, 17

Pediatrics

~~~~~~

Ever since I was seven or eight, I've known that I wanted to become a doctor. It started with my annual visits to the pediatrician—over the years, I began to admire her so much. She was successful, had a family, and loved helping others. I specifically remember, in the car coming home from a checkup one afternoon, telling my mother that I wanted to become a doctor and that I'd even decided on my specialty. She told me, as good moms do, "You can be anybody you want to be if you set your mind to it."

I did, playing doctor rather than anything else with my friends and asking only for medical books as gifts, year after year. I still have the encyclopedia-like manuals, with highly detailed information and illustrations on human-body systems, diseases, diagnoses, particular organs. Then a recent experience put life in perspective and made it clear to me, in a grown-up way, that becoming a doctor was truly my purpose in life.

Earlier this year, my mom was robbed and assaulted by a complete stranger, in broad summer daylight, two blocks away from our apartment building. This part alone was a shock: We'd been in the neighborhood since I was two, it's really quiet, there's barely any crime, and the streets are particularly safe because many old people live around us and are always watching what's going on. I look up to my mom like crazy. I'm an only child, and my parents got divorced when I was very young, so my mom and I are very close. She had such a terrible childhood, in a poor town in Brazil, where she had to work on tobacco fields with her grandfather while somehow taking care of her ten brothers and sisters. She moved to the United States when she was in her twenties and has worked so hard to make a good life for herself and me in New York.

I wasn't even home when it happened. I was at my father's house in New Jersey. It was mid-afternoon, and all my family was over for a party when I received the phone call from my stepdad. I went into another room. I remember him saying, "I don't know how to tell you this, but Mom has been attacked and she's in the hospital. Can you get here as soon as possible?" I was completely stunned. I remember going into the living room, hysterically crying and screaming that I had to leave *now*. My father drove me home, and the whole time I was so scared and so angry at myself for not being there for my mom when she needed me most.

By far the most terrifying experience in my life was walking into the hospital room and seeing my mom lying there so helpless and beaten. She'd been sick before—she has glaucoma and has had hemochromatosis (too much iron in the blood)—but I'd never seen her in a hospital before. She was conscious when I arrived, but so tired and weak that she couldn't even lift her head. I sat by her side and cried. I couldn't believe this had happened. A while later, two doctors came in and told my stepfather and me that my mom had fractured her skull and a blood clot had formed in her head. They also said her heartbeat was irregular and that they would have to do more tests before they could tell us anything in terms of treatment.

After twenty hours of waiting in emergency, my mom was finally moved to the sixth floor, where she shared a room with an old Italian woman who had broken her leg walking down the stairs. The woman was delusional and I had to listen to her talking to herself while I sat by my mom's bed for hours each day. Also, our neighbor Elaine, who'd been a friend of the family's for many years, happened to be four rooms down from my mom. She had a heart condition and was very ill. I'd visit her some days and tell her that I was praying for her to feel better; she said she'd pray for my mom, too. Elaine passed away a few days later.

School hadn't started yet, so the routine was that I'd go to the hospital in the morning with my stepdad and we'd stay until visiting hours were over. He was dealing with it all better than I was. He had faith that she was going to be OK, but I wasn't so sure. For lunch, we'd usually go to the pizza parlor across the street. Then we'd get my mom some soup or something she was craving, because the hospital food wasn't good at all. I felt so helpless.

But I knew my mom was a fighter. I'd study her, study my medical texts, study the doctors, and sometimes sit on the ledge of the hospital window and look out into the Bronx. I'd see the cars going by and all the buildings and wonder, with all those families, how this could have happened to mine. It was sunny, so nice out the whole time my mom was in that bed, which seemed like a sick joke, summer going on without her.

I never again want to sit helplessly in a hospital. Since I can't exactly start med school yet, I've been volunteering at a hospice once a week. I talk to patients, feed them when they need help, and keep them company, because most of them are all alone. And all of them are dying. This may sound depressing, but it really isn't. The patients are so full of life. They tell me great stories about themselves. There was this one man with cancer who would get so animated when he'd talk to me about when he was younger and friends with a priest who swore a lot, and would help build houses for the poor. He'd also tell me how cheap things were back then. He even got well enough to leave the hospice, which is always good to see.

I will never forget the image of my mom in the hospital. It haunts me every day. She's better now, still weak at times—sometimes so much so that she can't leave the house—but getting stronger. On days when she feels up to it, we go shopping in the city and out for lunch, just the two of us. At first she was terrified just to go outside.

Then she was terrified to walk around anywhere by herself. And who could blame her after being attacked like that? But now she's not that scared anymore. She loves our quiet neighborhood nearly as much as she ever has, where all the old people call me "Doc" and are keeping an eye out for her recovery.

Anna Saxon, 17

The Management

~~~~~~~

Every teen girl gets her fair share of bad jobs. Mine is in a pizzeria, as a waitress, server, busser, runner, and about anything else you can imagine. At normal, nice restaurants, people are hired and assigned to a specific job, like serving. Not me. I get a whole variety of things that I have to do, including answering the phone *every* time it rings, cleaning toilets, filling small cups with boiling sauce to put in delivery orders, and kissing my boss's ass.

I have a new boss now at this job, who's OK. But before him was his brother, the most entertaining and psychotic boss I've ever seen or heard of. (We've been told he's off taking an extremely long vacation.) When he got drunk, which was a lot, he got seriously irritable. He'd drink himself to the point of passing out and do absolutely no work. He'd overpay all of the waitresses as a result of an inability to count while wasted. He'd also sleep quite often in his office on a set of three wooden chairs. Sometimes late at night, when only teenagers from the movie theater come into the pizzeria, he'd go up to them, totally drunk, and meow in their ears. Yes, a boss whose business relies on kids scared them away. One time he'd gone (drunk, of course) to the neighboring store and bought children's sunglasses— bright red frames, for a face no bigger than a five-year-old's—and stuck them on his very large head. Hulking and six foot five behind his baby shades, he then proceeded to strut around the restaurant, making cat noises at customers while sneaking shots of Sambuca out of pizza sauce cups behind the counter. And he had an amazing ability to contradict himself within one sentence: He'd tell me to stay up front to help other workers, then immediately tell me to go in back to fold pizza boxes. After asking me to do the first part, he'd yell at me for not doing the second. "Red!" he called me, for no reason more creative than my hair, "I told you to stay up front at all times!" I was actually fired by him once while he was completely wasted and then hired again about twenty minutes later. It makes absolutely no sense.

Another thing about this boss is that he's Bosnian. Don't get me wrong—I have nothing against people from other countries or Bosnians—just *this* Bosnian. He wasn't the only one, either; he brought in whole groups of them, like six or seven at a time. They'd stand around in the back, smoking, drinking, and talking loudly in Bosnian, a language you completely *cannot* understand. You'd only know they were saying something about you when they looked at you with their glaring drunken eyes and laughed.

As any waitress would understand, you have to be very nice to the customer so they'll come back, and so you'll get a good tip. When you're nice to people and they're still mean to you, it's very frustrating. Like for example, you bring someone the wrong dressing for their salad, and instead of laughing about it and asking for a different one, they get far too angry and yell at you. I hope anyone who reads this, anyone who has done this before, will seriously consider never doing it again. Every time anything like this would happen with a customer, my boss would somehow find out. Then, for twenty minutes in his tiny little smoked-filled office, I had to hear about how I'm a terrible person and a professional failure and I "can't possibly be serious" about my "career."

Bottom line, every pizzeria—every restaurant job, every job as a teenager, I suspect—is like this to some extent. But I can guarantee that not a boss out there is like my former employer. Thank god he was replaced, however marginally better his brother is. But now I can actually relax and occasionally try to enjoy myself at work. My new boss drinks less, or at least does it more quietly, with fewer Bosnian friends and no cat outbursts.

I wish my story would serve as an example for people, so they know how *not* to act: as the boss, as the customer, as a decent human being. Still, even though that boss made my first restaurant job miserable, I'd have to say he contributed to my growth as a human being. So thank you to my ex-boss, who will remain unnamed: You taught me about the type of person that I never want to be.

Apiarian Days

~~~~~~

*T*he glare of stage lights beats up on my poor bespectacled retinas. Below me, flashbulbs spark and shudder. Seven hundred people are documenting my every move. My armpits are sweating. I open my mouth to say something . . . No, not just yet.

I square off with the microphone. I move it up. I move it down. If only I could move it away. Up again, close enough. My breath, deep and labored, reverberates through the amplifier. How embarrassing. I have nothing to fidget with unless you count the big yellow placard dangling from my neck.

A woman at the foot of the stage peers at me over her reading glasses. "Samantha, we're going to have to ask you to start spelling the word now."

Taking a deep breath, I close my eyes and pray the walls won't cave in. "Diapason. D-I-A . . ."

The only things missing from this scene are a lit cigarette and several shotguns aimed at my person. But this is no execution. This is the Scripps Howard National Spelling Bee.

Sitting in our station wagon, I waited. Outside, the damp chill of a February island evening made the warmth of the car all the more comforting. Across the road, windows glowed in the early dark. I watched my father disappear into a house, there to retrieve a spelling bee study guide. Another homeschool parent had ordered a package of them in an attempt to encourage students in our community to compete in the

Martha's Vineyard Regional Spelling Bee. I was in seventh grade and figured it would be a piece of cake.

My father returned to the car and handed me a small multicolored booklet. I leafed through it. My stomach lurched. More than 9,000 words. *I have to study this? Terrific.* Thus began a three-month odyssey.

That little terror-inspiring chapbook was the *Paideia,* from Greek meaning "to educate the child." It's peppered with words like *siphonapterology, kamelaukion*, and *effleurage*—words you'll hope to never come across again in your life. Yet over the months of studying, you form a strange bond with the book, a kind of Stockholm syndrome. *Paideia* is your captor and your friend—the only friend you'll ever see if you are studying hard enough.

A few weeks into the memorization process, our homeschool community held its equivalent of a schoolwide bee. I championed on *hurricane*. Easy enough, but there were miles to go, starting with the regionals.

Sedulously trudging through *Paideia*, I wrote down each word three, five, even ten times in my spiral-bound notebooks. Every speller has a way of breaking the monotony of study. Some invent memorization games, others create flash cards. Mine was doodling in the margins and downing cans of Diet Dr. Pepper. I also resumed an old habit: nail-biting. Beginning and intermediate words, no problem. But there was an enormous gap as far as the advanced went. The day before the regionals I spent eight hours slumped before the computer, guzzling soda and listening to the online *Audio Paideia*. I went to bed with Hamlet-like resignation, certain that I would fail.

The next morning, four other contestants from Martha's Vineyard and I assembled in the function room of the island's ritziest hotel, the Harborview. The order in which we would spell was selected at random. I was number one. *An omen? Perhaps.* An audience of eighty-some children in damp raincoats shuffled their way into the room,

including my own sizable fan club. After much speechmaking and formal introductions, the competition began.

And, twenty-five minutes later—lightning-fast by regional bee
standards—it ended.

"Burglary. B-U-R-G-L-A-R-Y."

"That is correct. Samantha is our champion!" Applause.

*That's it? Burglary? How could they? ALL THEY GAVE ME
WAS A STUPID EIGHT-LETTER INTERMEDIATE WORD?! Thank
goodness.*

I was congratulated, photographed, flower bedecked. And then,
thud! The grand prize was dumped into my lap: *Merriam Webster's
Third New International Unabridged Dictionary,* the bible of the National Spelling Bee. *U*nabridged, "More than 475,000 entries." At
home, I weighed it on the bathroom scale: fourteen pounds to study,
plus a few extra ounces of "words most likely to appear in the first
round of the nationals." Was I going to have fun or what?

If *Webster's Third* is the Bible, Spellingbee.com is the Talmud.
Word lists, rules, foreign languages, and more, all of which I followed
religiously. I filled notebooks, I pressed onward.

As May loomed, preparations for Washington began. Mom made
plane reservations. I studied. New clothes were bought. I studied. I
had no idea what other kids were doing. I studied. To my chagrin, the
dictionary fit into our suitcase.

It was Memorial Day weekend, the most frenetic time of year for
Washington, D.C. Despite the crowds, we ran the full gambit of patri-
otic sightseeing, from the spire of the Washington monument to the
Tomb of the Unknown Soldier. I worried about my own burial, on
national TV. I could not stop spelling.

"Monday, May 28th—Mandatory Assembly for Spellers and Official
Escorts . . . 1 to 2 p.m." Thus read the *Bee Week Guide* I'd received
during registration at the Hyatt Regency. In addition to the schedule
of events, the *Guide* featured photographs and mini-biographies of
each of the 248 contestants. There were public schoolers, home-

schoolers, and kids from parochial schools; Hindus, Christians, Jews, and Muslims. Practically all were geeks in their fields: science nerds, math whizzes, musicians and thespians, Tolkienites and Trekkies, a vibrant nerd community bound by words.

The hotel's Independence Ballroom was the official location of the bee proceedings. Here we all gathered, with parents and guardians, to learn the rules and regulations. The grand prize would be a $10,000 grant, a collegiate-size reference library, and one enormous gold cup.

That night, settled into our prepaid hotel room, I hyperventilated. I don't normally hyperventilate. All I knew was that the nationals were tomorrow and I was short of breath. Mom told me to go breathe by the open window. The air smelled of car fumes. I climbed back into bed and have no idea when or how I fell asleep.

"Smile!" The next day I posed at the microphone as if it were an un-scary place to be. My parents snapped a couple photos. I stepped down. A few dozen other spellers posed as well, then walked offstage to be nervous someplace else.

Round one was divided into two groups: spellers numbers 1 to 123 competing in the morning, and 124 to 248 that evening. I was number 220. As the time neared 7:00 p.m., 124 shell-shocked kids in T-shirts and shorts took their respective seats on stage. On each chair we found a bright yellow placard displaying our name, number, town, and the local newspaper sponsoring us. We slipped these awkwardly over our heads and sat down. Some kids prayed. Others fidgeted. Still others yawned and couldn't care less.

The first victim was summoned to the mike. Dr. Alex J. Cameron, bee pronouncer, was stationed at the post he'd held annually for more than twenty-one years. Assistant pronouncer Jacques Bailley sat be-side him, dictionary at the ready. Lucky 124's word was *siccative*. She nailed it.

Each speller had a different technique. Some spelled in their heads. Some mouthed the words, made faces, or pretended to write on their hands. A few threw caution to the wind, spelling the word right up front. Some said please, others demanded answers. Nearly all asked for a definition, language of origin, and to hear their word used in a sentence. Daniel, the boy representing Jamaica, always addressed kind, grandfatherly Dr. Cameron as "sir" and thanked him after every answer. Whatever their style, fact is, the more questions a speller asked, the more they were stalling.

Waiting was agonizing. I squirmed in my seat, blankly staring at the blood-red carpet. *Ding!* Whenever someone misspelled a word, one of the judges hit a small brass bell, the kind often found perched on hotel desks. The chime was a death knell for spellers.

Finally, the moment came. I arranged my feet on the masking tape "X" at the back of the stage, waiting for a fellow Massachusetts resident to finish spelling. *He got it right!* I gave him a high five. I slunk up to the microphone, summoning every ounce of concentration.

"Piccata."

Yes! I know that one, no questions. Dr. Cameron, I love you! "P-I-C-C-A-T-A" and no bell.

The press waited outside the ballroom like birds of prey for the round-one survivors. The moment I stepped out, a reporter whisked me off to be chewed over by her crew. I then returned to my room to collapse (and study).

The spelling gods continued to be kind to me the next day: rounds two and three posed *chalice* and *theomachy*.

Back in the hotel room, friends, family, and strangers had called to offer encouragement. My old elementary school sent flowers. Newspapers wanted to interview me, even the *Boston Globe*! Tomorrow was the championship, and I would be ready.

Morning came. I solemnly donned my official bee polo shirt, white cotton with the National Spelling Bee logo. Downstairs, the atmosphere was electric. Eighty-six kids in matching attire paced like nervous sheep. Today things were serious. We would be televised to more than 70 million households.

The crowd hushed. Photographers took their places. Miles away at home, our preprogrammed VCR began to whir.

Round four gave me a hole-in-one word: *shiatsu*. (I'd seen it weekly in an ad for a massage studio in our local newspaper.) Round five was *malaguena*, seemingly indecipherable until I heard the alternate pronunciation. I was on a roll. And then . . .

"Samantha, we're going to have to ask you to start spelling the word now." Trapped like a rat. I'd never even heard of anything remotely related to *diapason*. I'd burned through every trick: language of origin, usage in a sentence, even part-of-speech, the last resort of the truly desperate.

C'mon, think! It's a musical term, for God's sake! I'm a violinist! I should know this!!!!!

The judges were staring at me. I had to do it. "OK. *Diapason*. D-I-A-P-A-S . . ."

(*pause*)

(*pause*)

(*deep resonate sigh*)

". . . I-N. *Diapason*."

Ding!

"I'm sorry, that's incorrect. *Diapason* is spelled D-I-A-P-A-S-**O**-N."

My eyes welled up. My whole being felt crushed. With one vowel, one solitary *ding*, months of painstaking preparation were obliterated. Standing on that lonely islet of defeat, I exhaled. That was it. O-V-E-R.

The gentle arm of a staff member herded me backstage to the Comfort Room. There, some fellow bell victims laughed off their mischance over cookies and punch, others sobbed hysterically. Mom came in and hugged me, taking me up to our hotel room. Finally, I let myself break down and cry.

That day, after a gripping battle of wits, Sean Conley of Aitkin, Minnesota, was declared the bee champion with *succedaneum*, meaning "one who succeeds to the place of another." Oddly enough, Sean had placed second the previous year, meaning he was now "succeeding" into first place. The following year, I would attempt to upgrade my standing, but, alas, the fates were not as kind.

When you've been bitten by the spelling bee, you never quite recover. Every time I take the stage to play a violin sonata, I'm up there again in my bee-issue polo shirt, channeling adrenaline. And my fascination with words and the worlds they create has only gotten stronger since. I inhabit literary alter egos, donning sets of vocabulary, rolling words over my tongue, testing them, tasting them, choosing the right flavor from English's rich selection. I'm blessed by my apiarian—to use it, from Latin, in a sentence—memories. I carry the full diapason with me always.

Lindsay Erin Sellers, 19

Alone

∿∿∿∿

"We won't be home until after you're asleep." I glance hope-lessly at my parents' faces, conveying anguish with my eyes. I really should be an actress when I grow up. As I usher them to the door, act I concludes; act II commences. The character of propri-ety leaves the stage, and self-expression replaces it. Chinese takeout menus are scattered over the kitchen table, Alanis Morissette is blast-ing, and piles of neon miniskirts materialize on my bedroom floor. Dancing around, I completely test what it means to be unobserved.

It's a winter Saturday in my grandparents' home in Florida, and everyone else rose with the sun to get in a round of morning golf. Nestled under a purple comforter in the purple guest room that my grandmother designed, I decide instead to pass the day around the house—alternating sleeping, resting, and eating. When I finally haul myself out of bed, I put on a fresh pair of pajamas in lieu of real clothes (there is no one here to dress for) and sprawl by the pool. I paint my toenails a soothing mauve, put on some sunglasses, and lie down. My family will wake me when they come back and lunch is ready.

We went out for dinner tonight, to the neighborhood restaurant with my parents' neighborhood friends. It was fine. But no child knows this awkward brand of family friend well enough to act at ease, even though they've been briefed with details of your life. Surely they know I have a boyfriend. Less sure they heard about the C− on my chemistry midterm. Throughout dinner I feel myself acting again.

My table manners become formal, and I resist every urge to roll my eyes, even when asked what I want to do after college. ("I have many interests right now and I am waiting to see where they lead me." That's good, isn't it?) After the meal, when my parents inevitably invite the couple back to our apartment, I cite exhaustion and escape to my bedroom. I crawl into bed, full stomach anchoring me down, and in the darkness I listen to the giggles of my mother and the clink of ice cubes in my father's glass.

The storm was so severe that it took me two hours to get home after school. I strip off saturated layers, moving away from the front door. By the time I reach my bathroom, I am completely divested of books, bag, and uniform. I draw a bath, and the warmth envelops my body. After soaking for a while, I wrap myself in a terry robe and sit by the window, gazing out at strangers scampering on Central Park West in the rain. I am the only person in the world who is snug, and I count my blessings.

Let me explain. I love being alone, but I am not a depressed person, not a lunatic, not a hermit. I am a student and daughter and feminist and musician and athlete and friend. And I am tired. Only when I do not need to label myself for any audience can I truly relax. If time spent with others is time to learn and improve oneself, then time spent alone is time to relish what you already are.

It's an interesting pattern I've noticed: Even though I'm the one who loves to spend time by myself, I rarely initiate it. Solitude falls into my lap because the people in my life seem always to be leaving, while I stay. This is convenient because nobody questions why I so like being alone, a penchant that for some reason has negative connotations.

However it plays out, privacy is always gratifying. When I am alone I enter a state of utter freedom. I can do whatever I want, however I want, when and wherever I want. Selfishness rules, and there's no one to judge me for it.

My boyfriend just called to confirm our plans for the weekend. A train ticket has been booked, and he will be waiting for me around 5:00 at the station in Connecticut. I dread the visit. The idea of staying in his home—a crowded, foreign setting with parents and siblings and pets—is beyond off-putting. What will I do, as a humble guest, when he and his family begin to irritate me and I need to spend some time alone? Will I dash off to the bathroom and sit myself on the toilet seat cover, all the while knowing he's right outside, questioning—or answering questions about—my prolonged absence? I dial his number. Excuses and apologies pour forth with a life of their own. (Apparently I have a cold, a history paper, and a desperate need to spend all of the following day with my mother.) I hope it doesn't sound fake or contrived, even though it is both. I can't tell him that visiting simply doesn't afford me enough privacy.

A love of solitude may be hormonal. Or maybe, similar to a predilection for slamming doors and shrieking, being alone is a teenage desire. According to these theories, it is doubly normal for me.

But every once in a while, I do wish that a friend were there. Someone to tell me if one of those crazy fashion ensembles I've concocted could actually function outside my bedroom. Or someone to remind me that I really shouldn't put an aluminum dish in the microwave. Aloneness can be perfect, but sometimes it's nice to have someone around to tell you things you don't already know. And sometimes it's even nicer to have someone around to tell you things you do already know, like "I love you."

I plead, "Stay a little longer," I plead, trying to hold on to a moment that has already passed. She's the type of friend who I love against my better judgment. When I'm with her, I feel fun and have fun. But she's impossible to pin down—never calling, never e-mailing, never proposing dates. I drastically reshuffle my calendar in order to accommodate hers, and I never want her to leave. But she is in high demand. "I'm late already," she sighs tiredly, refusing to indulge my supplications. It hurts me whenever she alludes to other friends. I appeal further, but she simply must go. She climbs into the elevator (out of my life forever?). So I find myself alone again. The apartment is empty.

Media, Pop Culture, Johnny Depp, Freakdom and Fandom

Sarah Schelde, 14

What Truthiness Taught Me About Being (Un)Cool

~~~~~~~~

There's one philosophy, a guiding force in my life, that I believe in above all others. I will forever be talking about it, about him, even when no one at my nursing home wants to hear it anymore.

Lately, *Monk, Scrubs, Psych*, and various British imports have taken a backseat to a man I just happened to have come across while working out in front of *The Daily Show* one night. Stephen Colbert, whose show comes on right after Jon Stewart's, quickly (like all of my obsessions) caught my undivided attention.

All of Stephen's driving speeches and fiery passion, his influence over the faithful Colbert Nation, and his audacity to really use the free speech we have been gifted with wormed their way into my everyday life. His genius term *truthiness*, the state of something being true because you find it to be so, became my mantra. And the facts about Stephen—that he's the youngest of eleven kids, that he lives in Montclair, New Jersey, that he's deaf in his right ear—became better known to me than some of my friends' birthdays.

See, if there's anything Stephen Colbert has taught me—and believe me, there is a lot—it's that you have to believe your gut. This is really the essence of truthiness, or at least the positive application of it. On his first show, Stephen slyly defined the term as "What you want the facts to be, as opposed to what the facts are. What feels like the right answer as opposed to what reality will support." Since then, it's been used by everyone from Oprah to dictionaries, and often to describe events related to a worldwide plethora of modern politics. In my life, though, it's about staying true to what you believe in, whatever anyone else says.

I talk about his show all the time. ("Well, last night on the *Report*, Stephen said he has a hatred of bears. I never really liked them . . .") I once had to make my way through traffic in Albany during a parade to get my hands on his special Ben & Jerry's ice cream flavor right when it came out. I write a forty-three-year-old comedian's name all over my notebooks and preach the (faux) evils of Nancy Pelosi to kids who don't even know what the Speaker of the House does. No one at my school has heard of Stephen, and no one cares to hear about him from me.

But it's not like I'm new to being the weird one. While most of the girls at my school listen to Beyoncé and watch *Laguna Beach*, I pop in a Kansas CD and my *Strangers with Candy* DVDs. Who wouldn't love a show that stars a hilarious woman, Amy Sedaris, who's not afraid to make herself seem and look ugly on television? Amy also happens to be one of Stephen's longtime best friends.

To tell my truthiness correctly, however, I should talk about Harry Potter, which I was introduced to in third grade and which paved the way for all my obsessions to come. Would it be odd to say that these books have had more of an effect on my life than my parents or my favorite teacher? I've reached a place where I truly don't know how I'll be able to live without Harry, his friends, his enemies, and even his pets. Since the very first book, I've faithfully defended my belief in the face of allegations like, "Harry Potter is so stupid and *gay*," and "Today I heard J. K. Rowling died! Guess you won't get your little ending." In the past turbulent year alone, these petty words were the norm.

If it's about my personal habits, my idea of truthiness, I don't really care what anyone else thinks. But I've always been the crybaby when someone insults my friends, my family—or most important, my obsessions. I even exchanged heated words with my own friends recently, for pronouncing Colbert wrong repeatedly during chorus.

They insisted on saying the *t* and I, age fourteen, cried over a half-deaf middle-aged TV host who didn't know me and probably would never have to learn how to say my name.

While I may be the only girl at my school who watches *The Colbert Report* or *Monk*, I know something comes from this. Those who are afraid to do anything that's not preapproved by MTV or the "cool" kids are also frequently those who lack imagination. People who have a drive to do things their own way have a certain advantage, I suppose. Anyone can be an athlete or a businesswoman, a writer or an artist. But without some spark of creativity, of individuality, how will they run their race or sell their idea? Who, in today's ubercompetitive world, will choose (for a job, for romance, or for life) the girl who straightened her beautiful curly hair just to become cocaptain of the JV cheerleading squad? Isn't the imaginative tomboy who listens to Japanese music she doesn't understand just because it's funky like that, with some awesome beats, a more interesting candidate? Isn't that truly truthiness?

I know I may never reach my goal of being great friends with Stephen and a junior *Colbert Report*-er (a job that doesn't actually exist). But I'm certain I'll be able to squeeze my way into a dream college and find success in the real world, largely because of my quirks. You can't be steered away from your version of the truth, at least not if you want to make it farther than the same small town you grew up in, reminiscing about how you could have married that rich dude.

Appeal from an Angry Not So Emo

〜〜〜〜

My friend always writes in her blog about how when she wakes up in the morning, she feels great; she feels like she can face the day and then some. But by the time school's out, she can hardly stand up because of all the ridicule and drama she's endured. She's called "emo" and a lot worse and taunted constantly in the halls to the point of crossing the line.

Maybe this sort of harassment happens to everyone. I know it does to most of us. But it's not like you get numb to the abuse. It hurts to see it—and sometimes feel it—firsthand. See, I go to a school where if you aren't a jock or a cheerleader, outside of your circle, you aren't anything worth talking to. My circle has no definition, at least to us. We listen to everything from screaming metal to plain old rock. Mostly what we have in common is that we just like to hang out, we tend to have a sense of humor with one another, and we don't really try to make waves.

To everyone else, though, we're just "the emos" or some other mean name like "the mutants," and we're all the same, which isn't even close to being right. It's all set up so you wouldn't bother infiltrating another circle or getting to know anyone as an individual. The high school social hierarchy is the perfect evil recipe, preparing kids for lifetimes of intolerance and fearing anyone who's not like them.

The labeling, of course, causes a lot of hate and grudges, even fights sometimes. It makes it very hard for us to ever feel comfortable at our own school. We're always looking over our shoulders, wondering who will choose us as their next target. Someone just this week told me that "all" my friends are "sick and moronic" just because a few of them smoke.

The ultimate worst part about the whole harassment thing, though—in the halls, on the Internet—is that the school does close to nothing about it. My friend and her boyfriend had a photo of them posted on MySpace with a very rude caption (which I will not dignify by repeating here). The school administration was notified, yet we haven't seen them take any action at all. They didn't even ask the kids who'd put it up to take it down. Which raises the question: Do they really care? How long can they ignore the ugly attacks? Until someone gets hurt—or worse? I may sound a little dramatic, but it's the way I see it happening.

My sociology teacher told us that there was a philosopher who said something like this: "The only thing necessary for the triumph of evil is for good men to do nothing." If people are too afraid or too passive to fight against dislike of the unliked (someone who is different from you), it could grow into a Holocaust.

This might be going a little far. I mean, MySpace and genocide are two very different subjects, but hear me out. MySpace is a massive company that connects billions of computers worldwide through the Internet. Everyone has a computer. Could you maybe imagine Osama bin Laden sitting in his hole in the ground on MySpace, accumulating friends? Just kidding. Me neither.

But I'm trying to make a point. Bad things could happen if we keep promoting, or at least not punishing, discrimination against people who are different from us. With everyone—the government, the school administration, the teachers, our parents, the people we look up to—so worried about their personal political or social status, they forget how to treat one another. This is what turns into war. And I'm talking about now, here. Iraq comes into it somewhere, but it's not the only war America's got going on. The government vs. citizens, whites vs. blacks, gangs vs. gangs, parents vs. children. The school vs. emos. If hate can turn into war, then maybe it can grow up to be something much, much bigger.

Grace Habegger, 16

The Depth of Depp

~~~~~~

One's greatest goal as an actor is to find inspiration. We need something to help get us going and figure out what it really means to be put in someone else's shoes. Johnny Depp showed me just how to do this. It's incredible how one person's view can completely affect and change you, and it's miraculous what Johnny Depp has done to me.

Acting brings me joy and helps me to escape from the sometimes harsh, shallow, and sad realities of the world. It can make you live and breathe a life opposite from your own and believe it with all your heart. You become that character by pulling it out of yourself. I never fully realized all of this until Johnny Depp.

I've been fortunate in my acting training and the roles I've received—starting small with church shows, school and community productions, then eventually with Minneapolis and St. Paul musical theater companies. I've worked with many Broadway professionals, and it's been an unbelievable experience. (Proving that he was born with theatrical skills and intelligence, Johnny Depp has never trained in acting and didn't even finish high school.) But I used to have such a false interpretation of the Broadway and Hollywood life I would live, thinking I would be rich and it would all be so glamorous. As I moved on from those middle-school days, however, I realized that's not exactly how it goes. I came to notice that there were many more important aspects of life than being rich and famous. The qualities and talent I've found in Johnny Depp—the way he loves his family, his living in France, the fact that his acting has never been about fame, money, or stardom but about the work—have helped me stick to the belief that if we're too impressed with someone else's life, then our own will just pass us by.

Really the first time I saw Johnny Depp was in *Edward Scissorhands*. I was a young girl, just starting out in acting, and I remember thinking he was so gentle and sweet. Plus, I was immediately drawn in by those deep brown eyes; I'd never seen eyes like that before. And I was fascinated by this character with scissors for hands who appeared to be so bizarre but really had the most dear heart and tender spirit. But I had no idea who the man behind the makeup was. Then one day I was watching television and saw those beautiful brown eyes again. His character was swinging back and forth on a chain, sporting long chestnut hair and a tall black top hat. I was curious, intrigued like I rarely am in front of the TV. I ate it up, watching him slide across the floor, make rolls from a diner dance with his forks, even cook grilled cheese sandwiches using a clothing iron! I thought he looked adorable, and the scenes were unforgettable. I found out this was Johnny Depp, playing the part of Sam in the wonderful movie *Benny and Joon*.

Then, when the first *Pirates* came out, I was just enamored by his swaggering persona and slightly feminine yet attractive way of portraying Captain Jack. That's when I really fell in love with him—for his wit and his beautiful face—but not even close to how I am now. Since I saw the second *Pirates*, a year or so ago, I've gotten more into him as a professional inspiration and as a person. I looked up his biography online, and I began collecting pictures, interviews, everything about the Johnny Depp lifestyle. I made a checklist of his films so I wouldn't risk missing any. I have all the DVDs. I watch them over and over again. I just cannot get enough of him!

I had always adored anything related to Peter Pan, so when I heard about *Finding Neverland*, I thought, Peter Pan *and* Johnny Depp? You cannot get any better than that! I bawled my eyes out at the end of the film and just wondered, how does he do it? How can he make his characters so honest and believable? He is just incredible.

When the second *Pirates* was coming out, I began preparing for the big midnight premiere, getting all dressed up in pirate attire (alongside an Orlando Bloom–crazed friend of mine). We drove to the theater with *Pirates* music blasting and talked in pirate lingo all night long. After seeing it, I could not get Johnny's unique ways, his humbleness, his mysterious dark-featured face out of my head. Just recently, for my sixteenth birthday, I received a life-size Jack Sparrow stand-up poster for my room, which of course I'm absolutely enthralled with. (You can see my parents are cool with my whole Johnny Depp obsession—although at first they thought it was a little crazy and overdone, and were always saying things like, "Oh honey. He's our age!" or "But he has kids and lives in France.")

I have friends who love and appreciate Johnny, but I've never met anyone who feels the same as I do, and I don't think I ever will. Everyone has a fixation. Mine just happens to be Johnny Depp.

There's a quote from Johnny I recently came across online that has helped and inspired me more than anything else as an actor: "In every part you play," he said, "there's a certain amount of yourself. There has to be. Otherwise it's just not acting. It's lying." That is absolutely brilliant. *Wow* is literally all I can say to that.

And I love the risks he's taken in his career. Johnny showed me that no matter how weird or different the person you're playing is— Ed Wood, Willy Wonka, Raoul Duke, Bon Bon, to name a few—you must pull it out of yourself. Like he said, if you only pretend, then you're lying. I'm now willing to play more eccentric characters, the mad ones, the ones I would have been put off by before my understanding of Johnny.

I also agree with what he always says—and did—about not wanting to live the Hollywood life. Johnny once said in an interview, "France and the whole of Europe have a great culture and an amazing history. Most important though is that people there know how to live." I've spent three summers in England and visited France twice, and I've found the same thing. The people there unquestionably do know how to live, and I grew quite accustomed to the easygoing, mellow existence that's so different from here. I just know I'll live in Europe someday, staying far away from the fast-paced and shallow Hollywood life just like Johnny does.

His amazing dedication to his family astonishes me, too. I knew he was truly this way after I heard about his seven-year-old daughter, Lily-Rose Melody, being in the hospital for blood poisoning, and how he hardly left her side the whole time. He's said this about his daughter's birth: "It was as if I was born that day, it was really like having some fog lifted from my eyes and suddenly meeting your reason to live."

In so many Johnny Depp interviews, he mentions how interested he is in people, how curious he is about what makes them tick. You see, I've never experienced any real tragedies in my life, so watching, talking, and working with people who have gone through these things is also a way to, for a short instant, step into their lives. I'm endlessly intrigued and moved by people's stories, too, especially when it's a misfortune of some sort, because that's the complete opposite of my life. Johnny's also said that if he weren't an actor, he'd be a writer, which is one of my choices as well.

I know I'll meet him one day, I just know it. I will make it happen. More than anything, I just want to talk to him. I've even practiced what I'll say. And I wouldn't come across as a crazed fan but as a friend to him. I want to further my knowledge about his inspirations, go deeper into religion, talk about the places he'd most like to visit, what languages he'd like to speak, and when he came up with his theories on acting. I would love to have him as kind of a mentor, as other actors have done for him, like Al Capone in *Donnie Brasco* and Marlon Brando in *Don Juan DeMarco*. I bet he'd love to help someone new as well. Then, hopefully, I could star in a movie with him! Yes, that would be my dream. Johnny Depp has inspired me more than anyone else. I look forward to my future in the performing arts and hope that he and I will be able to work together someday.

Olive Panter, 16

Play

~~~~~~

I grew up on music: Frank Zappa, the Beach Boys, the Mamas and the Papas, the Jam, Captain Beefheart, Bonzo Dog Band, the Isley Brothers, Brian Eno, Curtis Mayfield, pop, punk, soul, rock, funk. You name it, I heard it. My parents constantly poured music into the house, from radios, turntables, tape players, and the now almost-obsolete CD player that was made readily available to the public when I was about five. The music I listen to now is heavily influenced by that which was forced upon me as a kid. Beulah is the Clash meets Buddy Holly meets the Shangri-Las; Nicole Atkins is Cass Elliot without the death-next-to-sandwich or heroin attached to her reputation; and Voxtrot is basically ripped straight from the poppy rock record sleeves that used to be stored in my dad's old studio. On road trips we'd listen to "Bus Stop" by the Hollies on repeat as per my request. Funkadelic and Luscious Jackson regularly seeped out of boom boxes on my mother's desk. She'd be designing whatever book or magazine she was working on that month, and I'd sit on the ground a few feet away, drawing. Both of us would vaguely sing along.

My life has centered around music for as long as I can remember. That's not to say I don't enjoy other things. I draw, I read, I silkscreen, I sleep, I paint, and I love doing them all. But no matter how proud I am of an illustration or how great it feels to be so deeply engrossed in a book that light slips into darkness without my realizing it, music inevitably makes me feel even better. It gives you pleasure that can either lead you to the nicest nap possible (recently experienced in a car with the entire *Pink Moon* album on repeat) or the ultimate high (Animal Collective on the iPod at the Morgan Avenue subway stop at 2 a.m. in good company).

And it's not only that *I* love music. It's the fact that everyone loves it. It doesn't matter how old you are, where you're from, what your bedroom looks like—I can guarantee that every single person has a piece of music that they enjoy. The fact that there can exist some composition of tones that one person adores and another abhors is astounding.

I've found that there are two types of people in the world: those who share their music and those who keep it away from everyone else. I make mixes nonstop, with every song I love, for people I care about. Even Alvin and the Chipmunks have been known to rear their adorably fuzzy heads. There should be no shame in music.

The best part is when someone's taste in music comes as a surprise. My grandmother is a wonderfully brash, Jewish white-haired lady with a penchant for Barry White. My badminton teacher—the stereotypical female P.E. type, close-cropped curly hair and a heavy Brooklyn accent—asked me if I listened to WFMU, a commercial-free, dorky, and awesome independent music station here. She said her son had gotten her hooked on it, and I've been making her CDs ever since. For her yoga classes, I gave her some Iron & Wine, Elliott Smith, Mountain Goats, Nouvelle Vague.

Then there's my infamous Christmas mix. Despite being raised in a nondenominational household, I have a verging-on-creepy obsession with the holiday. The Hallmark version, not the Christ-is-born Sunday mass version. When I put it to music, there're the standards (Burl Ives, Bing Crosby, Eartha Kitt) and the covers (Hellogoodbye, the National, Sufjan Stevens, Death Cab). And then there are the teeny bit embarrassing songs that make the CD. Alvin's charming flat note that he manages to make sound sharp simply because of his voice? Wonderful. And then . . . there's a Hanson song. The brothers who everyone thought were girls. That's about as shameful as it gets.

It's easy enough to follow trends and listen to what everyone else is listening to. It's easy enough to let your true aural attractions fall by the wayside, lulled by Top 40 radio or watching *TRL*. But every once in a while you'll be in a restaurant or a store, and you'll hear a song that you've never heard before, and you realize that if you could hear it again, your life would be a little bit better. Last time this happened to me, it was "16 Military Wives" in a Thai fusion restaurant that otherwise played *the* most pretentious hipster music. And while, yes, I am exaggerating what a single song can do, "16 Military Wives" has cheered me up countless times. Plus, Colin Meloy is a walking, singing dictionary, so every other phrase in every Decemberists song leads me straight to look up a new word, which excites me to no end.

I've been singing virtually since birth. I played piano for a year, quit, attempted to learn the guitar three times, quit three times, and am, with the fourth go, finally getting the hang of it. But I've learned the key to success for those who want to make music but are not interested in actually learning an instrument: If it's in any way possible (and it usually is), sing. So many singers could barely stay on key but are revered as most influential or at least most fun musicians: Lou Reed and Nico. Adam Green and Kimya Dawson. Or better yet, learn five guitar chords. It worked for the Ramones, Nick Lowe, Saturday Looks Good to Me, Art Brut, the Arctic Monkeys.

I'm lucky to have grown up with insanely supportive artist parents, surrounded by relatively famous musicians and music that isn't some guy whining about his girlfriend leaving him for his best friend, accompanied by twangy gee-tar. I can't count how many times my mom has yelled at me for *not* being in a band. "You're in high school! That's when you're supposed to be rock and roll. You're going to move out and have to pay rent, and it'll be harder and harder. Do it now."

About a year ago, I realized I could probably manage it. I can. I'm doing it. Two bands, one, Euphoria People, is a cover band, but only of terrible 80s songs. "I Saw the Sign" and "I Want to Know What Love Is" have never sounded better than when in wispy, girly harmonies with hip-hop beats in the background. We're basically Co-

coRosie with lots of hopping and jazz hands instead of musical genius. The other, slightly newer We Are Thor is pretty much cliché pop rock but with better baselines and faux-Russian techno drum. And it's creepily fun. I feel as if it should almost be illegal, I get such a rush while singing. Even better? I'm good. The bands are good. Even better than being good? Being complimented by people who suspected you'd be terrible then found it to be entertaining—or "cute" that you were even trying.

I adore music. I'm good with music. I can handle music, unlike a lot of other things. I know that I need to be completely immersed in it for the rest of my life. And that's probably enough for me to make it.

Just Watch

You want to know what my problem is? You want me to spell it out, writing the words, because saying them is too frightening, too embarrassing to admit in front of people who'd see it as oh-that's-so-weird (back away slowly)? My problem is TV. My problem is the wedge it proves to be, the slow nudge that inexorably pushes even the closest people apart. Take me, take my family.

Take me, age five-ish. TV was a gift, something you got when you were sick or it was hopelessly rainy outside and you had nowhere to be, either today or tomorrow.

Take me, age ten-ish. TV was the whole rebel deal, the whole hey, guess what, I-watch-TV-when-my-family's-out-of-the-house-aren't-I-just-the-most? The whole innocent puppy-dog eyes as Mom felt the warm sides of the TV when my younger sister and I were too slow to turn it off.

Take me, age fifteen. Take the way we started renting movies-moviesmovies every weekend. Something exciting coming up? Hey, let's watch TV! TV was no longer the proud rebel cause—that was trying to undermine the school system. TV was what you watched when no one was around, a false company when you felt you would SCREAM without anyone to talk to. TV was what caused the incessant headaches. TV was whatever you never brought up in real life because you dreaded discussions, loved talk shows.

Take me, age sixteen. TV is what someone unerringly turns on whenever they're in the den, when they'd rather be wrapped up in a world of bad news, of drama and fluff and *That's So Raven* and *The*

Colbert Report. TV is the news before dinner, the wheedling for car-
toons or soaps (or, in my case, the Food Network) after, and movies
before bed. TV is family time, how we connect, rather than the board
games, the card games, the tickle sessions, and the role-playing via
Simba and Barbie and Horsey and Bun-Bunny and Panda and all
those stuffed animals, whatever we had lying around before puberty.

You want to know what my problem is? Every night, the TV, when
I'm trying to do my homework (sometimes late, if I'd been at school
for ages for so-called queer club or the literary magazine or Young
Democrats or tutoring or drama). So I turn on the computer and plug
in headphones to drown out Lou Dobbs or Anderson Cooper or Phil
of the Future with the love that is *RENT, Wicked, Aida*, Steely Dan,
Queen, the Beatles, Joni Mitchell, or some other musical genius. All
this, just to focus on whatever essay or Web quest or chemistry work-
sheet I have—in front of the fire, in front of the TV. The brainrotter
box, sucking my attention through my toes as I try to work.

You want to know what my problem is? It's not just the whole dis-
traction during the ritual that is homework. It's that wedge. It's that
not chatting with friends when the phone line could be busy. It's
that loss of togetherness, the collective isolation, the absorption in
the superficial parts of life. The how was your day that really means
how much are you going to be on the computer tonight. How much
are you going to be away from the family, not in front of the TV? It's
the whole need to be together—something I love, something I thrive
on—but in a totally uncomfortable, distant, *STFU, I'm watching TV!*
sort of way. It's stifling, wilting. The TV channels our minds (the ones
that should have 734027345627834601738456092846773 thoughts going
on at once) into the singleminded, false, and high-color world we
compare our lives to in increasingly alarming increments.

There are people all around shouting to be heard—take Niger,
take world hunger, take anything of that sort. If they're not on the
TV, not tonight, then we don't think of them. Who cares about
the starving, the oppressed without their own channels? We focus
on Brangelia and Britney and Kevin and Dolly Parton's tits and

less-than-perfect singing voice on the Oscars. The media doesn't cover gay bashing, not really, not since Laramie and Matthew Shepard but omigod, troubles with Pat Robertson? Quick, quick, cameras over here! We really must focus on whether thus-and-so got a nose job, rather than GIVE A DAMN. Karl Marx said that religion was the opiate of the masses. Well, Mr. Marx! We have this oh-so-*shiny* new development. It's called the television, and if it isn't religion, then I don't know what is.

Even as I'm writing this, Dad is watching *MASH* and turning the volume up. I overcompensate with *RENT*'s "Today 4 U" on headphones, literally killing my eardrums. I'm unable to concentrate because the lyrics are right on my brain, coupled with *MASH* dialogue that manages to slip in anyway. My thoughts are tied into two tracks, neither of which corresponds with this, with writing, with processing anything of my own.

You want to know what my problem is? I keep complaining about this imminent destruction of creativity and communication, and yet I do nothing about it. I'm just sitting here, shouting at the top of my lungs in unintelligible whispers, wanting, no, *expecting* someone to read my mind and turn off the TV. I'd like someone to take out Clue or Monopoly or Apples to Apples or Risk or Stratego and get the family to do *something* together besides looking in the same general direction with the same unfocused eyes.

My problem is that I hate this but I do not get up to select a board game. When I leave the room for some quiet, I can hear the TV from across the house, even with doors closed in between. But the worst part is that I can hear the silence—between my mom and my dad and my sister, and between them and me. I can hear the lack of speech, the empty chatter of the newscasters enthralling my family. The machine I've turned to for company is the machine that is isolating me right now.

The World and What's Wrong (Sometimes Even What's Right) with It: Battle Cries

Ms. President

〰〰〰

E*xtraordinary.* That word always sounded unusual to me. It means above the ordinary, of course, but it sounds like you're just extra ordinary. Like you are really bland. Plain. Tofu. You see, when I was little and people used to say, "Wow, Dani! You sure are quite extraordinary," I used to think they were saying, "Wow, Dani, you're really boring!" It was a beautiful moment when I understood the real meaning.

I was about six years old, and I had just attempted to braid my friend Missy's hair. Since I was an inexperienced braider, I didn't know what to do with the flyaways. So I decided to put them into their own little braids. When we showed my mom the crazy arrangement, she had this look of astonishment and said, "You are an extraordinary child." That's when I got upset and told her to stop calling me that because I definitely did not want to be on the same boring level as tofu. She picked me up, placed her smooth hands on my burning cheeks, and explained, "It means that you have something very extraspecial about you that ordinary people don't."

Since then, I have taken up the cause of making sure that every single girl in the world understands the "extra" part within themselves. I started with Missy, who had always been a little neglected. Her hair was messy, her face dirty, and her clothes never matched. On my new mission, I'd tell her that her hairdo didn't matter because she could run really fast. What I saw of her face was that her eyes were so pretty. And even if her clothes didn't match, she was still fun to play with.

As a child, every night when I was supposed to be fast asleep, I'd sit up in bed and create a small party with these little girls that were all my age, which was three or four at the time. Queen Eloise of the Ocean had a huge castle that was made up of seashells and seaweed and surrounded by water that was full of cute little animals, like dolphins, otters, and brightly colored fish. Ms. President Heatherina was the leader of the sky; she flew all day with the birds and laughed with the sun. Patricia the Space Girl lived on the moon with outgoing aliens who jumped and raced and waved to the humans on earth. What happened to these girls? Truthfully, I just don't know.

I do know that there are a lot of things thrown at teenage girls these days. Like the media. They tell us we have to be a size zero, and what do even the prettiest of women promise us we can look forward to? Plastic surgery! Famous teens lead us to think it's cool to party, do drugs, and go around wearing no underwear. Aren't these the kinds of things that drive girls into feeling cheap about themselves?

Disease and war are huge, too. With today's technology, weapons of mass destruction threaten the lives of thousands, even millions! They make a girl wonder if she'll even make it into womanhood. When the Twin Towers in NYC were attacked, it scared me so bad. For weeks I had nightmares about thousands of burning planes flying into my house and exploding it. I was in second grade. During school recesses, if I heard a plane, I would look up and run as far away from it as I could get. I can hardly imagine how life is now for girls in schoolyards in Iraq, where bombs explode every day and families are ripped apart. It's like one of my many nightmares, except they can't wake up from 24/7 terrorism fear.

And what about the religious and political leaders of the day, who seem more interested in their own financial or personal gains than in the welfare of others? Who can we trust, and who can we believe in?

I think I have the answer. It's you, it's me, it's us together, as a generation who can find the extra in each of our ordinary lives so that we can make a positive impact on the world we live in.

I would like to believe that Queen Eloise grows up to be a global-warming activist. Ms. Heatherina will become the first woman president. Space Girl Patricia will lead the expedition to walk on Mars. Though their names may change and their personalities become more lifelike, I believe these girls are out there somewhere. I believed in them then, and I believe in them now.

In life, there are two roads you can take. You can be the follower or the leader; the inspired or inspirer; the supported or the supporter. You can choose to let others control your life, or you can choose to believe in your power to make a difference. When someone gives you that you're-worth-nothing look, you should return it with a smile instead of the same. Honestly, it throws them off guard. Real-life scenario: I'm an actress in both the L.A. and San Francisco markets. At one audition (a really BIG audition for one of the major studios), there were a bunch of girls waiting to be called in to meet with the casting director. One was gazing at each and every other girl in the room, giving that nasty stare. I watched them, one after the other, return her look. So, when it came my turn, and that girl glared at me, I just smiled at her. She was sort of astonished—and then she giggled, one of those pure-hearted, innocent giggles that girls rarely share with girls they've never met. It was contagious, and soon everyone in the room was laughing. See, you don't have to be well known to have a strong on others. Ordinary girls have the power to be truly extraordinary.

I am going to stop global warming and be the first woman president. The person to walk on Mars will be me. I am going to be one of those anonymous extraordinary women who inspire so many people. I will be a successful surgeon at a very good hospital. I am going to bring food and medicine to Africa. I will lift the veils from teenage girls in Iraq! I am going to be your biggest cheerleader, because I think all girls should believe in themselves.

All around the world, teenagers, especially girls, are dealing with things that other generations never had to deal with. I spend a lot of time reading up on girls my age in other cultures, trying to find some sort of connection. I've made many new friends from Australia to

Alaska and from China to Peru, even though I haven't actually had a conversation with any of them.

I know that some girls want to speak up but are, with good reason, afraid to. I understand that some girls aren't allowed a voice, so I speak for them. To my displaced sisters in Darfur, Sudan, who are beaten and raped by militias, some even left for dead, I speak out to those who abuse you: Stop this evil of using rape as a weapon of your war! I speak for my sisters around the world, more than a million in Africa alone, who have been subjected to genital mutilation. To the leaders of your villages: End these harmful and cruel procedures! I cry out for my sisters who are sold into sex slavery, and those whose hands bleed from harvesting crops out in the hot sun all day. I fight for their rights. Give them education and safety, not fear!

To my sisters in Europe and the USA who are homeless or hungry, or who will cry themselves to sleep tonight: Be strong. You are not alone, we are all in this together. Your potential doesn't change whether you have black hair or brown hair, blond or red, if you speak Mandarin, Spanish, English, German, or Swahili.

It reminds me of the imaginary world of my childhood bedroom. My friends from around the world are real, too, like you who are reading this. If we young girls could all accept this—and each other as friends—now that would be extraordinary.

Cammi Henao, 13

Once in a While

~~~~~~~

Sometimes things we don't expect to happen do happen. September 11, 2001, was one of those things. I was still living in Colombia and hadn't even been to the United States yet—but my mom was there visiting my dad, who'd gone ahead to try to find a job and a house. We were getting ready to move there.

I was staying with my grandmother, in her apartment in Cali, and I didn't like it. I missed my mom! Then, one morning just before I was supposed to go to school, my mother called. My grandmother looked terrified. I knew something bad had happened. She told me to turn on the TV to the news, and at first I didn't want to: I was going to be late to school.

It was amazing in a terrible and sick way. Replay after replay of the majestic towers crashing down over and over and over again. The thing was, my mom and dad weren't in danger—they were in Chicago. But so was the Sears Tower, right? The tower you think of as tall even before you think of the ones in New York. I became completely terrified something would happen to my parents, who I was all of a sudden sure were at the top of Sears Tower.

It took my mom twenty extra days to get back to Colombia before they thought it was safe. In her absence I'd seen all of the horrible pictures, all the dead people. My eight-year-old mind went into crash mode and couldn't register why people had done this. No one could ever explain this to me, no one. I was suspicious about any out-of-the-ordinary behavior and ordinary behavior. I became certain that the next person around the corner had come to blow me up.

I was scarred for life, but no one even noticed because I acted completely normal, getting ready for school, helping out around the house. Before America became my home country I tried to learn everything I could about how 9/11 happened and why. I was only eight, but I could read advanced stuff, and my parents had been taking me to English classes in Colombia, so I understood the language.

Facts could help me, or so I thought. No way. I learned about religious conflict, Al-Qaeda and why they had attacked the United States. But nothing could explain to me why these people could think they would get a special place in heaven through this horrible act. This was a crime against humanity. I read and read—and remained completely confused and terrified.

It took my mom five months to convince me that I would not be hijacked on that plane to Chicago. Going to the airport was a pain. Not only was I leaving my country, my friends, and everything I knew and loved, but I was completely terrified of getting on a plane. My mother had to drag me, screaming, all the way to the gate.

We made it safely and settled into an American life with my dad. But even now I'm terrified to get on a plane. Six years have passed, and my defenses are up immediately at anything suspicious I see: a person with a weird look on their face, a lumpy bag, anything at all. I get this feeling of dread. People in this organization were capable of killing themselves and thousands of others—why couldn't they do it again? I knew they weren't going to rest until we were gone forever. The world will never be the same. I will never be the same. That's why I wrote this, to try to be the same again.

I mourn for the people whose dad, mom, brother, sister or aunt, children, little innocent defenseless babies (BABIES!) had been killed. The one who'd just fallen in love, the one whose birthday it was, the one who was pregnant with twins. I still cannot understand, and I cannot put this in the back of my mind and think that forgetting about it will help. I CAN'T. On that day, I swore that when I got older I would try to help confused kids like me about September 11. Because it's not going away. It belongs to us and it is a tragedy we cannot fix.

When I didn't get it back then, the entire act just stood there like a lump of oatmeal that no one would eat. It's still there, only grosser and more solid now.

This year, my little baby sister was born in America. And every single day I wish that nothing like September 11 occurs again in any country, any place. I know many kids who just don't care—who didn't care on that day, who shrugged and sighed when the teacher tried to explain. It's why I chose to do my Social Studies project on the attacks: Sometimes people don't care, even though they should. While my partner and I were rehearsing our presentation in front of my brother, he interrupted to ask, "I'm just wondering why would anybody do anything like this?" I told him that no one can understand.

Burning in Heaven

I am the victim of a happy childhood.

My father never stumbled home after Friday's payday, breath stinking of booze and evil, five o'clock shadow as dark as the circles under his bloodshot eyes. My mother never forgot to take her medicine, never drowned the dog in the inflatable pool out back as the neighbors peeped through the blinds and wondered whether to call the police. My brother never ran away to join the army or marry his pregnant girlfriend.

Instead, I was born on the wealthy side of town. My parents, it turned out, were very nice people, with college degrees, savings accounts, blue jeans. I was not afflicted with any life-threatening diseases or deformities. My hair was pleated just so. I ate the right amounts of fruits and vegetables. Visits to the doctor came annually, where I was informed that I was in the fiftieth percentile for height and weight.

And so, when the night was at its deepest, when the whole world was sleeping, I prayed for calamity: fire, tsunami, genocide. I wanted to feel my insides squirm and threaten to come out, my heart beating against my rib cage.

In second grade, we began to learn about the Civil Rights movement. While the peace marches were nice and the bus boycotts well organized, nothing could quite equal the injustice of the dogs, the water hoses sending little black bodies sprawling across the streets of our textbook. As Martin Luther King's birthday approached, our teacher, face overflowing with compassion, turned to the one black boy in the class.

"Jason? How does this make you feel?"

I waited, breath caught somewhere between my throat and my stomach. Here, *here* was a casualty of war, a boy who had faced *trials*. Here was a boy who knew the gleaming red eyes of adversity and refused to yield.

"I dunno."

I wanted to slap him back into consciousness, to holler in his ear until he told us of his misery. What an abject waste of blackness, of a chance at martyrdom! This boy had faced the fire and refused to show us his burns.

That night, as other girls' Barbies got pregnant and married Ken, mine escaped the Holocaust, a rogue Nazi on her arm and a bounce in her step.

Zoe Mendelson, 16

Places of Worship

~~~~~~

I hope you can appreciate my view and know that nothing here is objective. It's all diluted with Zoe, one teenager in a materially based society. At sixteen, I am constantly fumbling to define my identity. Something primal in me keeps trying, considering words like *mainstream* or *rebellious* that make me writhe, either way. But at least it forces me to continuously survey myself, and among my findings, inevitably, is my Judaism.

Sunday school is a staple of American Jewish childhood. I should know because I went to five different ones. There was one at the exclusive, affluent synagogue my family couldn't belong to because there was a seven-year waiting list, and one within a hippy-dippy, crunchy, small community. Their version of Sunday school involved the rabbi's wife taking my three preteen siblings and me into a separate room, where she would guide us through "mental journeys," which we found utterly hilarious. At services we sat on colorful pillows on the floor and people played bongos. We read Native American scriptures sometimes. They signed along with prayers, even though there were no deaf people in the congregation. When I decided I wanted a bat mitzvah, I worked with their rabbi—a man named Mark who went by Menachem with a *cccchh*—once a week for five months to learn my Torah portion. I loved it because Menachem was patient enough to answer every what-does-Judaism-think-of question. He was in his twenties but he had a long beard and soft nature that suggested wisdom, so I trusted everything he said and thought he was awesome. He made my bat mitzvah a great experience, even if I was embarrassed to do sign language on stage in front of my friends.

My family recently joined another fancy congregation so that my youngest brother, who's six, could start going to Sunday school. He went once and hated it. He only went that one time. A few weeks later we got a report card in the mail, telling us how smart and wonderful my little brother is, and how well he participates and plays with others.

The hypocrisy was killing me. How could a religion based on the concept of *mitzvoth*, good deeds, have congregations so expensive, services so strict or silly?

I've learned to take what I like and leave the rest with my Judaism. I don't believe that any people are the chosen people, but I do believe in *mitzvoth*. I think Jews should have a state but cannot bring myself to support Israel and its brutal military actions. I mostly identify with my Judaism through culture rather than specific beliefs. I'm content to search for hidden *matzo* at Passover and hear stories about my relatives. Last year I started a Jewish club at my school. We used to do silly things, like draw on *yarmulkes* and watch *Seinfeld*. But recently we got involved with the high school counterpart of Hillel. Every week now they bring pizza and some kind of much more planned activity.

My father is unequivocally proud to be Jewish. He idolizes his grandfather, whose pinky ring he wears, and beams when he tells stories about the strong people his grandparents were. Quite simply, I think he's proud to be Jewish because they were Jewish. It's a little more complicated with my mom. She's a peace-and-love hippy of sorts, though not as crunchy as the people at Menachem's congregation. Her parents raised her Jewish as much as it meant bagels on Sunday mornings and apple picking on Rosh Hashanah.

My father's daughter at age eight, I defaulted to supporting Israel as soon as I knew what it was. I was even his comrade at rallies. And all I really knew of Judaism was the story of Passover: that God had led the Jews out of Egypt to Israel. The way I understood it, Jews had been there ever since.

As I came to learn that this was not nearly the case, I became wary. I understood—and my mother filled in the blanks—what I hadn't been taught in Sunday school. When the Jews claimed Israel, they forced out thousands of Palestinians, whose families had been living on the land for generations. And what justification was there to offer? That thousands of years ago a god—not even the same god that you believe in—told Moses that this land should belong to the Jews? This is not sufficient explanation, and it brought me to a moral conflict.

Every time I read about another suicide bombing there I am enraged. But I'm equally enraged by reports of the Israeli army's atrocities. Though it was far less publicized than Hezbollah's attacks, Israel's bomb raid of South Lebanon was, among other things, unnecessary. It's been difficult for me to sustain my pride in Judaism and this supposed Jewish homeland the way my father has.

Two summers ago, I spent a week with a group of twelve Israeli teenagers who'd been direct victims of the conflicts described above. Every one of them had lost a parent or had their home destroyed or had been in a bombing at a café, a bus to school, the mall. A program with the Jewish United Fund flew them into Chicago and planned a week of fun activities with American kids as hosts. We took them to Navy Pier, WhirlyBall, all of the museums, the zoo, and Great America.

Knowing what I did about them, I expected the Israelis to be very withdrawn and quiet, maybe bitter. But I couldn't have been more wrong, and I found myself forgetting that they were terror victims. They were energetic, outgoing, and fun. They cracked a lot of dirty jokes to show off their English. They pretended to teach me how to say "I like your top," and instead had me calling whomever I addressed "a fat whore." We got along great. Living in a country where you're constantly in danger, it must be hard to let loose. But they definitely did here.

I got particularly close with one girl, Rhotem. She was so beautiful in the classic Israeli way. She was a little bit quiet, but super witty, and she made me laugh with her commentary on all things Americana. She pointed at the sign on the McDonald's at Navy Pier that reads "McDonald's: The Future" and said with her thick accent and a grin, "This is em, a little bit scary, no?"

One rainy afternoon, when the group all went to see *The Incredibles*, Rhotem became so uncomfortable. I was sitting next to her, and every time I looked over she had a completely straight face and wide eyes. I couldn't imagine why; it's just not that kind of movie. When I asked, she explained that loud noises make her uneasy. This shook me up. Tragedy had never seemed tangible to me until then, maybe because I'd never been so close to it, or maybe because Rhotem was so much like me. She started crying a little bit, so I took her out into the lobby. She told me a missile had flown right into her living room and that she and her family had survived only because they happened to not be home. Even so, she knew she was not unscathed. That she could not enjoy a simple movie was heartbreaking. As we sat on a bench, in a room full of flashing lights and vending machines and arcade-game explosions, I started to wonder how much perspective I could really have.

Sometimes it's crucial to have emotional, highly personalized accounts of history; they can be far more important than names and dates. History is made of lives upon lives and of cultures. It's also made of great minds—and of average minds. Mostly, though, it's these average minds that fill space and time, the people who create and consume culture, the people who go see movies and have families. The incredibles.

Danielle Norman, 16

Repeat

~~~~~~

I wonder why the human race is so stupid. We march around the world, pretending we own the place—building, changing, controlling. When a volcano explodes, a hurricane drowns a city, an earthquake buries countries, we are powerless but won't admit it. We settle anywhere that will sustain life and command the elements not to disturb us. Over and over we are confronted with the awe-inspiring forces of nature, but our only response is a quick burst of worldwide sympathy and aid, followed by a neat tally of donations whose numbers are then used to assist in elections.

Billions of dollars were sent to the Hurricane Katrina victims, relief was prepared. Before that, newspapers were flooded with survival stories and pleadings from tsunami victims. Yet now, what seems like so long after these horrors, the zealous spirit to help has been lost. The influence of humans does not extend to controlling the weather. But we are given the decision of what to do, of how to repair others when disaster strikes and long after it is over.

We refuse to learn from history, fighting over the same things over and over again. Starting at a young age, with small, repeated bickers over the same toy, this continues far into our lives. We fight in junior high then high school over friends and boyfriends. If we lose, we go back for more and hold a grudge that will poison everything else. The world fights wars that are so similar to each other that you learn a few, you learn them all. Europe fights over royalties, and the phrase "thousands dead in the streets of Paris" can be played on a tape recorder on a loop. America has entangled itself in a war that is now being compared to Vietnam.

Yet we continue on. We think of ourselves before others, and then we are shocked when we see the statistics of people going hungry. We send millions of dollars in aid across the ocean and turn a blind eye to those starving in our own community. People wonder how a parent can physically harm a child, and yet some will shout and swear at their spouse in front of a little one they think doesn't understand. Why do we feel sympathy for those with tears streaming down their TV faces but can't see the pain of a weeping soul right next to us? We place judgments without understanding what goes on behind the doors of someone else's home, or what struggles they hide inside.

In the past we have enslaved fellow men, forcing them to bend to our will. Denying them the very right that we fight for daily and demand for ourselves. Even now, though not quite as literally, we have enslaved those who are not considered wealthy. They live without a living wage. Many families are unable to afford insurance and therefore doctors. The elderly are bound by complicated forms of Medicare and insurance policies that make no sense.

We run our lives with hypocritical statements. We get angry with and punish people if they do something we don't like. Then we turn around to do the exact same thing to the next person we see, from back-biting friends taking revenge on each other to politicians who can't keep their self-respect high without shooting others down. Civilized countries balk at the inhumanity of war. But we broke the rules we'd set to prevent violations of basic human rights. Prisoners are kept for years without knowing what they've been charged with—no chance at a trial or a lawyer, violating the very thing that sparked our country into being.

We try to fix the small things that will disappear with time, ignore the harder problems no one wants to face. Leave them for the next generation to deal with. Debt mounts as someone else's problem, economies are teetering, and politicians are pulling up long-dead or nonexistent problems to distract us. In high school, one-week flings are treated like the real deal, and before you know it, choices lead you to have to make it the real deal. Our government applies Machiavelli's "the end justifies the means," defending a patched-up job in Iraq with the accomplishment of a goal unrelated to why we began the fight.

Now, after I'm done writing this, and you're done reading it, we will all go out into the world and do the same thing we have been doing for hundreds of thousands of years. We will be humans. We will close our eyes once more to the pain of the world because it hurts too much to see it. Because we are afraid we might see a little of that wrong in our own life. We are afraid of what we can't control, what we can't solve, and what we don't understand. I wonder why this cycle goes on and on, spreading through generations like some mutated disease. I wonder why we allow it all to happen.

The Border

~~~~~~

As an immigrant and a teenager, being ambitious, cultured, outspoken, creative, enthusiastic, caring, and a self-starter has come at a very expensive price—tears and blood. Being Mexican in an American high school is difficult, as is going back and being so-called American in Mexico. What the two countries, maybe all countries, seem to have in common is that the person who's different is an enormous threat to society. What you want to do is fit in; it's just easier that way. It used to be like that in my little world, but not anymore. I want to be unique. Original. It will define my personality and make me successful. It will remind me what I've accomplished. I'm writing in a language I came very late to.

My story began on a rainy Friday in April when I was born, a little Mexican girl in Bellevue Hospital, New York City. Everyone in the hospital knew I was a different kind of child: I was the biggest newborn there, and my father had dark skin and was sixty-five years old, while my mother's skin was light and she was only twenty-nine.

When I was two, my family decided to move from New York to Mexico, because my father was retired and feeling tired of the city. He also wanted his daughters, my older sister Micheleluce Oralia and me, to attend a private Catholic school and get the best education possible, one he wasn't able to afford in the United States.

So, I grew up in an extremely wealthy society in Sahuayo, Michoacán, where I studied ethics, morals, and Catholicism. The school encouraged its students, the most privileged children in the city, to do community service: Our teachers explained that we as Catholics should always be kind and generous to those who aren't as fortunate. When I was ten or twelve, I started realizing how much I enjoyed helping others and feeling the need to change the world. I always thought it unfair that other kids had to work at my age. I also began to notice that individuals who didn't have an education were paid a misery but worked twice as hard as people who were well schooled. I became aware of the importance of getting an education, not only because it would help to provide a great income, but also because I did not want to be a human being who was ignorant and fooled by appearances.

My house in Mexico was luxurious, and we had many expensive objects. I counted shopping as a hobby, took vacations every six months to the nation's most popular and beautiful regions. I learned to play the piano and the violin, to paint, to read literature, to recite poems. My father, an artist and musician, felt the need to show us the beauty of those things. He was also a lawyer, an engineer-electrician, a seaman, and a veteran of World War II, Korea, and Vietnam. He played golf and tennis. He spoke Spanish, English, French, and Patwa.

In my eyes, my father was more than perfect, and I grew up being as ambitious and curious as he was. I graduated second in my class, with a 3.9 GPA and all the signs of a rising star. I won several poetry competitions, I was president of my sixth-grade class, and I was chosen to join La Escolta, a group of students who would carry the Mexican flag at public events.

At home in my privileged neighborhood, though, I'd notice people staring at my extremely dark-skinned father. Most of our neighbors were of fairer European descent—and their ignorance made them assume that my father wasn't educated or that he was some kind of evil man who was involved in illegal activities. Later on I realized that most Mexicans in my city were extremely racist. At times some of my neighbors weren't allowed to play with me. The parents would OK me for their kids' company only after they found out my father was

French, which they took to mean wealth and sophistication. All of a sudden, plenty of racist Mexicans would feel the need to become my dad's best friends.

When I was thirteen, my world collapsed. My family and I moved to New York City. My father, then seventy-eight, had been diagnosed with a cancerous tumor and was entitled to free veteran's care in the United States.

I arrived without knowing how to speak, read, or write English. I was placed in regular-to-slow classes here instead of in ESL, which would have helped me to learn the language and transition faster. I went from the honors track in Mexico into classes where I couldn't comprehend a word, with students who refused to learn or care about their future. I was thrown in with kids who had spent time in juvenile prison, were pregnant, racist—and mean to me. I never thought that being Mexican or coming proudly from both Aztec and Mayan heritage would create such problems.

Crying hysterically and feeling depressed were a part of my every day. I was broken. I had no real friends, and my grades and test scores were lower than I ever dreamed they could be. I would try to read and I wouldn't understand. I felt like I was completely losing touch with myself and the world. To make matters worse, my grandfather, who was so close to me, passed away in Mexico; with my dad needing to be near the hospital I couldn't go back for the funeral. Life was nothing but difficult and the pain was unbearable.

The second semester of my sophomore year, two years after we'd moved, I hit rock bottom. I was destroyed, and I didn't even have my own room. (I had to share with my sister, and we had our differences and totally dissimilar taste in everything.) I wasn't used to living in a small, one-bathroom apartment; back in Mexico we had four bathrooms. My family didn't go on trips anymore, and no one seemed to care about me or my situation. I realized I was in denial—I couldn't admit that I would not be returning to Mexico, where life was full of promise and a bright future. I kept thinking about how ungrateful I used to be there, and it was excruciating how much I missed my friends who I'd known since I was three. Meanwhile, they were having the times of their lives. I wasn't there for their Quinceanera parties, after all the dreams we'd had about turning fifteen together. I wanted to see my grandmother. I wanted to be that honor-roll student I always was. But it seemed impossible. I was alone. I had support from no one.

One day, also in tenth grade, I was looking through old pictures and couldn't even recognize myself in Mexico. I was ashamed that I'd let two years pass in America feeling nothing but depressed. I'd lost sight of my dream, which was to help other people, make change, perhaps be a world leader. I was painfully slow at coming to it, but I had to accept that my life was happening in a different place, and I had to take action. I had to leave the big baby I was in New York back at Bellevue. I started teaching myself English and signed up for more challenging courses that semester, including AP classes in U.S. history and Spanish literature. I got involved with the YMCA's Global Teens, the Lower Eastside Girls Club, and the N.Y.P.D. Explorers. I started getting used to the New York City life: taking trains and buses, using elevators, eating pizza, celebrating the 4th of July. I started appreciating the chance to meet people from all backgrounds, teens with different sexual preferences.

My father is doing well, the cancer in remission for years now, though he was recently diagnosed with Alzheimer's. My world has come to include tall buildings, gangs, and violence. It's all made me very open-minded, though. Because I understand what it is to suffer—to be on the other side of the community service equation—I'm even more strongly committed to working with people who need help, those who are sick and can't afford health care, oppressed indigenous populations, elders, students who are struggling, underprivileged children, immigrants. Gandhi said, "You must be the change you wish to see in the world." For me to achieve this, the next challenge is to get the best education out of the rest of high school as I possibly can, then onto university. Because I don't want to be ignorant like some racist Mexicans or certain American teenagers.

Kathleen Hicks, 18

Bodies of Water

~~~~~~

I magine living on an island, not really worrying about what's going on in the world, and then you wake up one day to see the things you see in the movies happening in real life. I live in Hawaii, which I admit is no excuse to have been checked out from events separate from my own little land mass.

I was just getting ready for school the day it happened. (Only it had already happened in our time zone, at around three in the morning, September 11.) I walked into the living room and saw my mom and dad not saying a word and just staring at the TV. My mom was still wearing her pajamas, even though she needed to get to work in half an hour. I was just about to ask what was wrong when I saw it: a plane hitting the first tower. And then the second one came. The station just kept playing it over and over again. How could something like this happen to one of the world's strongest nations? I watched dumbly, I didn't understand.

All day at school people couldn't stop talking about what had happened, and almost every classroom had its TV on to the news. I remember coming home and sitting on my bed and just tearing up, knowing that so many people had died for no reason whatsoever, and thinking about all those families who'd said good-bye to loved ones just hours before and wouldn't be able to see them ever again. As the days went on, I started to feel even worse for the people who didn't know if their loved ones were alive or dead.

9/11 means that no one can get away with living on an island, pleading ignorance and isolation. 9/11 means the end of the United

States as I've known it. 9/11 means the end of the easy in, easy outs of flying on a plane—of the simple crossing of bodies of water to connect with others.

It still makes me mad to think that the U.S. government knew about the mounting terrorist threat, yet didn't do a thing about it. All those innocent people, just going to work one morning, living their lives on their island, were victims of the U.S. government's stupidity.

The date will always be one of the single saddest days in history. 9/11 means that I will know at least two of the daughters whose fathers were sent to Iraq and died in duty. 9/11 means seeing more and more Hawaiian soldiers being deployed to the war. 9/11 means that they will be my relatives. More and more and more of them.

The Dial Life—and Him*

It was overwhelming, the forced taste of fermented grapes out of an absurdly large goblet of wine. Full enough to satisfy a congregation, wiped at the mouth repeatedly, however unsanitary, on a priest's holy robe. I kissed a gold-plated icon at the hands of an old Romanian. I watched from between worshipping legs as each walked up, in line, to the altar. Romanians speaking loudly, kissing one another aggressively, even violently at times, and discussing their plans to bring loved ones to America. This was always a concern, and I was aware of it even then, at the age of five: how to mesh the old world with the new. The fitting of pieces, the rise and fall of communism, the rise and fall of our lives, these were Sunday mornings. The appeal of the weekly trip lay solely in the location of the Greek Orthodox Church, on New York City's Upper West Side, so close to the carriage horse bridal path. If I was lucky, I would see one or two of those majestic beings and retain their image through the incomprehensible chants. Soon enough, however, I grew too old to be pressed into going, too big for the horses, too cynical for the talk that surrounded me.

Those were my first run-ins with religion, and my experience was not wholly negative. The church had an amusing quality to it: There was always something to look at, touch, or attempt to break apart. Everything was old and everything was gilded. The smell of city air never seemed cleaner and crisper than when leaving an overcrowded room sealed with all too many smells, old woods and burning wax,

*Title taken from Emily Dickinson's poem "A Clock stopped—Not the Mantel's"

strong perfumes to disguise age. In truth, I had no sense of the importance of being there. All I knew was that it made my father happy, and that there were rewards: a trip to the toy store, a pastry in hand.

At age five, I started attending a small French academy on the Upper East Side, a beautiful landmark building with angels sculpted in the ceilings. It was a school designed to be as diverse as possible. There were children from countries I had never heard of, speaking languages I struggled to recognize. My father had spent a year in political asylum in Paris, and having married my mother, a Romanian and a francophile whose French was fluent, decided that I should be raised trilingual. I brought lunches that smelled unfamiliar to the children of France or its colonies; I spoke Romanian to my governess, who picked me up daily from school. In hindsight, I belonged there, perhaps nowhere else.

I soon came to realize that the French were devout Catholics. At the request of my parents, I took catechism once every other week for five years. I had a little best friend named Celine whose mother, Viviane, taught the classes. When I was about eight or nine, Viviane introduced my family to the French Catholic church, and we stopped attending the Romanian Orthodox one. I think my parents, like me, were ready for a change. Religion had always been important to my father; he'd clung to it during the darkest moments of his life, living in Romania under the communist regime. How could I oppose his wishes? Besides, there was no reason to question this religion; I had no reason to doubt anything. God was there, behind an unexplained, unquestioned mechanism that was life. I woke in the morning and breathed in deeply, just as those around me did. I believed, until the day the air thickened.

Celine's house was frighteningly perfect, organized and regulated by some unseen system. At Christmas, her grand piano became the stuff of dreams, a stage for an entire mountain of movable vacationers surrounded by cotton snow. Electric skiers made their way up and down a mountain and colorful trains circled. I knew Viviane was the force behind this yearly structure, personal and intricate. During the year, her house maintained the same warm, clean smell, as if its rooms had never known or seen a mess. It was enough to make you never want to leave.

Celine sang beautifully, much like her mother, and was a quiet favorite of all who encountered her. Viviane had a gift, and although we tend to say that of many, she really did have a glorious voice. It was as if God had created her as a worthy medium for his hymns. The cruel joke, however, was that Viviane was sick. She was sick, and I could not have possibly understood with what at the age of eight, nor was I expected to know why headscarves regularly enveloped her skull. However, it seemed rather odd that she should be sick when I was being preached repeatedly, from Viviane and my family alike, that God watched over the good. Did God not watch over our health? Who then did we attribute our state to, our lives, our breaths, if they were not of his making and of his taking? Religion's inconsistencies had begun to bother me, but I brushed them aside in favor of being a child, in favor of believing in my unconditional safety—that denial of mortality we uphold for as long as we can.

Celine spoke nothing of her mother's illness, and neither did I. I never openly questioned discrepancies until I was ten, when doubt and a sense of pending doom stirred inside of me. Then, it became a trial. My parents fought my sound logic, and much to my sadness, they eventually gave in. They admitted that certain things, such as sickness, surpassed pure religious explanation. I had won when all I'd wanted was to be reassured.

Viviane soon stopped teaching, and we were handed substitutes at random—pious Frenchwomen who desperately clung to rote diagrams and stories to guide us through. My father began to take Celine and me to school, along with her younger brother, as Viviane could no longer and her husband, as my father always put it, "had his hands full." Celine and I met in her lobby every morning. The floor was checkered in black and cream marble, and as we waited for her brother to come downstairs, we jumped from square to square. Celine's laugh was infectious and rich; I longed to hear it as often as I could. We became like sisters, eating dinner in her kitchen together nightly. The undying mechanism seemed to be in full motion: Meals continued to include all food groups, and the house was as ordered as ever.

Viviane's visits to the school and appearances at church became less and less frequent, and we were asked by our teachers to pray for her nightly. When I'd show up for dinner with Celine, Viviane would tend to greet me, inquire "How is your lovely mother? Where has she been traveling to?" then retreat to her room. Her clothes were refined but hung oddly on her, as if her body wasn't assigned to carry them. She was long and thin, her cheeks sunken, but she maintained an unpronounced beauty. She knew my family well, knew my mother's job had always required heavy traveling, and that my father, a writer, was frequently referred to as "best mommy-dad." At school he'd filled in for my mother on mother-daughter day.

My mother traveled, my father read. My household was nothing like Celine's. My home made no effort to appear perfect, my parents smoked and liked dark artwork. No one ate at the same time, and dishes, cooked by my eighty-year-old Romanian governess, had names that none of us could pronounce. I loved Celine's home for its look inside the lives in the movies, an apartment decorated in a color scheme. Balanced meals with such bland sides as rice, things I didn't enjoy but knew were necessary. My family had never made me do anything "because I said so" or "because you have to." This American sitcom language was beyond them, and my mother, father, and I were inseparable.

When I first asked my parents about Viviane's condition, my father replied, "She has a growth in her stomach," but not like a child, not an ounce of good. This growth was abstract and not a satisfactory assessment to me. I couldn't see or imagine it. Afraid to ask Celine, I turned to the only reference I had, the perfect family portraits on their walls. Viviane's hair, under scarves as long as I could remember, had been long and rich. It was terrifying to see her looking so vital that one could easily suspect effects had been used on the picture, at some extra expense. The next time I looked at Viviane, I was equipped with the saddening before perspective and could fully see how plagued she was. Her eyes watered, dissolved, and her every step was taken with effort. It became clear to me that she was cancer-stricken, but never that she could die. I continued to pray for her. I was not praying for a miracle; I didn't deem it necessary.

Viviane went into remission, and Celine and I went on playing tag in her apartment's countless corridors, soccer in her long hallway. At school, we were inseparable. We sat together at lunch and walked together in the park. Viviane became more present, and her singing at church regained its former renown. Although I never doubted that she would get better in the first place, I took this as proof that God existed. It fueled me to become a Catholic.

I wanted to be like Celine, and I wanted to be certain I was being protected under not only the right religion, but the right faction as well. I was tired of reminding myself what being Orthodox, my mother's religion, meant, and why I wasn't Catholic, the norm at my school. My father was Catholic, but having been divorced prior to marrying my mother, was forbidden to take communion. It seemed like a waste of time explaining this to my classmates, though, when I myself didn't understand the complex differences between the two. I decided to convert to Catholicism in the spring, and Viviane was to be my godmother. I walked down the church aisle and accepted my first communion at age eleven with Viviane by my side.

In truth, I felt nothing that day. Nothing of religion; rather, I was self-conscious and worried about how I looked in my white dress, makeup-less, with a daisy crown around my head. My family was so proud, and of what, I asked myself. I was embarrassed by the flowers I was holding, the fact that I was receiving communion with much younger girls, so late in the game. My focus was on anything but God at that moment, and I felt guilty. There stood Viviane, a woman who believed in him above all else, despite her hardships. And there I was, inspired by Viviane's recovery but also hugely relieved to no longer

be the black sheep of Christianity in my school. My guilt only wors-
ened with time—a guilt that I sought to rid myself of, only to discover
that it was a widespread element of Catholic teaching. Guilt of sin-
ning, guilt of doing too little, too much. I was promised to feel guilty
the rest of my life until, by some decision not my own, I would be
saved.

As I entered my teens, church became a social affair. My only goal
was to be there on Sunday, dressed to impress not confess. My father
often yelled at me in the morning, as my outfits tended to be twice as
revealing and my makeup twice as heavy as on weekdays. I sat separate from my parents and chatted away with friends all through Mass.
As it came time to take communion, I'd sloppily rise from my seat and
wait on line, making as much eye contact with the opposite sex as I
could.

I was a well-liked young woman, very outgoing and up on trends.
But that was what the school knew of me. At home, I was painfully
close to my parents and hated my mother's biweekly trips.

Nowadays, at eighteen, this still holds true. My parents remain
the most important thing to me, and my distaste for the hypocrisy of
the Church continues to frustrate me. I cannot bear to attend Mass,
even on holidays. I'm frustrated with my own vanity, with my inability
to feel free of judgment, even in a sacred space. However, in the past
I went because everyone was there—the boys, the girls, the old, the
young, the believers and the nonbelievers, and Viviane. She kept Celine under tight ropes, and I did not want to be considered a negative
influence. I didn't want to fall out of Viviane's favor. I did, after all, owe
her so much.

Just as Celine and I were getting ready for high school, Viviane's
sickness caught hold of her again, for the last time. By that point I understood the gravity of the problem and had a new sense of what Celine risked losing if Viviane should die. My mother was a vital part of
my existence, and I could not imagine how hard it would be for a girl
my age to lose such an essential figure. I began praying again, only

this time it was desperate pleading. I begged God to save Viviane, begged him to let Celine grow up with a mother. Viviane's appearances at church, though rare, suggested that she believed now as much as ever. And this is the heart of my struggle: I could never understand her doubtless devotion. Viviane continued to preach the word of a God who seemed to show himself so little. Never once did I see a grain of bitterness, even toward the very end of her life. I saw physical weakness, I saw her body failing her, but not her faith.

There is some truth, perhaps, in the romantic belief that the dying have a peaceful, admirable quality to them. They seem more constant and solid than the rest of us, their future being decided and purely a matter of wait. Viviane died one day in spring. I found out through a friend who put it bluntly, with no visible concern. I immediately collapsed on the street. I cried and slept through the rest of the day, feeling utterly tortured. Where was God, I wept angrily, helplessly. I couldn't bear to believe that it was for the best, peace at last, as did those around me. "She can't suffer anymore," said my mother. But why did she have to suffer in the first place?

There are moments when language fails us, when, unless you show me, I will not understand. These are the moments when God should descend to explain himself, reaffirm our faith, wave a long, transcendent hand. I had questions I could not ask my religious father; I was alone. God appeared so ready to let us suffer, to let us go. If he could take Viviane, wherein lay salvation for the rest of us? Why was I, frivolous, ungrateful me, still alive? I should like to know, now, why Viviane was stolen, prematurely, from all she worked toward, from all those who loved her.

I am aware that people struggle with this daily, and that I'm not the first, nor the last, to ask these questions. Books adorn the shelves on divinity, religion, *The Idiot's Guide to God*. We are all the idiots.

Celine and I stopped talking when I left for high school. I had never addressed her mother's death; I just didn't know how. I'd made new friends I thought I loved more, had more in common with. I saw her last summer, for the first time in years. I came up to her apartment to find her room a disorganized wreck, fully and painfully un-recognizable. The mechanism, it seemed, had stopped. Her mother's picture sat on the nightstand, as did a glass of unfinished water. Though Celine smiled and laughed her rich laugh, I wanted so much to grab her, ask her, "Do you believe, still?" I wanted to see if she took after her mother in doubtless faith, ask her how she had been, how she had *really* been. To make up for all those years we never discussed Viviane's sickness. But how could I distress her for the sake of my peace of mind? I couldn't, just as I could not bear to tell her that soon after her mother died, my mother had been diagnosed with the same illness and survived.

Many wonderful things have been said about Viviane, but in the simplest terms, she played by the rules. She married, had children, preached the word of God—and still died young. I cannot separate reason from my faith. From the moment we are born, we enter a system that relies on justice to work. It's as much innate as it is learned, this concept of fairness, the language we accord to those we admire, what we presume they *deserve*. God, I want to yell, "How *fair* is it that a beautiful daughter and son live on now, motherless?" But I know it's not a question of justice; there is not one ounce of it in the world.

I am not a defeatist, but I am often disappointed in the world's self-ishness, in my selfishness, in humanity's limitations, and most of all, disappointed in God for not taking a more active role in light of our shortcomings. I have lived my eighteen years as best I can and stand by a sense of stubborn hope. Why not be a no-nonsense preacher and ask, "God, Viviane was a productive citizen of the world and an influ-ential publicist for your abstract kingdom and teachings; why did you take her back?" In the corporate world, one would be dissatisfied with the way God chooses to market himself. He might want to consider getting rid of some of the bad guys first, according priority of exis-tence to those who deserve it, those who are active in maintaining and sustaining this odd planet that we find ourselves on. But that's still not enough.

Religion, and why religion? Why is it that we all struggle with faith, and all suffer some life-altering encounter with it at one point or another? We need to believe in something. Self-serving as it is, I want to believe that there's more to life than science can readily explain. I would like my romance, please—free of theories and interpretations, free of chemical effects or brain stimulators. However, I would also like doctors to save me should I fall ill: Evidently there is absolutely no guarantee that God will make you better.

I would like to believe that some things are beautiful for no other reason than that a greater power has made them that way. But I cannot be like Viviane; I cannot be at ease with everything. I cannot make peace with her sickness or my mother's. I accept it, move on, and am grateful for every day. I am not bitter, I am reasonable.

Is there room for reason in religion? Perhaps the problem is that the two already overlap and are nearly impossible to separate. Whatever the formula may be, Viviane seemed to know it and apply it flawlessly. But I'm not as strong as she was, or I am simply different. I am religious, yes, but I struggle. I am not a doubtless follower just as I am not a doubtless lover and perhaps never will be. But in the end, I want God, I *need* God. I need an impalpable, intangible non-answer, and that is reason enough to believe.

Emily-Nicole Johns, 19

New City

~~~~~

I understand that I am misunderstood. Who am I? Where? No place is like home, especially when you live in a city like New Orleans. Sometimes writing my thoughts to my insides is my only sanity. Do you ever think that if someone heard your thoughts they would really wonder about your head? I've laughed madly with the homeless on street corners and shared my stories with newborns in taxis. I wonder if this life is really all that we have and if I am really writing to someone who's alive.

I don't think we are silly for living in the future, writing children's stories on the ripped wallpaper and broken glass of my destroyed home. My home may look nothing like the rest of the dead's but all of my realities, everything I'd had to say, drowned in the floods of Hurricane Katrina. I am aware of the offense, mourning pieces of paper when all those people and pieces and people . . . Yet my boxes of crying sisters and cotton clouds were demolished, and my heart was crushed. I never wanted to write again. It all seemed too big to be true, and the only way to get through it was to live life with my hands pressed over my eyes, lumps in throat.

Sometimes when the sun came up it was like none of it had happened. Erase loneliness, erase doubt and guilt. Erase the truth and blind bad thoughts out with the day. Clean your face, wrap yourself in gold. But nothing seemed to work. I was drowning, completely out of air, suffocating at the filthy, wet hands that wrapped around my throat my junior year. Nature sent me down unfamiliar halls, packed with unfamiliar faces that seemed to stop talking as I walked past with my head down. The hatred was unbearable. The stinging whispers about the neighborhood I grew up in as a "sin city that deserved every drop of water they got" caused me to sew myself up even more. For the people in this new city, it was all about the shortened curfews and the abundance of colored people in town. In reality we were just abandoned children looking for a new place to call home for a while.

They ask questions—Did you lose everything? How does it feel to lose everything? Are you OK? Are you OK? Are you OK?—and they're tiring and repetitive. Each response from me is mostly that I don't know, but sometimes an acknowledgment that it's not at all what you think. On the phone in my closet, I cried over why this can't be easier, why this is hardly ever OK. My family left New Orleans. We moved, if it's still moving when there's no home to pack up, to Baton Rouge, about an hour away.

The first time I went back to the city, nearly a year after Katrina, I could hardly catch my breath. The pain from that look forward is perpetual and indescribable but so incredibly real. It builds up and up, and at some point you realize that every time you cough you're pulling the tide into your throat. Every time you breathe deeply to laugh you're running the risk of choking on a whole ocean. The city lost its lights and there were bridges and levees completely split in half. I walked through it all and thought, *At the end of this, I will know what matters the most.* And everything I saw made characters pleading to be put on paper, for rescue. I imagined the public phone booths floating by, carrying people grasping to handsets, cords. I assumed their last words were "I love you" and that by then they weren't all that scared. The food supplies were pointless. The gas masks were pointless. The story of everything, and still my hands were running away from paper. I'd become a multicolored mess.

As the months passed, I still felt incapable of writing. I wouldn't allow it because I feared what would flow. Without writing to lean on, I no longer knew how to speak or feel. I let a boundless tragedy take the one thing that I felt I could do wholly and beautifully.

I hid until the only person who mattered to me sent me a hand-written letter. She said, "You cannot hide forever, though you may try. I have heard the stories you tell. You can go out into the world and show others. They will feel less alone because of you, they will feel understood, unburdened. But to share with them you must wear shoes. You must go out and it will be harder. You must face jealousy and sometimes rage and desire and love, which can hurt most of all because of what can then be taken away."

So I undid my stitches and opened my eyes. I think that if I could just find the right kind of quiet, the right shade of stillness, I could write all of the poetry that crawls down my back like heat, and then I'd be able to find new ways to fill myself. My hair is getting so long, and I'm taller than we all thought I'd be, and I want to keep telling people these things so that I can't forget them. I think that's OK, like I'm preparing someone else to feed my story back to me when I need it.

This is my story. I am no longer away from home, and eighteen is not exactly what I imagined. Sometimes I can't think of anything to say. Sometimes I feel like I became too cynical too young. Because it's a big betrayal to realize that humanity is indifferent.

But it has enabled me to know exactly who I want to be. I'd very much like to be the young woman who, when you look at her, makes you feel like everything in the entire world is not only right but smil-ing at you. I'd like to wink at little kids and yell things about love in French. I want to be reckless with someone, pushing each other in front of buses and pulling each other back at the last minute, shout-ing, "I saved your life for love!" above the traffic.

I would like to live in an apartment in Brooklyn with old wallpaper and a refrigerator with plastic magnetic letters. I'll play my kids the songs that they were named from, like Jude or Lux, out of the exact tape deck that I'm listening to right now. I'll read them stories and not edit out the disturbing parts, because there shouldn't be good words and bad ones. I want to change names and repeat little wisdoms like "Things are only as permanent as you make them." I want to be the old woman at the head of the table telling those long, intricate stories while everyone either laughs or cries hysterically. I want to be like the lovers who die pressed in history's pages: mountains or martyrs or murderers. I never want to be forgotten. And I'll never stop telling you.

Carla Perez-Gallardo, 19

To Do

~~~~~~

I took psychedelics a couple of months ago, and the skies opened up for me to lick with my pink tongue, so I did. I touched the ground and I felt the stars fall into each little groove on the soil's surface. The trees swept their longing arms around my body, and their roots wrapped my thighs. The air moaned with glory, webs swinging from the beings above my head to the ground beneath me. Everything was connected. I think this is when I started believing that there is something I can do to make this world a place to be constantly in love with. I realized there is something to be scared of—but even more to be excited about changing, conquering.

The next day I figured out how I wanted to save (a part of, at least) the world. As college students, we're all faced with having to choose a major, a career path. This, along with some other revelations—in August I'd started seeing a gray ponytail hippie-therapist named Geoff—made me think hard about what I wanted to do with my life. For the longest time I'd had a quiet dream about being a printmaker in Vermont, or a writer. The loudest my dreams had gotten was a short-lived desire to be a museum curator. Then something opened up to me and allowed me to see my role: I need to be someone who helps keep the world sewn together, and finds others who want to reach those mountains in the sunlight. Together we can work as a community and through activism, education—the roles we, as students, teachers, farmers, parents, politicians play—we can establish a sense of responsibility and ownership of the world around us. Geoff fully supported the way I was thinking, reminding me that Jungian-based personality tests had sorted me as a Teacher Idealist.

Walking down the dirt road that day, after picking up a work-study paycheck from my job at the printmaking studio, the epiphany came: I want to start a high school or university. I know that this is ambitious, and that some would think the chance of it actually happening unlikely. But with my new desire to make change and *be* change, I was sticking to my story that nothing is impossible.

The school I envision—and I admit my visions are in their very vague, early stages—would incorporate physical labor to promote social responsibility. At my current college, I've experienced a great lack of awareness on the parts of financially privileged students: Some don't know how to do their own laundry or cook, or know what it feels like to work on one's feet for a day. My own education has encouraged me to believe that tending the land—literally planting seeds, sinking fingers into dirt, observing the growth and decay of plants—would make young people think more critically and progressively about the link between life and death, and about the power we have as individuals. Part of the curriculum would be testing the quality of soil and crops, and continually working to improve it. Students would work inside the buildings as well, cleaning and maintaining classrooms, cooking meals, serving each other. Parents reading this—don't fret! There will still be time for academics, but in all honesty I believe that they are second to the existing need for complete awareness of ourselves and the land around us. I also do not believe in college being a place where you go to learn how to get a good job. College should be—school should be—where you learn to be a good person, a whole human being. My school would work toward finding gentle ways of enforcing common social values. I don't mean to imply that it would have a dictator at its head, forcing thoughts down students' throats. I just mean that the school would be a place where change is born, where positive ideas can grow.

I think a lot of existing universities forget that freshmen (and even upperclassmen) are still young. We could do with reminders that leaders are needed, that a lot of soul and change are required to keep this world together. We're so close to danger. And it's too easy to forget that when global warming seemingly gifts you with a brilliant sixty-degree day in New York in late November. The sun hits your back and you're relieved to lose your coat, and the last thing on your mind is how unnatural and scary it all is.

When I really started thinking about making changes in the world around me, it was a world I'd been unhappy with for quite some time. I wasn't happy at school, at home, with my girlfriend, or with myself. I certainly had never been suicidal, but I was depressed—the kind of depression that engulfs you so suddenly that you scream into pillows on some days and on others it fades away slowly, unnoticed, like a bruise. And the feeling one has after the bruise fades and you're able to stretch that limb as if it is new filled my body and made me want to construct the world inside my head, a world of dreams, of clean water, air, of communion and fellowship.

I didn't mean to get so into the workings of my future university, and the ideas I've mentioned are in no way final or deeply thought out. They're simply what I find important to me right now. They're also what I can see being important to me for the rest of my life—as many, if not all, of the issues are not going to be disappearing on their own anytime soon.

There's a lot going on in the world. There are many things that need to change. I want to help. I am EXCITED.